Public

The Pastoral Letters of the American Catholic Bishops

Camilla J. Kari

A Michael Glazier Book

LITURGICAL PRESS
Collegeville, Minnesota

www.litpress.org

A Michael Glazier Book published by Liturgical Press

Cover design by David Manahan, O.S.B. Photo by Marie Boucher of PHOTOALTO.

1   2   3   4   5   6   7   8   9

Library of Congress Cataloging-in-Publication Data

Kari, Camilla J.
    Public witness : the pastoral letters of the American Catholic bishops
/ Camilla J. Kari.
        p.   cm.
    Includes bibliographical references and index.
    "A Michael Glazier book."
    ISBN 0-8146-5833-4 (pbk. : alk. paper)
    1.   Catholic Church—United States—Pastoral letters and charges. 2.
Catholic Church—Doctrines.   I. Title

BX1753.K344   2004
282'.73—dc22
                                                                2003018778

To my mother, Gabrielle Kari,
for giving me her admiration of education and her love of learning
and
in memory of Father Louis B. Hasenfuss, O.S.B.,
for his presence on my journey

Contents

Introduction   ix
  Pastoral Letters   x
  Research in Perspective   xii
    Historic Reviews   xii
    Commentaries   xiv
    Rhetorical Studies   xvi
  Pastoral Texts   xvii
  Overview   xix

Chapter One: Frontiers and Foreigners: 1792–1884   1
  Origins of the Pastoral Letter   2
    Establishment of the Episcopacy   3
    Setting the Pattern   4
  The Provincial Councils, 1829–1849   7
    Countering Calumny   12
    The Scope Expands   15
  The Plenary Councils, 1852–1884   20
    A Pause in Pastorals   24
    Ethnic Tensions   26
    The Pastoral of 1884   28
    The Suppression of Americanism   30

Chapter Two: The Twentieth Century: 1919–1980   34
  The New Century   35
  The New Organization   36
    Social Reform   38
    The Bishops' Program of Social Reconstruction   40
    The Pastoral Letter of 1919   42
  Between the Wars   46

World War II and Its Aftermath 49
  Materialist Prosperity 52
  The Activist 1960s 56
A New Mission 60

Chapter Three: The Challenge of Peace 69
  Inception 71
  Preparation 73
    Secular Consultation 73
    Four Versions 75
    Vatican Intervention 77
  The Public Responds 80
    Government Protest 80
    The Vatican 82
    Ideologies Polarize Debate 83
    Accounting for Press Coverage 86
    Public Outreach 87
  Opening Rhetorical Dialogue 88
    Public Argument 89
    The Technical Sphere 91
    Broadening the Audience 92
  After the Pastoral 94
    Education 94
    Effects 96

Chapter Four: Economic Justice for All 99
  Precedents 100
  Undertaking the Pastoral 103
    Consultations 103
    The First Draft 104
  The Lay Letter 105
    Preempting the Bishops 106
  Conservative Concerns 110
    To the Bishops' Defense 113
  Permeating the Public 114
    The Second Draft 114
    Ecumenical Support 116
    The Bishops Move to Center Stage 116
    The Vatican and International Reaction 118

The Third Draft   118
Arguments for the Public Square   119

Chapter Five: The Pastoral That Wasn't   122
The Best of Intentions   123
To Be or Not to Be   125
The First Draft   129
Innovation in Style   131
Papal Preemption   132
The Controversy Continues   133
The Second Draft   135
The Voice of the Vatican   138
The Third Draft   140
The Final Outcome   142

Chapter Six: Contributions to Public Discourse   148
The Work Continues   150
Contributions to Civic Discourse   154
Public Discourse   155
Moral Discourse   156
American Discourse   157

Notes   160

Works Cited   192

Introduction

ON APRIL 12, 1988, THE ROMAN CATHOLIC BISHOPS of the United States released their first draft of a pastoral statement about the status of women in the Church and in society. Since the expanded social and legal opportunities for women that had become available in the secular culture had not been extended to the institutional Church, the bishops' intention was to articulate a position for modern women that affirmed their worth and documented their obstacles. They had good reasons for confidence in facing this difficult task—their earlier efforts had resulted in a good deal of acclaim and had captured the attention of the general public.

Two of the bishops' recent pastoral letters had addressed secular social topics: *The Challenge of Peace: God's Promise and Our Response* (1983) and *Economic Justice for All* (1986). These topics represented a wide range of opinions and technical expertise. To produce them, the bishops had employed a new process of gathering input by inviting testimony from secular experts. They then wrote treatises on the moral perspectives of nuclear war and the economy, basing them on philosophical and theological rationales. Conservatives railed against the bishops for addressing topics outside their arena of authority, pundits claimed violation of Church and State, and the press avidly reported the resulting controversy, spinning the bishops into the headlines. Nevertheless, despite the opposition, the pastoral letters created a good deal of public dialogue, generated discussion in intellectual circles, and elicited approval from people of other faiths. So the bishops had no reason not to expect a similarly positive outcome for their new pastoral letter on women. Using an even broader process of gathering input than before, they established a commission, set up a series of hearings, and prepared to listen to their experts—ordinary women around the country. However, after a decade of attempts, eleven drafts written, and four published versions, a pastoral letter on women has still not been adopted. What happened? Why did this particular process of public discourse end in failure?

Probing these questions requires an understanding of the historical context of the American joint pastoral process. As this study will show, the bishops increasingly used pastoral discourse to respond to secular events, addressing a widening audience. Over the years their letters met with growing public response and acclaim, culminating in a shift that, in two centuries, moved American Catholic bishops to change their rhetorical orientation from the defensive posture of an alienated minority to one of confident social advocacy. The passage of time has also served to shift their voice from autocratic pronouncement to more participatory dialogue. The attempt to reach consensus, to initiate dialogue with lay persons, and to critique public policy all represent usages that were radically different from the rhetorical form of the joint pastoral letter from its inception. The phenomenon of such a dialogic process can be understood only in the context of the two-hundred-year span of the bishops' collective communication with the American public.

Accordingly, this study investigates the evolution of a particular rhetorical form, the joint pastoral letter of the American Catholic bishops. Its aim is to show that the expanding historical form and function of the pastoral texts emanate from the bishops' emerging justification of their role as contributors of a moral perspective on general social issues. Beginning with the initial pastoral, the study examines the entire corpus of published pastoral texts to trace the increasing influence on public policy that the bishops sought to exercise through this form. To establish the parameters of this study, this introduction explains the role of pastoral letters within the American Catholic Church.

PASTORAL LETTERS

Letters have been a hallmark of ecclesiastical communication in the two millennia since St. Paul's epistles exhorted and instructed geographically dispersed religious communities. Those letters served to educate the faithful few and persuade them to remain true to their tenets while living in a mainstream culture of non-believers. Like epistles, pastoral letters became a fundamental form of communication by individual Catholic bishops to the laity within their dioceses.[1]

In 1792 the Church in this new nation needed to create uniformity and to consolidate unity for worshipers within the growing union of states. Although French and Spanish missionaries had already established a presence on the continent, the Church, now an official organization of the fledgling nation, faced administrative difficulties in maintaining Roman practices in a Protestant society. To help them in this matter, the nation's Catholic bishops held a series of collegial meetings. From the onset it became customary to conclude each conclave with the issuance of a letter to the nation's Catholics. These joint pastoral statements, representing the collective voice of American Catholic bishops, began as a means of unifying dispersed Catholics in America.[2] The letters provided reassurance and instruction, asked for support, and admonished them to adhere to the faith while being served by only a few scattered clergy.

While Roman Catholics today constitute the largest single group of religious adherents in the United States, when this country began, Catholics were a tiny, feared, and disdained sect.[3] England's painful transformation into a Protestant society had created a legacy of animosity toward "papists," and English settlers imported the residue of that hostility across the Atlantic. When the nation's Catholic population bulged from the influx of European immigrants, their American bishops found themselves attempting to define a civic demarcation for American Catholics that encompassed the tension between preserving the faith and identity of Catholics within the Protestant mainstream, while encouraging their assimilation as loyal and responsible Americans. The success of that assimilation is attested by the transformation in the focus of the pastoral letters from promulgating religious practice to critiquing peace and justice policies. The bishops' pastoral commentary paralleled their growing confidence in the legitimacy of their moral contributions to the public debate on social problems.

An examination of the American pastoral documents reveals that a pattern of such increasing commentary on public policy occurred in stages. The bishops of the nineteenth century were preoccupied with the survival of the American Church in several ways: obtaining financial support and personnel to care for a vastly expanding frontier; defending themselves against both physical and slanderous attacks by a resentful populace; coping with ethnic rivalries among both laity and clergy; and providing a vast number of religious, educational, and social institutions to accommodate increasing throngs of immigrants. During the twentieth century the bishops turned their focus to secular and governmental issues, paralleling the increasing influence of the nation in global affairs. Like the government, the bishops became more organized and bureaucratized, which increased the frequency and scope of their statements. In the 1980s the bishops made significant modifications in their process, producing longer theological reflections on moral repercussions of secular policy. The annual production continues at present but has changed yet again through the turn of the millennium.

RESEARCH IN PERSPECTIVE

Previous scholarship on the American Catholic joint pastoral letters has been limited in its scope. While some historians documented the councils from which the nineteenth-century letters originated, and commentaries delved into the substance and flow of events surrounding the pastorals of the 1980s, neither of these fields has focused on an overview of the process of creating and disseminating these documents. A number of rhetorical studies have examined pastoral letters, but these looked at specific statements as persuasive strategies rather than as a communicative process.

Historical Reviews

A number of historians have focused on the context of the Church's experiences in the United States. General histories of the development of the Catholic Church in America, such as those by Theodore Maynard, John Tracy Ellis, Thomas McAvoy, Robert Leckie, and Jay Dolan, provide a narrative background for public events affecting Catholic Americans, prompting the bishops' response through the medium of the pastorals, but these histories rarely address the discourse itself.[4] Eminent Catholic historian Peter Guilday documented the events and proclamations of the Baltimore councils, held throughout the nineteenth century, meetings that convened bishops from around the nation and resulted in the issuance of joint pastoral letters.[5] As editor of the compendium of several volumes in which the pastorals are published, Hugh Nolan supplied historical material about the production of the letters through his commentaries introducing various periods of the pastoral texts.[6]

The shift in the twentieth century to a greater concentration on social justice in pastoral discourse has not gone unremarked. A number of historical overviews have focused on the contribution of the Catholic Church's perspective in debating societal issues. Walter Woods' dissertation surveys the totality of the letters from 1792 to 1977 from the perspective of moral theology, searching for characterizing principles that distinguish the Church's fundamental approach to dealing with public issues. However, he concentrates on statements issued between 1966 and 1977.[7] John MacInnis' dissertation examines the early pastorals for references to the religious education of children and the maturation of faith in his analysis of how the hierarchy exercised their pastoral responsibilities.[8] Gene Burns furnishes a sociological analysis of liberal Catholic ideology by examining the dynamics of the hierarchy's politicization as an outgrowth of papal interpretation of the Church's role in society.[9] For Burns, the change in the social responses of the bishops represents a rift in their pastoral tradition rather than the trajectory that will be depicted here. Still, he concedes a trace of continuity in earlier thematic elements evidenced in more recent statements.

Some historians have focused on the dramatic events of the early twentieth century, when a permanent organization of the nation's bishops was instituted. Joseph McShane's coverage of the bishops' 1919 "radical" program of commitment to social reform and labor issues points to the trajectory that places the contemporary letters within an American Catholic tradition of progressive activism.[10] Elizabeth McKeown has examined the tradition of American pastoral discourse. She represents pastoral statements as rhetorically creating an increasingly inclusive sense of "family" and the use by the bishops of metaphors and entailments that mark a broader sense of humanity.[11] Both of these studies contribute to a synchronic perspective of dynamic adaptation as the bishops increasingly participate in public life.

Several surveys have made the pastorals and other statements by the bishops the sole focus of their lens, resulting in assessments that read as ideological critiques of the bishops' efforts. J. Brian Benestad surveys the public issues addressed in the joint pastoral statements issued from 1966 to 1980, concluding that the bishops have been ineffective because they lack the authority to delve into secular issues and should restrict themselves to emphasizing personal conversion.[12] His critique conflates the application of Catholic social teaching on public issues with political activism. Phillip Berryman pairs the pastorals on peace and economics to argue that they represent resources for a new national agenda.[13] He attributes to the bishops a rhetorical expansion of the conventional boundaries of public dialogue about war and the economy. His chronology and review of the various drafts illuminate the changing texts and position of the bishops as harbingers of social reform. Michael Warner assesses the statements issued in the era between 1960 and 1986 and the forms of social teaching exercised by the bishops, in order to critique their lack of effectiveness in affecting public policy.[14] Revisiting this subject matter in 1995, he examines the entire pastoral output of the century (1917–1994).[15] He concludes again that the bishops should restrict themselves to religious matters, since the pastorals risk creating divisiveness among American Catholics and diminish the moral authority of the bishops. Timothy A. Byrnes also criticizes what he perceives to be their overt political advocacy and their alignment with a progressive stance as he surveys the bishops' forays into the political arena.[16] He does, however, acknowledge their shift to creating a national voice on a wide range of issues. A survey by David P. Schultz on the pastoral statements issued between 1919 and 1961 examines the bishops' pattern of emerging concern about social issues, which move from a peripheral matter to a central focus of the letters.[17]

The most specific histories that have direct bearing on the process of the letters have been chronicles about their production. Jim Castelli documents the unprecedented level of lay participation in composing the various drafts in his contemporaneous account of the development of the pastoral on nuclear arms.[18] Eugene Kennedy provides a similar narrative for the creation of the first draft of the pastoral on economics.[19] Philip Lawler provides an analysis of the chronology of production and the content of the peace pastoral. Subsequently, he turned his attention to the economic pastoral as a case study to describe the consultations, the drafting process, and the levels of authority that influence the bishops' decisions.[20]

Commentaries

Two particularly lengthy and controversial pastoral letters, *The Challenge of Peace* (1983) and *Economic Justice for All* (1986), sparked a great deal of public and intellectual debate, resulting in a number of anthologized commentaries. There have also been several dissertations on these topics. Anne Shepard's dissertation inquires into the process of drafting the peace pastoral by examining the bishops' commitment to the moral issue and their orientation to the technicalities it involved, but her interviews focused on the transformative self-education of selected bishops.[21] George Cheney's dissertation uses the peace pastoral as a case study for his examination of how leaders manage their organizational identity within institutional rhetoric.[22]

A number of volumes are devoted to essays that analyze, expand, or refute the substance of *The Challenge of Peace* or *Economic Justice for All.* The weight of commentary produced by these pastorals testifies to their contribution in provoking public discourse regarding the issues of nuclear arms and capitalism.

The peace pastoral generated the first series of monographs, edited by Philip Lawler (1983), Philip Murnion (1983), Charles Reid (1986), and Matthew Murphy (1987). These compilations offer scholarly insight into the historical, theological, philosophical, or technical aspects of their subjects. Others provide contextual analysis, such as James Dougherty, who positions the discourse in the context of pacifism and just war doctrine, and compares the American bishops' outspokenness to the cautious silence of their European counterparts.[23] These volumes constitute a symposium of voices that expound or challenge the bishops' ideas. According to Cardinal Joseph Bernardin, who headed the process of drafting the peace pastoral, the essays that comment on the religious and moral analysis from multiple perspectives mirror the consultation that the bishops solicited from experts in theology, technology, and political science during the letter's development.[24]

The economic pastoral also received copious commentary in books written by Thomas Reese (1984), Walter Block (1986), and Michael Novak (1993). Even more numerous are edited volumes of essays, from Jubilee Group, a British response (1985), proceedings of the U.S. Congressional hearings before the Finance Committee (1985), R. Bruce Douglass (1986), Thomas Gannon (1987), James Finn (1990), and Douglas Rasmussen and James Sterba, who conduct a debate in print (1987). These responses offer perspectives on the possibilities of the bishops' proposals for economic reform, contentions regarding the priorities of moral values and economic realities, and the bishops' desire to create a transformation of attitudes. In reference to the commentary produced by the economic pastoral, Douglass writes, "It has generated the first serious discussion of the relationship between religious belief and economic practice in American public life since at least the 1930's. . . . [T]his scholarly discussion is by no means confined to Catholics."[25]

The unexpected influence of these pastorals on non-Catholics can be assessed by the volumes produced by respondents of other faiths, an indication of both ecumenical responsiveness and public interest. Charles Strain includes essays by Jews, Catholics, and two groups of Protestants, mainline and evangelical, who were encouraged by the bishops' stance that the "public square" not be restricted to government.[26] Dean Curry focuses only on the latter group, evangelical readers who analyze the peace text in a holistic rather than selectively critical manner.[27] Charles Lutz similarly collects eleven Lutheran responses to the economic pastoral.[28] While differing on the specifics of the bishops' policy proposals, all were encouraged by the entry of a moral dimension into the military and economic realms.

The pastoral on the status of women that was to follow those on peace and economics was not adopted. Therefore, critiques of the document are limited to reviews of the various drafts that were issued. Georgia Masters Keightley (1988) links the minority role of women to the minority status of the laity within the Church.[29] Maria Riley critiques the pastoral as patriarchal.[30] Julie Fontenot performed a content analysis for her communication thesis, which identifies the rhetorical devices that addressed each of multiple audiences.[31] She concludes that the proposed pastoral was oriented toward American women rather than representing the views of the universal Church. Newspapers, the Catholic press, and various women's organizations provide the bulk of public response to the pastoral drafts.

Rhetorical Studies

Several studies discuss the role of American bishops as institutional rhetors. Carol Jablonski, refuting assumptions of grass-roots foundations for the rhetoric of social movements, points to the function of elites within an organization when a change is being fostered by an institutional authority.[32] She surveys pastoral letters addressed by individual bishops to their dioceses in the 1960s, examining their collective role as agents of change in implementing the modernizations of the Second Vatican Council. Jablonski concludes that the bishops, in order to function simultaneously both as innovators and as guardians of tradition, deal with the dilemma by presenting themselves as exercising traditional obedience to Rome in instituting the required changes in the liturgy. She provides a useful framework for looking at the maintenance of traditional authority in the face of innovation. However, in contrast to individual pastorals, the rhetorical stance of the bishops in collective pastorals appears to be less as agents of Rome than as innovators of domestic moral reform. Later Jablonski posits a need to develop theory on the rhetorical requirements for elites within their own institutions, suggesting that while the rhetorical patterns she highlights provide new dimensions to pastoral letters, they do not transform the bishops' public communication in any significant way.[33] This present book seeks to refute her claim by suggesting that, in fact, the processual nature of the letters' production underwent a radical transformation, influenced as it was by its American democratic context.

Another mode of looking at institutional rhetoric emerges from Steven Goldzwig and George Cheney, who address the way in which the peace pastoral shapes both internal and external audiences as well as the identity of the bishops.[34] The identification of rhetorical strategies that they present expands our understanding of the design and dissemination of arguments for public discussion. Their study examines the pastoral in light of the Church's conservative social positions and affirms the importance of context in assessing the transformation of pastoral discourse.

Cheney's exploration of rhetorical decisions made by the bishops in creating the peace pastoral provides a useful reference to the negotiation of "voice" in a corporate document.[35] Because the joint pastorals represent a collective rhetorical creation of discourse, Cheney examines not only the negotiation of their own differences but the multiple audiences whom the bishops had to consider. His conclusions verify this study's claim regarding the increasing expansion of audiences whom the bishops sought to address. Edward Sunshine also examines pastoral letters as a medium for creating consensus, and their rhetorical construction as moral argument.[36] He concentrates on three topics related to public policy: abortion, peace, and economy. His study also claims that the letters, besides addressing the public, functioned as an internal means of achieving coherence on these controversial issues among the bishops.

Likewise, J. Michael Hogan regards the pastoral letter on peace as an attempt at institutional management.[37] His perspective, however, differs from those of Jablonski, Sunshine, Goldzwig, and Cheney, as he claims that rather than managing change, the bishops write as a maneuver to contain dissent. Unlike other critics, Hogan sees the bishops, not as advocates of radical change, but as trailing behind the forefront of Catholic activism and attempting to control its extremism. Such an alternative reading contributes to the debate about the bishops' need to absorb and reflect highly divisive positions within the Church, a problem that plagues all the recent pastorals discussed in this study.

While all these studies contribute insights to the rhetoric of pastoral letters, they mostly treat the letters as single, static documents, not as a series of increasingly adaptive strategies. The studies appear to focus on the internal motivations of the bishops as rhetors rather than on the place of the pastorals in a continuum of broadening appeal to a pluralistic audience.

PASTORAL TEXTS

The texts of joint pastoral letters of the American Catholic bishops were first collected in a volume edited by Rev. Peter Guilday in 1923, as a record of, and a source for, ecclesiastical and social history. The proliferation of documents in the next decades necessitated a new version, and *Our Bishops Speak (1919–1951)*, edited by Rev. Raphael M. Huber in 1952, brought the previous volume up to date. After the bishops had reorganized as the National Conference of Catholic Bishops (NCCB), *The Pastoral Letters of the American Hierarchy, 1792–1970,* was produced by Rev. Hugh Nolan in 1971. Within a dozen years, however, the accelerated pace of producing statements meant that containing the accumulated material in one volume was no longer practicable, making it necessary to publish the texts in a series of volumes.[38] The collected letters are currently divided into six volumes.

As the amount of discourse has multiplied in contemporary times, a number of terms (letter, statement, resolution) are used to label the texts.

For the purpose of this study, substantive discourse issued for public dissemination, that is, statements not intended for ceremonial or administrative purposes or addressed to particular persons, will be considered a form of joint pastoral discourse.

Published by the United States Catholic Conference (USCC), the five-volume set of pastoral letters edited by Nolan, *Pastoral Letters of the United States Catholic Bishops,* can be considered the official version of the issued statements and provide the critical edition for the included texts. Since the initial documents were addressed to a lay as well as a clerical audience of American Catholics, they were written in English. Utilizing the original texts, Nolan's versions preserve the idioms of the era in which they were written.[39] Since the bulk of references to the texts of the pastoral letters themselves are taken from Nolan's compendium, this study refers to them by volume number and page only. Other citations to Nolan refer to the historical material surrounding the production of the letters, which Nolan provides as context in his introductions to various eras of the pastorals. The sixth volume has been edited by Patrick W. Carey. The joint pastoral letters are divided as follows:

Volume 1: 1792–1940   Volume 4: 1975–1983
Volume 2: 1941–1961   Volume 5: 1983–1988
Volume 3: 1962–1974   Volume 6: 1989–1997

The complex nomenclature that applies to the Church's hierarchical organization requires familiarity with the many terms used to distinguish its degrees of office. The words *Vatican, Rome, Holy See, papal,* and *Curia* all refer to the central function of the universal Church, located in Rome and exercising authority over all matters that overarch the bishop's functions.[40] A *cardinal* is the highest ranking office next to pope, but the pope and cardinals are all still technically bishops (the pope is the bishop of Rome). *Archbishops* preside over larger geographic areas and may be assisted by associate bishops. In this book the term "episcopal" refers to the domain of the *bishop,* who is appointed by the pope and is directly responsible to him. The area under a bishop's jurisdiction is called a *diocese* or *see.* Dioceses are further subdivided into *parishes,* which are served by a neighborhood church (and perhaps a parochial school) and staffed by *priests* who are under the direction of the bishop. This brief synopsis is intended to emphasize that the bishop is the central pivot of the Church's organization and directly under the jurisdiction of Rome rather than any national organization, a factor that has helped the Church to retain its global unity.

OVERVIEW

The purpose of this study is to provide a historical account of the rhetorical goals and practices of the leaders of a non-democratic institution, the Roman Catholic Church, within a democratic nation. In examining the corpus of joint pastoral discourse, it becomes clear that these statements manifest a rhetorical momentum that parallels the social history of the nation. The processes of producing the pastoral letters trace an arc of gradual and continuous transformation as they evolve from internal exhortative epistles to ecumenical public forums.

Scrutinizing the series of letters within the context of their historical situation reveals a pattern in which American Catholic bishops seek to transcend the separation of Church and State in order to transform American public life. This study will demonstrate that the bishops utilized pastoral discourse in response to historical conditions that can be summarized as three stages: first, through an association of Catholicism with nationalism; second, by an escalated attention to national policy issues; and third, through the development of a process of secular consultation that diverged from the traditional top-down communication of the Church. The history of American Catholic joint pastoral discourse traces a path of increasing American democratic influence and an expanding role within the public arena. As American Catholics became transformed from a persecuted minority into an assimilated, educated, acceptable presence, their bishops experienced a concomitant desire to contribute their perspectives on social issues.

Rather than a single textual analysis, this project represents a historical study of the construction of a series of rhetorical documents, in which changes were fostered by a shift in the bishops' rhetorical aspirations. The steps by which this occurred form the crux of this investigation. In this study the historical eras provide a context for illuminating the bishops' manner of dealing with issues in American public life by appraising episcopal responses that marked significant alterations in the function and scope of pastoral discourse. This will be followed by a close-up view of the process of the pastoral statements on peace, economics, and women, which will illustrate the apex of these trends and the reception accorded them.

Chapter One, "Frontiers and Foreigners: 1792–1884," provides an overview of the joint pastoral letters from their inception through the last of the series of Baltimore councils that produced the letters. The bishops of this period were preoccupied with the territorial and demographic growth of the Church, and the letters stressed maintenance of the faith in a physically challenging frontier. Anti-Catholic social sentiment was exacerbated by massive waves of immigrants of varying ethnicities. Throughout the nineteenth century the letters demonstrated the bishops' advocacy of American values as they sought to reconcile assimilation into American life while preserving the faith. The controversy of "Americanism" stemmed from the bishops' fervor for a progressivist perspective but brought censure from the Vatican and created a vacuum in pastoral production.

Chapter Two, "The Twentieth Century: 1919–1980," follows the dramatic shift in pastoral discourse caused by increasing acceptance of Catholicism by the American public. The bishops became emboldened to institute a standing national lobbying organization, resulting in a surge in the production of pastoral statements, beginning with a renowned statement advocating social reform. As the influence of the United States grew, so did the bishops' address of international issues, through the Depression, the Second World War, and its aftermath. The global upheavals of the first half of the twentieth century were followed by the social upheavals of the latter half. Legitimized by the Second Vatican Council (1962), a reorganized national organization dramatically amplified its voice in commenting on public policy issues, creating statements on race, farm labor, housing, and health care, among many other topics.

Chapter Three, "The Challenge of Peace," assesses the innovation established by the bishops' lengthy and complex pastoral examining national policy on nuclear arms. The bishops initiated a consultative process with lay experts, a significant deviation from previous proclamations. Opening the process to the public through press coverage, public meetings, and study groups contributed toward generating an unprecedented amount of commentary and critical response, gaining ecumenical support, and educating the laity on moral aspects of public policy.

Chapter Four, "Economic Justice for All," probes the extension of the elements surrounding the peace pastoral to the statement on capitalist economics. Like its predecessor, this pastoral utilized a sophisticated rhetorical form, created public furor, generated ideological dissension, and introduced a more participative style of production. This chapter examines the contribution to civic discourse derived from the ensuing public discussion and the challenge from those who would silence the bishops' public voice.

Chapter Five, "The Pastoral That Wasn't," deals with the bishops' next attempt to create a pastoral on the status of women, the four different drafts that resulted, the factors that contributed to ideological dissension, and the bishops' ultimate impasse. Although the elements of the rhetorical trajectory created by the previous pastorals were extended still further in this project, the inability to complete the pastoral raises questions about the limits of a democratic process in bringing about institutional discourse.

Chapter Six, "Rhetorical Contributions," weighs the contributions to civic dialogue, American discourse, and moral perspective offered by the pastoral letters. A review of the additional work of the bishops to the present provides an indication of the communicative lessons learned and applied.

Chapter One
Frontiers and Foreigners: 1792–1884 ═══════════════════

THE TRADITION OF ISSUING A JOINT PASTORAL LETTER from the bishops to all American Catholics began at the time of the nation's founding. The practice was begun after local clergy assembled at the First Synod of Baltimore in 1791 and followed each of their infrequent meetings—seven provincial councils held between 1829 and 1849, and four plenary councils between 1852 and 1884.[1] The letters were not a report of the formal, legal work of the councils, during which the bishops passed acts and decrees regarding Church governance in the new nation, but they did provide a public forum for the voice of the Church to reach its unwelcome minority population.

During this period the bishops used the pastoral letters for multiple, although circumscribed, functions. The rhetorical exigencies facing the bishops arose from the conditions to which Catholics were subjected in nineteenth-century America. Externally, as the Catholic population of the United States shifted from a compact nucleus of educated English families to waves of "foreign" Europeans, public suspicion regarding "papist" beliefs, behavior, and loyalties resulted in outbreaks of slander and riots. Geographic dispersion and ethnic diversity of Catholics diluted the unity of shared faith. Scarce financial and human resources limited the ability of the bishops to meet needs in their territories. This situation was further strained by the sheer size of Catholic immigration throughout the century.

This chapter will demonstrate that on one level the joint pastoral letters functioned as communication devices to inform and unify dispersed Catholics, exhorting them to retain their religious practices in a predominantly Protestant environment. However, the letters also had a wider public aspect in that they represented an indirect way for the bishops to address the greater American public. While explicitly addressed to Catholics, the letters also served to assure non-Catholic audiences of the Church's patriotism.

The letters became noteworthy for their defense of Catholicism's compatibility with American citizenship. While the bishops sought to preserve the faith, they also sought to advance its standing in American society by advocating civic assimilation. At the same time, the bishops used the opportunity provided by the public nature of the letters to insist on the civil rights guaranteed to the Church under the Constitution. Despite the public's characterization of Catholics as foreigners whose primary allegiance was to the pope, the bishops framed their Church in the context of American ideals.

During this period joint pastoral letters were stable in their rhetorical characteristics, maintaining consistency in style, form, purpose, and timing. The letters provided unilateral and paternal advice from the bishops to their congregants, and their persuasive intent during the nineteenth century was limited to matters directly affecting the American Church. Their exhortatory character, topical nature, and infrequent appearance all reflect the difficulties of frontier life and the strain of accommodating Roman Catholicism to the American scene.

ORIGINS OF THE PASTORAL LETTER

In order to properly comprehend the strain of being Catholic in the former English colonies, it is necessary to understand the political and institutional factors that created a strong and lasting hostility to the Catholic faith. The defining event that triggered England's break with the Church was precipitated by King Henry VIII's desire to marry Anne Boleyn. A request to have his existing marriage to Catherine of Aragon annulled was denied by Pope Clement VII in 1527. Undeterred, Henry had himself named the new head of the Church in England. During his reign, aside from his rejection of papal authority, religious practices were not radically altered.[2]

Reformers who desired to purify the new Church of England of its Roman trappings gained influence under Henry's son, Edward VI. His Catholic sister, Mary Tudor, intensified English hatred of Catholics when she succeeded to the throne in 1553 and, in her zeal to undo recent changes, persecuted Protestants. Elizabeth I, when her turn to rule arrived in 1558, followed a more moderate policy, seeking unity for the country. This did not satisfy "Puritans," whose goal was to purge religion of all "popish" pomp. As these strict Calvinists lost their influence at the English royal court, they emigrated to the colonies of New England, bringing with them their strong anti-Catholic bias.[3]

John Tracy Ellis points out that Jamestown and the Southern colonies, in spite of their theological differences with the Puritans, had similar charters prohibiting the presence of Catholics.[4] Suspicion toward, and superstitions about, Catholics became a pervasive element of American life. "It may be said that this transplantation of English religious prejudices to America thrived, though carried thousands of miles from its place of origin, and struck such enduring roots in new soil that it became one of the major traditions in a people's religious life."[5]

Unwelcome both in England and in any of the colonies, Catholics founded a haven of their own. Maryland was established after George Calvert, who was Secretary of State under King James I, converted to Catholicism in 1624.[6] The penal laws of England severely limited the civil rights of Catholics, including holding public office, so Calvert had to resign.[7] As a token of his services to the Crown, he was given a large land grant in the Chesapeake Bay region, along with the title Baron Baltimore. When he died in 1632, his son Cecil inherited the title and the proprietorship of the colony.[8]

In order to secure the right to worship for Catholics, the new colony's charter provided for freedom to all religions.[9] The first expedition landed in 1634, and religious liberty prevailed for a time. Maryland's Act of Toleration of 1649 legalized the informal acceptance of religious differences and welcomed a settlement of Puritans expelled from Virginia. However, as Protestants began to comprise the majority of the population, they repealed toleration in 1654, and penal laws were enacted against the Catholics who had founded the colony.[10]

Throughout the eighteenth century, when what Theodore Maynard calls "pressure" rather than persecution applied, laws in England and the colonies were in effect against Catholics.[11] England's Act of Toleration of 1689 had legalized all religions except Catholicism.[12] It should be emphasized that the bigotry against Catholics stemmed from cultural and political fears as much as religious dissent. Catholicism was associated with France and Spain, longtime English foes. Moreover, the pope was at this time not only a spiritual leader but a temporal ruler over the Vatican states.[13] Rumors of popish plots involving conspiracy with French and Indian allies to take over the colonies circulated.[14] Leckie adds, "In defense of the English settlers, it must be made clear that much of their hostility sprang from that deep, ingrained conviction that Catholicism was a foreign, anti-English and treacherous thing."[15]

Establishment of the Episcopacy

The suppression of Catholics in both England and America had eliminated the normal clerical hierarchy of the Church's organization. Well-born Catholic boys were sent to Europe for education, especially if they aspired to be priests. Therefore, between 1634 and the American Revolution, all the clergy functioning on the North American continent were missionaries who were supervised only by infrequent correspondence with their European superiors.[16] Once the war had ended, Rome proposed the idea of selecting a bishop to organize the institutional Church in the new nation.[17]

The clergy in America were apprehensive about such an action on several counts. First, such an appointment could antagonize their Protestant compatriots, especially given the Calvinist distaste for pomp and rank.[18] Second, the recent revolution in France had displaced many bishops, making it likely that Rome would appoint someone from France to the office, an affront to English sensibilities. Third, the sense of equality in America made the idea of a hierarchy an anathema.[19] However, since the Episcopalians had been able to appoint a bishop in 1787 without protest from the public, the American clergy accepted the idea of a prelate but were anxious to forestall the appointment of a French bishop.[20] Instead of imposing such an appointment, the Vatican granted the American clergy the unprecedented privilege of choosing their own bishop, an outcome attributable to John Carroll.

Carroll, a cousin of Charles Carroll, a signer of the Declaration of Independence, was a member of a wealthy and influential family that had prospered in Maryland. Both boys were educated abroad when Catholic education was outlawed in the colony, and John was ordained a priest in France.[21] Although living quietly in Rock Creek with his mother, he was appointed superior of the American missions by the Vatican in 1784.[22] Recognizing that a French bishop, the Vatican's likely choice, would be received with resentment by the clergy and suspicion by the public, Carroll wrote to Rome to request permission for American clergy to elect their own bishop.[23] Rome agreed, and it was Carroll himself whom the Americans chose by a vote of 24 to 2 at their meeting at the Jesuit plantation Whitemarsh (now Bowie, Maryland), in 1789.[24] Therefore, the first bishop of the United States was, fittingly, a native-born American who was also an enthusiastic patriot.

Setting the Pattern

The American tradition of issuing a pastoral letter to the nation's Catholics began after the new Bishop Carroll called a synod in Baltimore in November 1791, attended by twenty-two priests. The gathering foreshadowed the American emphasis on episcopal collegiality. "This Synod is in reality, the real formation of American Catholicism, the fusion of Catholic principles with American circumstances."[25] Following this, Carroll initiated what became the practice of American bishops at the conclusion of a national council, namely, addressing all American Catholics with a pastoral letter.

Although subsequent pastoral letters were all "joint" productions, that is, signed by, and considered to be from, all the presiding bishops, Carroll was necessarily the sole author of the first pastoral letter. The see of the bishop of Baltimore covered all the territory east of the Mississippi River except Florida.[26] Carroll remained the only American bishop until 1808, when the Vatican created Baltimore as an archdiocese, with Boston, New York, Philadelphia, and Bardstown, Kentucky, named as suffragan sees, subject to Baltimore but having their own bishops.[27]

Carroll's letter of 1792, which initiated the practice of two centuries of national pastoral discourse, established several characteristics for American pastorals. The letter was written in English, ensuring that it would receive the widest understanding by a lay audience. Carroll's native language was English, and he had a history of supporting use of the vernacular in the Mass.[28] Moreover, Bishop Carroll's ten-page message to the Catholic population of the new nation has the rhetorical characteristics of a letter. It begins with a salutation and an expression of benevolence: "To my dearly beloved brethren, the members of the Catholic Church in this diocese; health and blessing" (1:16).[29] Carroll's salutation is refreshing in that he avoids the usual practice of addressing clergy as "brethren" and the laity as "children." His democratic precedent of addressing both groups equally became a standing practice. The letter closes with a series of phrases from various Epistles before his signature, "John, Bishop of Baltimore," and the date, May 28, 1792 (1:127).

Carroll explains the impossibility of overcoming the obstacle of geographic expanse as his reason for the letter in his opening sentence: "The great extent of my diocese and the necessity of ordering many things concerning its government . . . have not yet permitted me to enjoy the consolation . . . of seeing you all, and of leaving with you, according to the nature of my duty, some words of exhortation" (1:16). The "duty" to which Carroll refers is the pastoral teaching authority of a bishop. Such teaching is not infallible, as a pope's *ex cathedra* pronouncement is, but it is considered authoritative, whether coming from a pastoral letter issued by an individual bishop or a conference of bishops.[30]

Carroll's letter typifies an American orientation in a number of ways. He emphasizes progress: obtaining "means calculated to produce lasting effects, not only on the present, but on future generations" (1:16). He addresses the financial needs confronting the Church: endowments for schools (1:18–19), support of the clergy (1:19–20), and provision of vessels, vestments, and buildings (1:20, 22). His pragmatic approach is evident even in his argument about the benefits of a Christian education, designed to appeal to natural self-interest: "You may be assured of finding, in those sons and daughters whom you shall train up to virtue and piety, by your instructions and examples, support and consolation in sickness and old age. They will remember with gratitude, and repay with religious duty, your solicitude for them in their infancy and youth" (1:17).

After noting in a general way the advantages of a religious education, Carroll appeals to his readers to support Georgetown College, from which "it may reasonably be expected, that some after being educated at Georgetown, and having returned to their own neighborhood, will become, in their turn, the instructors of youths who cannot be sent from home" (1:18). Since Georgetown might be expected to educate some young men interested in the priesthood, Carroll then turns to the need for a seminary to train native-born priests, who would be "men accustomed to our climate, and acquainted with the tempers, manners, and government of the people" (1:18).[31] Carroll, as head of the hierarchy, was forced to cope with the apprehensions of European clerics regarding democracy, as later voiced by a French bishop of New Orleans, William Dubourg: ". . . how contagious even to the clergy . . . are the principles of the freedom and independence imbibed by all the pores in these United States."[32]

Carroll's appeal to patriotic pride and his emphasis on American ways are not limited to the priesthood. He also points out that Christian education benefits the nation, "whose welfare depends on the morals of its citizens" (1:17). The letter closes with spiritual matters: the need to attend Mass despite the difficulties of distance (1:21), the need for prayers (1:24–26), and the establishment of a feast day for the diocese (1:26).

As a member of an old Maryland family and a patriotic American, Carroll recognized that the institutions of the Church needed to conform to the spirit of America to be accepted. The American characteristics of the nation that Carroll sought for his Church were its nationalistic spirit, its independence, and its separation of Church and State.[33] He continually emphasized the unity of the American Church, encouraging the clergy to put aside their European connections. He informed feuding factions to "strive to form not Irish, or English, or French congregations and churches, but Catholic-American congregations and churches."[34] Carroll's strategy called for avoiding undue interference from Rome in American ecclesiastical affairs to preserve a public perception of independence and to assure Americans that Catholics could be loyal to both simultaneously.[35] In a personal letter Carroll vented his frustrations with the meddling of European bishops in

American issues: "How any of these Prelates . . . could determine themselves to interfere in an affair so foreign to their concern, and to which they are so incompetent, is a matter of surprise."[36]

Carroll's concerns for the fledgling Church encompassed its internal well-being and its accommodation within American society. These themes would be promoted in the subsequent pastoral letters of this period. In this first American pastoral, Carroll emphasizes the maintenance of the Church in terms of financial support for clergy, attendance and contributions at services, and education with the intent of fostering future clergy. However, in his other writings he introduces a theme that succeeding pastorals would elaborate, namely, that the nation would gain from the "preservation and increase of true religion, for the benefit of our common country, whose welfare depends on the morals of its citizens" (1:17). Carroll lays the foundation for a concept of reciprocal benefits between the faithful who sustain democracy and a nation that protects its diverse worshipers. The mutual relationship between individual salvation and the good of the nation would become a notable component of future pastoral letters.

THE PROVINCIAL COUNCILS, 1829–1849

Carroll's pastoral letter guided the fledgling American Church for almost four decades. The four additional bishops who were appointed in 1808 met with Carroll in 1810 and produced a letter dated November 15, 1810. However, none of the volumes of collected pastoral letters include this text, because it merely repeats the decrees passed during the meeting in 1791. The War of 1812 hampered the ability of clerics to travel and meet. Interim proclamations dealing with the specific problems of particular dioceses were issued and so were not national in scope.[37]

The resources of the Church were strained at this time by the exponential growth of land area resulting from the nation's acquisition of western territories. Additional bishops were being appointed to serve the expanding population. John England, bishop of Charleston, recognized a need for uniformity of rules and practices among the nation's multiplying dioceses. In letters he repeatedly requested Ambrose Maréchal, who, as archbishop of Baltimore, held the highest, most senior position among the American bishops until the appointment of the first cardinal later in the century, to summon a council.[38] England's petition to Maréchal carried on Carroll's pro-American stance by posing a series of arguments that aligned the Church's communal customs with the democratic norms of the nation:

> Because the usual mode of a Synod is more congenial to the old canons of
> the Church. Because the usual mode of a Synod has been prescribed by the
> last general council. Because the usual mode of a Synod has been found most
> beneficial in those places in which it has been followed. . . . Because the
> usual mode of a Synod is more in accordance with the spirit of our national
> institutions, and because it is the mode which will best please the flock and
> insure their support to its resolutions.[39]

The lapse in councils, and therefore of pastoral letters, was caused by
fractures in the unity of the Church. Maréchal resisted convening the bishops because he was afraid of the havoc that might be caused by the friction
among the nation's Irish, French, and German bishops, discussed below.
Bishop England succeeded in having a meeting called only after Maréchal's
death in 1829, when James Whitfield became his successor. As a result of
England's persistent efforts, a series of provincial councils was scheduled to
meet every four years in Baltimore, beginning in 1829.[40]

Specific issues regarding the clergy and the laity confronted the bishops
during this period, providing the impetus for the bishops to take the unusual step of producing two pastoral letters after the first Baltimore Council of 1829. This proved to be the only time that different letters were
prepared for the clergy and the laity.

The need for a separate pastoral letter to the clergy stemmed from the
difficulties caused by some of the priests who had arrived in America. The
United States had become a convenient place for bishops abroad to relocate
recalcitrant priests. These men created dissension here that the bishops felt
needed to be addressed without bringing it to the attention of the laity.
Maynard comments on the frequency of the occurrence:

> In almost every instance an uninvited cleric . . . lands in America with ap-
> parently excellent references from his bishop or superior [in Europe]. . . .
> He is accepted . . . because [of the] dire need of priests. . . . Having gath-
> ered a party, he sets himself up against his bishop. This leads to a suspension.
> . . . Several times we hear the threat to set up an "Independent Catholic
> Church of America."[41]

Another issue that created factions among clergy was ethnicity. The
anti-clericalism of France's revolutionaries caused its clerics to flee to this
country in numbers disproportionate to the French-speaking population
here. The aristocratic French tended to be assigned to minister to the large
numbers of proletarian Irish arriving here.[42] But the ability to preach, so
prized by Americans in general and the Irish in particular, was hampered

by the language barrier. Therefore, by the time Ambrose Maréchal had become bishop, the antagonism between Irish and French cultures was strong.[43] The Irish were resentful of the Gallic dominance of the hierarchy and appealed to President Jefferson, who chose to stay out of the fray.[44] French-born Archbishop Maréchal, in turn, complained to Rome about the behavior of Irish priests in America, whom he characterized as troublesome, intemperate, poorly educated, and causing scandals.[45] Bishop England, himself from Cork, asserted in 1835 that Franco-Catholicism hampered social acceptance of the faith:

> I am daily more convinced that the genius of this nation and the administration of the French are not easily reconciled. Besides this, one of the strongest topics of prejudice against our religion is that it is a foreign Religion, and it is not American, that it is the religion of strangers, of aliens. . . . The French can never become Americans. Their language, manners . . . their dress, air, carriage, notions and mode of speaking of their religion, all, all are foreign. . . . They make the Catholic religion thus appear to be exotic.[46]

Disputes between German and Irish clergy were caused by cultural differences in liturgy and administration. Each used their own language during services, and the organization of their churches and schools differed. Already by 1789 the German Catholics of St. Mary's Church in Philadelphia felt discriminated against by the Irish and started their own parish, Holy Trinity.[47] The Germans, who tended to settle in rural Midwestern areas, were prosperous and desirous of retaining their language and customs and of educating their children in German-language parochial schools. Their pastors, whom they brought with them, shared decision-making with the laity.[48] Unlike the Germans, the Irish tended to be poor laborers. They did not become property owners, had no objection to public schools, and had a tradition of stern clerical authority. The Irish felt superior to other groups because of their fluency in English and began to rank as the most numerous among Catholics in Eastern urban areas.[49] These cultural differences between the three major ethnic groups comprising American Catholicism indicate the rapid shift in population from the predominantly middle- and upper-class Anglo-Catholics at the time of the Revolution.[50]

Seeking unity and uniformity, the bishops issued a pastoral letter to the clergy (1:50–56) in October 1829, addressed to their "reverend cooperators and brethren" (1:50). The letter calls for proper behavior both in public and in private. The bishops remind priests of the need to develop their inner lives through prayer (1:52–53), meditation, reading Scripture (1:54–55) and study (1:56), and also admonish them to be mindful of the public eye (1:56–61):

> We live in the midst of a world that scrutinizes our conduct with habitual
> jealousy; the most perfect among us are liable to have their very best actions
> misconstrued, their sayings misinterpreted, their motives unappreciated,
> and their imperfections magnified and blazoned forth to public observation.
> It is natural that this should be the case, because since we are established as
> censors of the conduct of others, human nature urges upon them the inquiry
> into our own demeanor (1:58).

The clergy are implored to consider their effects on a wavering believer: "Let
the dignity of your vocation be made manifest in your conversation, in your
attire, and in the becoming gravity of your conduct" (1:60). The letter to the
clergy is specific to those in ministry, encouraging them to be pious in per-
forming the liturgy (1:62), to be virtuous, and to "be meek, be charitable, be
courteous, be kind" (1:64), and in effectively teaching the young (1:64–65).

The pastoral letter to the laity (1:35–49) addresses them as "children in
Christ, the Laity of the Roman Catholic Church in the United States of
America" (1:35). The letter refers to current conditions and issues and creates
opportunities to praise the nation. It reviews "the vast tide of emigration
which . . . has swelled our population. . . . Large acquisitions of territory
which had been occupied by Catholic nations, were made to the south and
the west" [referring to the Louisiana Purchase], enabled by "our admirable
civil and political institutions." This growth has created an "utmost want of
a sufficient ministry" (1:35–36). This reference to a shortage of priests leads
to an exhortation regarding the religious education of children (1:38–41).

Midway through the letter, however, the bishops turn to a defense of
their Church against anti-Catholic attacks and the "misrepresentation of
the tenets, principles, and the practices of our Church" (1:41). There was a
resurgence of bias against Catholic "papists" during this era, exacerbated by
the influx of two million Irish, whose rowdy shantytowns crowded Eastern
cities.[51] The prejudice against newcomers by "nativists" was expressed with
invective and rumors of strange practices. Maynard writes: "The adherents
of Nativism honestly believed that the Catholic Church was by its very nature
a persecuting and bloody affair, and that it was already planning to introduce the Inquisition into America. Everything they saw seemed to confirm
their dread."[52]

In their pastoral the bishops depict the pervasiveness of false beliefs
about their faith:

> The mind of the very infant is predisposed against us by the recitals of the
> nursery; and the schoolboy can scarcely find a book in which some or more
> of our institutions and practices is not exhibited far otherwise than it really
> is, and greatly to our disadvantage: the entire system of education is thus

tinged throughout its whole course; and history itself has been distorted to our serious injury (1:41–42).

Such falsehoods not only contaminate schools, the bishops said, but " the public press, the very bench of public justice, have all been influenced by extraordinary efforts directed against us, so that from the very highest place in our land to all its remotest borders, we are exhibited as what we are not, and charged with maintaining what we detest" (1:41). The bishops go on to relate efforts to establish a religious press to counteract such public misinformation and caution their "dearly beloved children" to read the Scriptures, but to use only versions sanctioned by the Church (1:41–43).

After these sections the bishops address the pressing problem of trusteeism, although the term is not used and the references are oblique. The prohibition against the Catholic Church being recognized in law by the states did not allow for corporate property ownership.[53] Therefore, control of physical church property was in the hands of a lay vestry, or trustees, a common practice among Protestant denominations.[54] Local Catholics would establish a congregation, purchase property, build a church, and wait for a priest to be assigned to them. Inevitably, such a disjunction between ecclesiastical authority and control of physical resources resulted in clashes and disagreements between pastors and their boards.[55] Some trustees went so far as to claim the prerogative of choosing and dismissing their own pastors, even their own bishops, as Protestants did.[56] This problem began as early as 1789, when the Philadelphia Germans selected a priest for their new ethnic church and then presented his name to Bishop Carroll. He rejected their right to elect a pastor, although he later made the appointment.[57] The issue of lay control would continue to plague the bishops throughout the nineteenth century.[58]

In this pastoral the bishops remind readers of the unchanging nature of Church law, alluding to their right to make all pastoral assignments (1:44–45). The issue is depicted slightly more specifically in following paragraphs:

> Yet there have been found amongst you, men who, not fully acquainted with the principles of our church government, either presumed to reform it upon the model of those who have separated from us, or claimed imaginary right from the misapprehension of facts and laws. . . . [D]isastrous schisms have thereby occasionally arisen (1:45).[59]

Near the end of the pastoral, the bishops remind Catholics to be diligent in regard to duties involved in practicing the faith, in spite of "the sneer of the unbeliever" (1:47–48). They close by advocating that Catholics project a non-judgmental, non-violent stance, "not only in your civil and political, but also in your social relations with your separated brethren" (1:49). Such encouragement of civil accord marks a distinguishing theme in national Church policy that can be traced through the pastoral letters of this era.

Both the letter to the clergy and that to the laity close the same way, dated October 17, 1829, and signed with the given names and titles of six bishops. Both address concerns arising from their distinct constituencies, and both are similar in length. Both admonish, exhort, and encourage good behavior and pious practice.

The Second Provincial Council of Baltimore, held in 1833, was once again called only at the insistence of Bishop John England. Although the 1829 council had specified that another meeting be called in three years, Archbishop Whitfield of Baltimore kept procrastinating. Bishop England petitioned Rome directly, asking the Vatican to intervene. Rome complied and ordered a council to convene for the purpose of providing uniform legislation for all the dioceses (Maynard, 1:223–224).

The letter (1:67–81) that emerged at the conclusion of the council allows the bishops to provide "some words of admonition, as the token of our affection, the evidence of our solicitude, and the fulfillment of our duty" (1:67). Although there is a passing reference to the legislation passed during the council and forwarded to the Vatican for approval (1:67), the letter is oriented to spiritual matters.[60] The bishops seek to center readers on the future of their souls: "Our journey is to the portal of the tomb; beyond which there opens the expansion of eternity" (1:66). They discuss the human inclination to evil and the role of grace, prayer, Scripture, and the sacraments as aids to salvation. Clerics are reminded of their obligation to recite the Divine Office (1:72–73): "Bear with us, then, beloved, if we seem over earnest in exhorting, in persuading, in compelling to this most salutary, most necessary, most profitable regularity in your daily meditations." The call for vocations to religious life is framed as an appeal that simultaneously invokes progress and independence: "We cannot be always, we should not be, when we can avoid it, dependent upon other nations for our ministry. We desire to see your children prepared to occupy our places" (1:78). The letter closes with reminders about the rules of abstinence (refraining from eating meat on Fridays and, at that time, most Saturdays) and abrogates the obligation to fast on certain feast days (1:78–79). Eleven bishops signed the letter on October 27, 1833.

Countering Calumny

The threat to the Church in the decades before and after the Civil War from the hostility of the nativist movements is evident in the pastorals of this period. "Nativism synthesized into a movement of opposition to minorities on the grounds of their being 'un-American.'"[61] Part of Bishop England's intent in convening the council of 1829 was to emphasize the American nature of the Church. However, the plan backfired. "Although the council's purpose was to quiet nativistic fears its effect was exactly the opposite, for the assembling of the American hierarchy in all its glory was a sight which caused grave concern among the simplicity-living Americans."[62] Moreover, the publicity surrounding the trustee scandals harmed the reputation of the Church, because Protestants, not understanding the Church's centralized organization, sided with laypeople on the issue, framing a scenario in which a democratic congregation confronted an authoritarian clergy.[63] These episodes kept the Church in the public eye and added to anti-Catholic momentum.

While the 1829 pastoral had alluded indirectly to anti-Catholic sentiments voiced in the press, the letters became more frank in reporting incidents against Catholics as events worsened in the intervening years. Ray Allen Billington points out that the revival movement then underway also contributed: "The whole country was under the influence of a wave of religious excitement; Protestantism suddenly became a thing to be venerated and protected, while Catholicism, as an antagonistic system, was proportionately resented. Those who attacked it became crusaders in the popular mind and were assured a large following."[64]

Publications such as *The Protestant Magazine* and *The Anti-Romanist* had only one purpose, succinctly expressed in the first issue's editorial entitled "The Protestant Vindicator and Defender of Civil and Religious Liberty Against the Inroads of Popery" and written by its founder, Rev. W. C. Brownlee: "With the deliberate conviction that Popery ought always to be loathed and execrated, not only by all Christians, but also by every patriot and philanthropist; we shall endeavor to unfold its detestable impieties, corruptions and mischiefs."[65] Articles with titles such as "Priestcraft Unmasked" appeared in the regular press, and publications from England bore such titles as *Female Convents: Secrets of Nunneries Disclosed* and *Master Key to Popery*.[66]

Although such tracts contributed to anti-Catholic hostility, verbiage turned into violence near Boston on August 11, 1834. A mob set fire to a convent of Ursuline sisters in Charlestown, which housed a prestigious academy for girls. While firemen idly stood by, the sisters and their sixty students (many of whom were well-to-do Protestants) managed to escape.[67]

The public's fascination with the mysteries of convent life created a market for exposés purporting to reveal salacious details. The best-seller of the genre was the *Awful Disclosures of the Hotel Dieu Nunnery of Montreal*, written in 1836 under the name of Maria Monk. Claiming to have escaped from the convent, she "revealed" life there as involving sexual orgies, secret tunnels, strangled newborns, and executed nuns, horror stories that appealed to the prejudice and prurience of its readers.[68] Disclosure by Monk's mother that the nearest her daughter had come to a convent was a stay in a Catholic mental asylum did not detract from the book's credibility. Nor did reports by deputations of Canadian and American Protestant ministers who visited the convent in question and found that it in no way resembled Monk's description.[69] A later lawsuit revealed that the bulk of the manuscript was written by a Rev. J. J. Slocum and other clergymen, who seized an opportunity to profit from the public's interest and gullibility.[70]

Given these circumstances, the bishops utilized the pastoral letter of 1837 (1:82–114), issued by the Third Provincial Council, as a forum of protest. This letter represents a change from a previous inward orientation to the needs of faith. The bishops use it to mount a defense of the Church in light of recent events. The pastoral is an explicit fulmination against the abridgment of freedom of religion resulting from public desire to suppress and discredit their faith. The bishops make clear their intent to frame the anti-Catholic behavior as anti-American and unconstitutional: "They cannot despoil us without ensuring the general ruin" (1:83). They lament the consequences of the virulent bias: "The affection of fellow citizens is destroyed, the offices of charity are neglected, the kindly intercourse of neighbors has been interrupted, suspicion, jealousy, and hatred have succeeded to confidence, mutual respect and affection; the demon of discord has usurped that station where the angel of peace abode" (1:82). They marvel at the gullibility of the public: "How can it be possible for men of reading and sagacity to be duped at this side of the Atlantic by charges refuted in Europe more than a century since. . . . [They should be] disbelieved by every one who has the most moderate pretensions to information" (1:84).

Counseling patience and acceptance during this time of trial (1:85–87), the bishops then give considerable space to the incident of the burning of the Ursuline convent, the subsequent acquittal of the arsonists, and public rejoicing over that verdict (1:88–89). They protest the government's reneging on its initial promise of reimbursement after the arson, a decision based on the court's decision that because Catholics bore allegiance to the supremacy of the pope, they were not citizens of the commonwealth and therefore forfeited compensation (1:89–91).

The bishops then turn to the publication of calumny. No specifics are mentioned, but the reference to Monk's book and its scandalous claims is clear:

. . . charges whose falsehood was exposed by American Protestants, the impossibility of whose truths was attested by Canadian Protestants, and whose imputation was indignantly rejected by both. Yet has the world witnessed those charges again brought forward with unblushing front, by obscure imposters of the most vile description . . . beings in whom it was hard to say whether vice, or recklessness, or insanity predominated, and those charges . . . pertinaciously adhered to after the demonstration of their absurdity, by men whose station supposes intelligence and integrity (1:91–92).

The bishops bemoan the public's "voracious appetite" for the "obscene libel" of "lascivious tales" and "immodest fictions" of books on sexual escapades in religious houses, about which the bishops say, "We should . . . cease to be astonished at the credulity and delusion of many of our fellow citizens" (1:92).

The remainder of the letter turns from current events to spiritual matters and support of Church institutions:

We are gratified by the spiritual progress of numbers, but deeply affected by the negligence of too many who, however sound may be their faith, yet do not reduce their principles to practice. We are aware of the many difficulties which exist, because of the fewness of clergy, the remoteness of churches, the sparseness of the flocks, and a variety of other causes (1:95).[71]

The bishops distinguish piety from sinlessness: "Religion is not satisfied with the mere rooting out of vice, there must be efforts to do positive good" (1:96). Perhaps as an antidote to the prevailing defamations of Catholicism, they elaborate on this theme by enumerating the virtues a pious person contributes to society, the state, neighbors, and family (1:97). Reminding readers of the importance of faith and the sacraments, the bishops liberally cite both Old and New Testament passages (1:98–104).

Before concluding, the bishops return to a familiar list of problems: the construction and furnishing of churches (1:105); troublesome trustees (1:105–107); contributions to support clergy (1:107–110); and popular support of the Catholic press, education, and the orders of sisters who taught, nursed, and performed social work (1:110–112). The letter concludes with a particular message to the clergy that is composed entirely of various passages from the Epistles (1:112–113).

The Scope Expands

Circumstances required the bishops to comment on external issues again four years later, in the letter following the Fourth Provincial Council in 1840 (1:115–139). The message begins with a positive progress report: two new bishoprics,[72] the establishment of seminaries, convents, and churches (1:115–116). The statement reports as good news the absence of events—while no compensation was received for the burned convent in Massachusetts, neither had there been any more "acts of barbarity" or efforts to sully the reputation of Church and clergy. The press and pulpit continue to defame Catholics, the bishops write, but prayer, not anger, is the appropriate response (1:116–118).

The long-range strategy of the bishops in advocating education is evident in the attention it receives in the pastoral. The bishops refer to the need for "aid in defraying expenses" for parochial schools, which at that time, as today, were also patronized by non-Catholics: "In many instances also, they who belong not to the household of faith have discovered the advantages which accompanied the system of education in our schools and colleges; they have often been more industrious to profit by them than you, for whom they were principally intended" (1:118). With a forward-looking perspective, the bishops complain about families that scrimp on their daughters' education, "a mistaken and thriftless economy, which led them to keep their children, especially females, at an inferior school of less cost" (1:119).

A long section is devoted to the problem of Bible versions used in the schools (1:119–126). This issue contributed to the growth of the parochial school network in the United States. Although intended to provide religious training, the establishment of parochial education was also a response to the fact that public school students were compelled to read the King James version of the Bible and to learn Protestant theology. Such practices, along with the use of textbooks that denigrated Catholicism, about which the bishops had complained in 1829 (1:42), caused them to claim that public schools were violating the separation of Church and State. The reason is not surprising, since, as David O'Brien points out, "[T]hroughout the country Protestant clergy often took the lead in organizing and supporting the common schools, recruiting the teachers, and naming superintendents."[73] Bishops of major cities fought battles with local school councils.[74] Therefore, the theme of Catholic education would become a question of preserving the faith of a minority and would be reiterated through all the pastorals of this period. Preservation of the faith is presumably the same motive for the bishops' passage warning about the problem of mixed marriages between persons of different faiths and requiring that offspring of such marriages be baptized and educated as Catholic (1:128–131).

The letter of 1840 is significant because it expands the scope of the letters in its treatment of several themes, trends in secular society, politics, and social issues. The tendency of the bishops to address areas outside the Church is becoming evident. The joint pastoral of 1840 extends not only to the arena of domestic affairs but to foreign events as well. Previous letters had focused solely on issues involving the Church in America. For the first time, reference is made to a situation abroad, in this case the actions of the King of Prussia and his unjust treatment of Catholics. The bishops report sending letters of support to the persecuted hierarchy there (1:131). This foray into international affairs foreshadows a movement that would later gather momentum.

While it is likely that previous mention of financial aid sent to the American Church from Europe was suppressed to avoid the appearance of foreign control, the bishops for the first time here gratefully acknowledge the role of benevolent societies in Austria and France in assisting American missions (1:137–138). These lay missionary societies in Europe contributed crucial monies to support frontier clergy throughout the nineteenth century.[75] Such assistance heightened the interest of Catholics abroad in pastoral news from this country.

The Americanization of the Church constitutes a distinct theme in the letter of 1840. The bishops link patriotic values as motives even for Christian education and the need for clergy: "America must gradually become independent of foreign churches for the perpetuation of her priesthood. At present, the tide of immigration is too copious to prevent our dispensing with the aid of an immigrant clergy" (1:128). Such comments indicate the continued stress created by ethnic differences among the clergy.

While the bishops had defended Catholic patriotism and citizenship in previous pastorals, they had refrained from political commentary. In 1840, while still neutral, they do articulate a sense of responsibility for civil involvement:

> Whilst we disclaim all right to interfere with your judgment in the political affairs of our common country, and are far from entertaining the wish to control you in the constitutional exercises of your freedom, we cannot in justice to ourselves, refrain from addressing to you a few observations equally demanded by the love we bear to our civil and political institutions, and the obligations of morality (1:133).

Assuring their audience that among themselves "our own views . . . are as little in harmony as are your own," the bishops entreat, "avoid the contaminating influence of political strife . . . and be assured that our republic can never be respected abroad, nor sustained at home, save by an uncompromising adherence to honor, to virtue, to patriotism, and to religion"

(1:133–134). The pastoral of 1829 had advocated toleration toward those of other faiths, and here again the bishops emphasize the need for harmony in social relations, even amid the dissension of the electoral process. The bishops link the morality of religion with the practice of civil behavior, commencing a significant practice of fusing these two arenas of public life and exhorting unity rather than discord.

In this pastoral of 1840 the bishops introduce an element that will be characteristic of their future discourse. Although always anxious to defend their American civic identity, they do not neglect their pastoral role as Catholic moral teachers. In this statement they establish the practice of contesting American preoccupation with material success: "The pervading temptations of our land are the pride of luxury, the speculations of avarice, the love of riches, the ordinate desire of gain. . . . [B]e content with moderate acquisitions of honest industry" (1:134).

Prior to closing, the bishops allude to a prevailing social issue of the day—the temperance movement (1:135–137). "We neither feel ourselves warranted to require, nor called upon to recommend to all our flocks, a total abstinence from a beverage the sacred Scriptures do not prohibit. . . . We, however, do commend the resolution of those persons who . . . having no need of their use, abstain altogether from ardent spirits" (1:136). The passing reference articulates the bishops' perspective on the hotly political debate over temperance, a stance that exacerbated resentment against Catholics by reformers. The Church's reservation in joining major social reform efforts of the day emphasized its alienation from Protestant advocates for social reform. The suspicion of the Church about being co-opted by causes associated with rabid nativists caused Catholics during this period to remain outside most movements except labor reform. The fact that the pastoral felt obliged to articulate and defend its stance on temperance indicates that external pressures were penetrating the institutional Church and creating a need for justification of its policies.

Seventeen bishops signed the brief letter of 1843, after the Fifth Provincial Council (1:140–148). The pastoral depicts a Church membership assaulted by external forces. The bishops react by providing exhortations regarding the importance of religious instruction, the prohibition of belonging to secret societies, and the dangers of intemperate drinking (1:141–144). While these themes are repeated from the previous letter, the bishops expand their scope by adding a paragraph about the scandal of divorce and a section on the bishops' authority that responds to unspecified instances of insubordination (1:145). They air their grievance against charities that require participation in Protestant services:

. . . the consciences of many in dependent situations are aggrieved by vexatious measures adopted to coerce them into conformity, under the penalty of wanting bread, and that in various public institutions attendance at Protestant worship is in many instances exacted of Catholics, notwithstanding the liberty of conscience which is guaranteed by the constitution to all citizens (1:141).

Such statements reveal the prohibition for Catholics of the period to be visited by chaplains in institutions such as hospitals and prisons, which in turn spurred the establishment of parallel Catholic charities.[76]

The letter of 1846 (1:149–155), following the Sixth Provincial Council of Baltimore, turns from events at home to focus on Europe. It vaunts high-profile conversions to Catholicism then occurring among English intellectuals (1:149–151). Changes in the political climate in England had resulted in the Emancipation Bill of 1829, which repealed penal laws enacted in 1688 prohibiting Catholics from the right to vote, to hold office, and to attend university. However, these new freedoms had also deepened anti-Catholic fervor on both sides of the Atlantic.[77] In their pastoral the bishops reiterate the compatibility of patriotism and obedience to the pope (1:152) and express their appreciation for money received from the Society for the Propagation of the Faith. The pastoral closes with a reminder about exercising temperance and dedicates the American Church to Mary.

The letter of 1849 issued by the bishops of the Seventh and final Provincial Council refers to the wishes of Pope Pius IX for reorganization of the American hierarchy. The two topics of the letter are confined exclusively to news about the papal exile[78] and Italy's confiscation of Vatican properties in Europe, and an explanation to the laity of the Pope's desire to define a new doctrine regarding the Immaculate Conception of Mary, the unique circumstance of her birth without original sin. (This letter anticipates the official declaration of the doctrine, which was made by Pius IX in 1854.)

The subdued and brief nature of these letters may reflect the bishops' desire to refrain from attracting public attention in the light of recent events. Three days of rioting in Philadelphia had occurred after Bishop Francis Patrick Kenrick was granted permission for Catholic students in public schools to use their own version of the Bible. In spite of his reliance on the protection of municipal authorities, shots were fired, and two churches and dozens of Irish homes were burned in May 1844.[79] In New York, Bishop John Hughes was seeking public funds for parochial schools because the King James version of the Bible was compulsory reading in public schools. That city escaped similar consequences only because Hughes took it upon himself to arm and station Catholic men around each church.[80] The letters may also reflect a loss of vitality, as the bishops confronted civil unrest, ethnic dissension, and limited resources for burgeoning populations in the waning days of the provincial councils.

THE PLENARY COUNCILS, 1852–1884

The provincial councils had been functional forums for the bishops as long as dioceses were subordinate to Baltimore, but as the number of dioceses increased in response to the swelling population and geographic expansion, a more formal and encompassing convocation became desirable.[81] While provincial councils dealt with matters pertaining to a single province, the nation had outgrown such an arrangement, and legislation passed by a plenary council would apply to all the dioceses of the nation.

The Americanization of the hierarchy continued to be an issue during the mid-nineteenth century. Convening at the First Plenary Council in 1852 were six foreign-born archbishops, seventeen foreign-born bishops, but only nine bishops born in the U.S.[82] The chief prelates of a number of major cities were of Irish birth, as was Archbishop Kenrick of Baltimore, who was considered the leading U.S. theologian and who turned down the opportunity to become the first American cardinal because he felt it should be a native-born American.[83] The Vatican delayed naming a cardinal for the nation until 1875, when the first holder of the title became John McCloskey, archbishop of New York, who was born in the U.S. (1:167).[84]

The pastoral letter of 1852 (1:173–184), issued after the close of the First Plenary Council, maintains this nationalistic emphasis. Like earlier letters, the pastoral is arranged topically, beginning with a reference to episcopal authority conferred by this national council (1:173–175). That the issue of ownership of Church property continues to plague the bishops is evident in their insistence that gifts for divine service or maintenance of the clergy, once given, are no longer under the control of the donor (1:175–176). The central focus of the letter is on the territorial expansion that necessitated stretching already thin resources to provide sacraments and essential instructions to both rural immigrants and those on the frontier:

> The wants of the Church in this vast country, so rapidly expanding in population and prosperity, impose on us, your pastors, and on you, our children in Christ, peculiar and very arduous duties. We not only have to build up the Church, by the preaching of the Gospel, and the inculcation of all the virtues it teaches, but also to supply the material wants of religious worship in proportion to the unexampled rapidity with which our flocks increase (1:177).

Hospitals, schools, missions, orphanages, and seminaries are mentioned as being in urgent need, and sections are devoted to the critical need for priests (1:178–179) and schools (1:179–180). An extended exhortation to convince Americans of Catholic acceptability by advocating civil and orderly behavior is especially poignant in its tacit acknowledgment of the conditions under which Catholic immigrants lived. Poverty, drinking, and disorder had become associated with urban ethnic enclaves in ways distinct from those of earlier rural settlements.[85] Therefore, the letter reminds Catholics to be aware of how their actions affect social acceptance of their faith:

> Show your attachment to the institutions of our beloved country by prompt compliance with all their requirements, and by the cautious jealousy with which you guard against the least deviation from the rules which they prescribe for the maintenance of public order and private rights. Thus will you refute the idle babbling of foolish men, and will best approve yourselves worthy of the privileges which you enjoy, and overcome, by the sure test of practical patriotism, all the prejudices which a misapprehension of your principles but too often produces (1:181).

Similar exhortations are given in specific addresses to the clergy: "To our action, even more than to our words, do the faithful look up for the rule they are to follow, the example they are to imitate" (1:182); to women religious, "the flower and ornament of the Church," who are "to keep their lamps filled with the oil of good works" (1:182); and to the laity, "our joy and our crown," to live as good examples in order to refute public calumny (1:183).

The pastoral of 1852 focuses on the survival of Catholics in terms of protection from nativists and provision of the sacraments and instruction in the faith, to the exclusion of social issues. The notable restraint from involvement in social reform movements by the bishops was based on their preoccupation with the civic and economic survival of their members.[86]

In spite of the growing political tension over the abolition of slavery, the pastoral is silent on the subject. Reasons cited for the Church's disengagement from public debate in the ongoing controversy over slavery were the Church's position that gradual emancipation was a preferable solution, individual bishops had opposing stances in support of their own regions, and the bishops did not want to take a position on political questions.[87] There was also at that time no doctrinal support, encyclical, or specific social teaching of the Church that gave the bishops precedent for opposition.[88]

For Peter Guilday, the Church refrained from participation because of the movement's nativist leadership: "The anti-Catholic and Abolition movements may be said to have walked hand-in-hand."[89] Robert Emmett Curran concurs that Catholics in both the North and South associated the abolition movement with nativism but characterizes the bishops' aloofness as a defensive strategy: "Self-preservation became a priority. The bishops as a group concentrated on private behavior rather than social ethics. Except for the area of public education, the bishops foreswore any activity that could be deemed political."[90] Ellis characterizes as wise the freedom of political action left to Catholics by the hierarchy, given the opposing alignments of bishops, the Catholic press, clergy, and residents conforming to the loyalties of the communities in which they lived.[91] The silence of the bishops on the topic of slavery can also be seen as a rhetorical strategy of demonstrating loyalty to American ideals by declining to dictate political positions for their membership, as well as an acknowledgment of their own inability to reach consensus. Other denominations were splintered by opposing stands over slavery; Catholic focus during this period remained on establishing uniformity and avoiding schism.

The pastoral letter of 1852 concludes with directions for its public reading in all the churches (1:183), the first time such direction was provided; it indicates the desire of the bishops that their statement be accessible to all their members, including the illiterate.

The Second Plenary Council had been scheduled for 1862, ten years after the previous council. Because of the Civil War, however, it was postponed until 1866. At the end of the war, Martin Spalding, archbishop of Baltimore, named as the papal delegate to preside over the council, moved quickly to convene in order to reinforce the unity of the American bishops and to replace the nation's rudimentary code of canon law.[92] Rome had submitted a list of concerns to be dealt with: providing uniform ecclesiastical discipline, filling episcopal vacancies, implementing the legislation of previous councils, dealing with priests not attached to a place or group, educating seminarians, establishing feast and fast days, and care of former slaves.[93]

At the meeting held between October 7 and 20, 1866, at Baltimore's Cathedral of the Assumption were seven archbishops, thirty-eight bishops, three abbots, and more than a hundred theologians, the largest ecclesiastical assembly in the history of the American Church thus far. President Andrew Johnson himself attended the final session of the council. The ability of the clergy to remain largely disengaged from the recent hostilities and the assistance they provided to both sides of the conflict had helped to dissociate them from the bitterness left by the war.[94]

The work of this council was focused on creating ecclesiastical legislation that would provide consistency within the entire nation. "The Baltimore Council of 1866 gave . . . the opportunity to express the teaching of the Church in a form more accommodated to the American scene. . . . In form, approach, and selection of topics, the doctrinal portions of the conciliar decrees reflected the concerns of the Church in the New World."[95]

The pastoral letter that followed, however, barely mentions the new legal codes. Instead, it opens with a long peroration on the authority of the bishops and the need for obedience to them (1:185–190), emphasizing the binding nature of plenary decrees and the bishops' authority to define "the truths of faith" and resolve controversies. The letter goes on to assert their prerogative to warn "the flock of Christ by seasonable admonitions, against whatever might interfere with the purity of Christian morals, and by rebuke and reprehension, when they are found necessary for the correction of abuses" (1:190). Such a statement strongly asserted the collegial authority of the bishops; they could go beyond narrow internal matters to comment on broader social and material conditions affecting moral life. The bishops then assert this new authority to make the following statement: "Hence, when we warn you, either collectively, as in the present instance, or singly in our respective dioceses, to avoid secret societies and all associations which we deem unlawful, you cannot, on the peril of your souls, disregard our admonitions" (1:190).

Pastoral custom continues with a refutation of nativists:

> The enemies of the Church fail not to represent her claims as incompatible with the independence of civil power. . . . So far are these charges from fact, the authority and influence of the Church will be found to be the most efficacious support of the temporal authority by which society is governed (1:191).

The letter laments that while some states have allowed Church ownership of property, many others continue to deny such rights, an "expression of mistrust of ecclesiastical power, as such" (1:192).

Means of coping with exterior conditions is also evident in sections dealing with marriage and the regulations regarding divorce ("successive polygamy"), consanguinity ("founded in well ascertained physiological principles"), and mixed marriages ("the danger of perversion, to which the Catholic party and the offspring of such marriages are exposed" [1:196]). Similarly, the pastoral warns that religious books must be certified by clergy as free from error, thus calling for a Catholic press (1:197–198). Concerns are expressed about the education and delinquency of young people (1:199–200), "the want of zealous priests" (1:200–201), and amusements of the laity, including dances, fairs, and picnics, which "are fraught with the greatest danger to morals" (1:202). Supervised Catholic associations and societies are offered as wholesome alternatives (1:203). Nuns, clergy, and emancipated slaves merit brief paragraphs prior to the conclusion (1:203–205).

The inability of the bishops to respond with a definitive plan for ministering to the nation's newly emancipated slaves proved disappointing to the bishops' contemporaries, as well as to subsequent generations.[96] European interest in the aftermath of the Civil War indicated that this concern had created widespread interest. A. Niedermayer, a European observer who produced a report of the 1866 council for those Catholics of Austria and Germany who were providing financial help to the American missions, hints at the interest and frustration over the question of former slaves:

> We have every reason to believe that the Negro question was one of the principal topics of discussion at the Council. But we can learn no details . . . much as we may desire it. Only in general terms does the pastoral letter speak of the new field . . . that has been opened up by the emancipation of the great Negro population of the South. The fathers think also that a system of gradual emancipation would have been more beneficial.[97]

Catholics of other nations were interested in the activities of the American prelates, because "American Catholics will, as far as numbers are concerned, take first rank at all general Catholic councils."[98] Niedermayer's acknowledgment of the significance of the American Church while it was still mission territory presages the international influence that it would come to have.[99]

A Pause in Pastorals

Only three pastoral letters were produced in the second half of the nineteenth century. The first preceded the Civil War in 1852, while the second followed the war in 1866. However, as decrees became uniformly codified, the urgency for bishops to convene in council eased. Delay in holding meetings was also occasioned by the daunting nature of travel as the nation grew. Territorial expansion to the west created formidable obstacles in terms of distances and time. For bishops of the western frontier to attend meetings in Baltimore required "four weeks of constant traveling for one week of hasty deliberation."[100]

However, there were other reasons to account for the lapse in addressing the laity, factors that involved Church politics both nationally and internationally. One element that may have contributed to a reluctance to call a national meeting stemmed from the antipathy to foreigners that confronted each immigrant wave. As immigrations began to shift from English and

Nordic settlers to more "foreign" southern and eastern Europeans, the influx caused a resurgence of anti-Catholicism, organized under a nativist group, the American Protective Association (APA). Public knowledge about pastoral letters was widespread enough for anti-Catholics to understand their significance, so much so, in fact, that the APA published fabricated pastoral letters alleged to be from the American hierarchy to their membership. The purported letters called upon American Catholics to form a "Papal Party," whose purpose was to "plot and labor for the absolute supremacy" of the pope. While less virulent than the Know-Nothing Party, its political counterpart earlier in the century, the APA, besides issuing the false pastorals mentioned above, also tried to pass off a papal encyclical purporting to exhort all Catholics to rise up at an appointed time and claim the country for the pope.[101]

These trends created in the bishops a desire to avoid drawing public attention to themselves and their Church. When John McCloskey was named archbishop of New York in 1864, he wrote to Martin Spalding, archbishop of Baltimore, "I hope we have no cardinal's hat in this country. We are better without one."[102] Ironically, McCloskey was named the first American cardinal in 1875.

The American bishops feared that the introduction of a cardinal and the new doctrine of papal infallibility that had been recently defined would fuel anti-Catholic sentiment. However, their deeper troubles came instead from a different source—their own Church.

During this period, despite coping with the heavy demand for religious and social services at home, the bishops were diverted, and divided, by tensions preoccupying the international Church. Several trends occurring within both the American and the universal Church were exacerbating factionalism. As with slavery, by avoiding meetings the American bishops were protected from directly confronting the opposition and hostility that they were experiencing. This antagonism stemmed in part from two schools of thought regarding the future of the Church, both in Europe and in the United States.

After the burst of nationalistic uprisings in Europe in the mid-century, the Church began to lose its role as a center of influence within the new civic states. Bismarck was waging a *Kulturkampf* ("culture war") in Prussia to disentangle the Church from German life.[103] Italy was under the secular control of Victor Emmanuel.[104] Some French and German intellectuals considered papal authority to be a bulwark against these growing movements toward nationalism and secularism and advocated a strong and infallible papacy to preserve the political order. The growth of this "ultramontane" movement (stressing close and central control by Rome over internal Church affairs) led Pope Pius IX to call the First Vatican Council in 1870. It became clear that the purpose of the worldwide council was to affirm the dogma of papal infallibility, which means that the Roman pontiff, by virtue of his supreme apostolic authority, cannot err when he defines a doctrine concerning faith or morals to be held by the whole Church. The liberal bishops of France and Germany found themselves allied with the American contingent and the Austro-Hungarian bishops in opposing infallibility, but their numbers were too small to affect the vote.[105] Fifty bishops showed their disagreement by abstaining from voting.[106] Thus tensions between an authoritarian papacy were colliding with increasing expressions of independence by European and American prelates. To be both Catholic and American was not, after all, very compatible, creating the uneasy posture of being "too Roman for the native Protestants and too American for Rome."[107]

Ethnic Tensions

Dissensions among the various ethnic groups comprising the American Catholic Church had not subsided with the passage of time. The eventual eclipse of French bishops by Irish prelates, especially in the urban centers of the East, was not an experience granted to other Catholic groups with significant population growth. Few Polish, Italian, Mexican, French Canadian, or Slav bishops were appointed, despite the percentage of their populations. For Germans and French Canadians, preservation of their language was a crucial component in preserving their faith.[108] German migration toward rural areas in the Midwest, where their native tongue was used in schools and churches, contrasted with that of the Irish, who eschewed farming and preferred the industrial cities of the East and whose native language was already English.[109] In spite of their number (two million by 1900), Germans were eclipsed by Irish because the latter's integration was fostered not only by language but by the permanence of their migration (returning home was not an option) and by the great numbers who entered religious life.[110]

The emphasis on assimilation found in the pastoral letters throughout this period is a reflection of the Irish-dominated episcopacy and is at odds with German and Polish preferences.[111] O'Brien points out, "A policy of Americanization was far more attractive to the dominant Irish-American wing of the hierarchy than it was to people from continental Europe."[112] Moreover, Irish Catholicism was characterized by what Jay Dolan calls a "hierarchical model," which had a submissive laity and an authoritarian clergy, unlike the German and Polish "congregational" model, which had an active laity with a cooperative clergy.[113] The Irish model of church as "pray, pay, and obey"[114] or "hatch, match, and dispatch" (referring to the basic rites of baptism, marriage, and burial)[115] tended to color the view of the American Church as a monolithic institution.[116]

Different views about the parochial school system (extremely important to the Germans) versus making accommodation with the public schools (acceptable to the Irish) became a field of battle.[117] The clash led to appeals to Rome for separate national churches for Germans, Poles, Slovaks, and Lithuanians.[118] Europeans (because of the funds they sent to assist the American missions) and the pope became embroiled in the fray. In the end the parochial system of education prevailed, but without being made mandatory for Catholic families. National churches were denied, while ethnic parishes were accommodated, with deleterious consequences: "As these parishes proliferated, the common elements previously experienced by Catholic parishioners regardless of their different European backgrounds were weakened."[119]

These issues reflected the changing nature of the American Church:

> During the course of the nineteenth century, Catholicism changed from a small, relatively homogeneous community in terms of nationality and class to a large, radically diverse population made up of people from at least twenty-eight nationalities situated at various levels of the social and economic hierarchy. . . . Unity in the church had been a keenly sought-after objective since the middle of the nineteenth century, and the increasing fragmentation of the church only intensified this rage for unity and order. This meant not only unity of belief, but also a uniform standard of religious practice.[120]

The reluctance of American bishops to confront their lack of internal unity had caused them to avoid calling a convocation since the 1866 meeting. The Third and final Plenary Council of the century was finally initiated by the Vatican, which wanted the American Church to organize its various regulations. As a non-Catholic country, a number of exceptions had to be made to standard Church law, requiring constant appeals to Rome and creating delay and disorder. Thomas McAvoy speculates that Rome was also influenced by the recalcitrance of the Americans on the infallibility issue, even though they afterward had all signed a letter of fidelity.[121] Besides seeking to test their loyalty, the Holy See was prompted by the 6.25 million Catholics in the nation by 1880 and their resulting ethnic tensions, numerous appeals from American priests against their bishops in struggles over authority, and the clear reluctance to convene a council.

As early as March 1883, American bishops visiting Rome were questioned about domestic problems; in June of that year they were summoned to a meeting to be held in Rome in November to set a council agenda. Seeing this as an opportunity to "Romanize" the American Church, the Vatican presented a distinctly Roman set of proposals, which the Americans were able to reframe in American terms.[122] Because of this, the bishops had no choice but to brave the lack of harmony within their ranks by convening a council in 1884.

The Pastoral of 1884

Finally assembled together again after nearly two decades, the bishops focused their council work on national rules for Church conduct and doctrinal uniformity. The legislation created was called "the Magna Carta of American Church life."[123] It was characterized by the London *Month* as having "so much comprehensiveness, so much largeheartedness . . . such a thoroughgoing practical American character stamped on every line."[124] However, this work, while acknowledged in the pastoral, was not elaborated upon.

The opening sentence of the century's final pastoral begins with a reference to the unusual time span that has elapsed since the previous joint pastoral was issued:

> Full eighteen years have elapsed since our predecessors were assembled in plenary council to promote uniformity of discipline, to provide for the exigencies of the day, to devise new means for the maintenance and diffusion of our holy religion, which should be adequate to the great increase of the Catholic population (1:209).

This statement capsulizes the intent of the nineteenth-century pastoral letters —pragmatic, dealing with current issues, and concerned about accommodating the swell of immigrants, in terms of both resources and assimilation. Fitting Catholic immigrants into American life was a two-edged sword. Civic patriotism was a theme repeated by the Irish authors of the letters, who simultaneously guided Catholics away from secular values. The introduction also contrasts the dramatic revolution from frontier to factory within the century. An almost lyrical passage evokes the nation's changes: "The wilderness has exchanged its solitude for the hum of busy life and industry . . . forests have given way to cities" (1:209).

The bishops then inform their readers about the Vatican Council that had been held fifteen years previously and explain the doctrine of infallibility that had been adopted. Although the letter refrains from revealing their opposition to the measure, they manifest their concerns about its effect on the American public through an effusive repudiation about doubts of their loyalty to the nation versus the papacy: "We think we can claim to be acquainted both with the laws, institutions, and spirit of the Catholic Church, and with the laws, institutions, and spirit of our country; and we emphatically declare there is no antagonism between them" (1:215).

Lengthy and solemn, this pastoral (1:209–240) focuses on institutions and social forms. A section on the growth of the Church and its institutions attests to the massive changes the Church has undergone:

> The clergy and dioceses have multiplied; the hundreds of the faithful have increased to thousands and to millions; her churches, schools, asylums, hospitals, academies and colleges have covered the land with homes of divine truth and Christian charity. Not yet a century has elapsed since the work was inaugurated by the appointment of the first bishop in Baltimore, in 1789 (1:218).

To staff these immense enterprises, the bishops logically turn to the need for learning among the clergy and financial support for their training and maintenance. The education of the laity is also addressed: "Popular education has always been a chief object of the Church's care; in fact, it is not too much to say that the history of civilization and education is the history of the Church's work" (1:222). The bishops stress the importance of home life, the sanctity of marriage, and the importance of good reading as a basis not only for morality but also civic order: "Teach your children to take a special interest in the history of our country" (1:228). Temperance, which the Church did not categorize as a law of God but a virtue pleasing to God, is not required of Catholics.[125] Moderation is encouraged, as workers are told to avoid "drinking places on Saturday night" and "the practice of selling beer or other liquors on Sunday, or of frequenting places where they are sold" (1:232).

This peroration on the bad habits of workingmen leads to a discussion on secret societies, which reflect "the universal tendency to band together in societies for the promotion of all sorts of purposes. . . . They may band together for carrying out evil or dangerous as well as laudable and useful purposes" (1:233). The letter goes on to lament the need for secrecy but carefully avoids a blanket condemnation by quoting from the Second Plenary Council: "Care must be taken lest workingmen's societies, under the pretext of mutual assistance and protection, should commit any of the evils of condemned societies " (1:236).[126] As an alternative, the bishops discuss societies in which they desire to promote membership—parish confraternities, charitable associations, and temperance societies. They seek especially "to guard our Catholic young men against dangerous influences, and supply them with the means of innocent amusement and mental culture. It is obvious that our young men are exposed to the greatest dangers, and therefore need the most abundant helps" (1:237).

This pastoral reflects an anxious concern for the daily life of Catholic laborers in industrial America. Dealing with the pragmatic issues of drinking, labor organizing, and education are all attempts to steer people through the dangers of hopelessness and violence and to ensure maximizing opportunities for the following generation.[127] The letter seeks to guard the faith of the laity, but it does so in a tone that is fully cognizant of their environment and pressures. The bishops demonstrate a focus on social reform within the private lives of their own members, placing the onus of responsibility on their own behavior and forms of socializing.

Hugh Nolan calls the pastoral of 1884 "probably the most important" of all the Baltimore pastorals but is unclear as to his reasons.[128] Certainly the pastoral was highly influenced by, and reflective of, the strictures emanating from Rome. Previous pastorals reflected a rhetorical balance in which the bishops' attention to civic adaptation was paralleled by concern for their congregants' spiritual welfare in the midst of American cultural mores. In this letter the bishops once more reiterate the pastoral themes of parochial education and "double allegiance," the doctrine of cooperation between Church and State. However, in this case the tone is didactic, creating a stronger sense of separation than assimilation, perhaps reflecting the bishops' need to placate Rome. The bishops condemn rationalism, "teachers of skepticism and irreligion," who seek to undermine morality and foster unbelief (1:211). International affairs are referenced by the Church's compromised position in Prussia and Switzerland. Obedience to papal teaching authority and infallibility, clerical support, and the education of clergy and support of seminaries are exhorted. Written in a collective voice, the letter attempts to mask the growing friction among a group of powerful prelates, conservatives pitted against progressives, in a struggle that encompassed not only the bishops of this nation but their relationship with the Vatican.

The pastoral letter of 1884, signed by Cardinal James Gibbons of Baltimore, was to be the last produced until 1919, due to continued opposition between American liberal thinking and Rome-centered conservatism. The culmination would be the express condemnation of American enthusiasm by the Vatican and a subsequent silence that lasted until the following century.

The Suppression of Americanism

The issue of intellectual freedom in the Catholic Church originated with German liberals during the mid-1800s, when universities began to merge theological inquiry with new scientific developments. Their resulting method of applying objective investigation in the prevalent spirit of rationalism to the interpretation of scriptural texts was adopted by English scholars. This advance warred against that of the neo-Scholastics, who promoted a revival of medieval studies and advocated submission to traditional Church teaching. The *Syllabus of Errors,* promulgated by Pope Pius IX in 1864, listed eighty ideas, including rationalism, naturalism, forms of socialism that subjected the family to the state, and capitalism oriented solely toward profit. The Pontiff also excused himself from reconciling with "progress, liberalism and modern civilization."[129]

In the meantime, a coterie of bishops began to develop an understanding of Church that originated in the United States and was imbued with the Puritan sense of America as a beacon to the world. In this concept, the separation of Church and State was upheld as a model of ideal freedom for both institutions. Additionally, a new historical consciousness promulgated a sense of progressive development through time, which applied also to the Church. This contrasted with the static immutability that had always been its hallmark. The progression would, by implication, require adaptation— to modern society. The archbishop of Peoria, John Lancaster Spalding, articulated the stance that "the Catholic church must fit herself to a constantly changing environment, to the character of the people, and to the wants of each age."[130] A particularly American concept was that of an immanent God acting in history and revealed through humanity's development. Movement and change through time were therefore the fruition of God's kingdom.[131]

Some of these ideas had their origin in the writings of Isaac Hecker, a mid-nineteenth-century American convert (and founder of the Paulists, an order whose mission focused on communication), who argued that Catholic theology was not responsive to the times and culture of the world. Authority should not be the central focus of religion, and without reconciliation with contemporary demands for freedom, widespread conversions would not occur. It was the task of Catholicism to connect the aspirations of the age and of human nature to universal revelation, a dynamic task that called for science, freedom, and progress.[132]

Supporters of this concept were distinct and easily identified. Besides Spalding, who was the force behind the establishment of Catholic University, John Ireland was the best known prelate.[133] Archbishop of St. Paul, Ireland was a prolific speaker and national figure, proclaiming, "[T]he Church must herself be new, adapting herself in manner of life and in manner of action to the conditions of the new order."[134] Close associates in these beliefs were John Keane, bishop of Richmond, who became the first rector of the new Catholic University, and Denis O'Connell, who headed the North American College for seminary training in Rome. Cardinal Gibbons of Baltimore remained more neutral due to his position as unofficial leader of the hierarchy, but he supported Archbishop Ireland in spirit.[135]

This desire to mold the Church to modern life was an attempt to articulate a purpose of mission for the Church beyond its mere presence. These men were not seeking to rebel against Rome but were struggling to reconcile their American views with a Roman sense of a transcendent Church, aloof from place or time.[136] Ranged against these mostly Irish and zealously nationalistic liberal bishops were a group of equally dedicated conservatives: Michael A. Corrigan, archbishop of New York, Bernard J. McQuaid, bishop of Rochester, and most of the German prelates. These men were more "Roman" than American, defending the authority and order of an institution in no need of modification and highly suspicious of anything smacking of concordance with Protestant American thought. Because they saw the secular world as contaminating and materialistic, they were wary of government and other institutions.[137] Thus the tensions among ethnic groups, while it continued, coalesced into theological and ecclesiastical ideologies.

The separation between these perspectives became more concrete and hardened after the council of 1884. As Dolan says of the bishops, "Conflict was inevitable, and for the last fifteen years of the nineteenth century, liberals and conservatives engaged in a series of bitter controversies."[138] The issue crossed the Atlantic, exacerbated by the French, for whom it fueled their own divisiveness. The tempest began when a biography of Hecker was translated into French, preceded by a preface extolling freedom and democracy's effect on the Church. This created an ideological furor in Europe. Labeled "Americanism" by the French and brought to the attention of the Vatican, Catholic intellectuals waited to see if the Vatican would condemn Hecker and his sense of democratic progression.[139] A letter by an American observer emphasized, "All the continent is now palpitating with these two ideas. The newest effort of the enemy . . . [is] to assert that the whole movement is towards Protestantism."[140] The enemy in this case was conservative Catholics.

The furor eventually required Pope Leo XIII to comment. In his apostolic letter of January 22, 1899, *Testem Benevolentiae,* addressed to the American bishops and people, the Pope expresses his desire "to put an end to certain contentions which have arisen lately among you, and which disturbed the minds, if not of all, at least of many, to the no slight detriment of peace."[141] Pope Leo specifies that such modifications are determined only by the universal Church and not by the will of the individual:

> The rule of life which is laid down for Catholics is not of such a nature as not to admit modifications, according to the diversity of time and place. . . .
> [I]t has never disregarded the manners and customs of the various nations

which it embraces. . . . But this is not to be determined by the will of private individuals, who are mostly deceived by the appearance of right, but ought to be left to the judgement of the Church.[142]

He goes on to take issue with Hecker's notion of immanent spirit, repudiating any sense of "Americanism" that calls for a Church different from the Roman model.[143] Thus the "culturally affirmative impulses" within the Church were quashed.[144]

The condemnation was a devastating blow to the progressives. While the liberals sent letters of submission to the Pope, privately they commented on the exaggeration that had been applied to what was primarily a social concept of religion.[145] Following the debacle, professors in seminaries and theology schools were compelled to take an oath of anti-modernism. The resulting chill on American Catholic intellectual inquiry persisted long into the twentieth century.[146]

Chapter Two
The Twentieth Century: 1919–1980 ═══════════════

FOR THE PAST CENTURY, AS THE VOICE OF THE INSTITUTIONAL CHURCH in the United States, the bishops asserted the ability of Catholics to balance the obligations of citizenship with the demands of their faith. By the First World War, American Catholics had built a proud record of military service and patriotic support in several conflicts. Therefore, the bishops felt able, in spite of continued nativist hostility, to legitimize their collective work through creation of a permanent office in Washington, D.C. This national presence and the cultural absorption of Catholics into a nation that was becoming a global power served to advance the bishops' aspirations for pastoral discourse to new dimensions. Social reform characterized documents of the early decades, the war years immersed the pastorals in international affairs, and the social activism preoccupying the nation was reflected in the pastorals of the 1960s and 1970s. Although the thrust of the pastorals was still fragmented, this era established themes that would be brought to fruition in the 1980s.

The irregular convening of councils in the nineteenth century had limited the bishops' output to a total of eleven documents. As seen in the previous chapter, those pastorals were encyclopedic commentaries on a variety of pressing topics dealing with Catholic adaptation to American life. With the advent of the twentieth century, significant changes in the frequency, scope, and style of the pastoral letters occurred.

This chapter explains how a new style of pastoral discourse materialized to provide commentary on American national policy. The pastorals of the new century take a different tack from earlier ones, which were effusive about patriotism and exhorted preservation of the faith. In contrast, the letters of the new century turn from a defensive stance to an offensive one. After the First World War, the bishops felt emboldened to broaden the scope of their discourse to encompass more than their views on the morality of American norms; now they began to directly address aspects of national public policy. The bishops of the twentieth century emerged from a long period of silence and showed a new confidence in their public voice.

THE NEW CENTURY

The previous chapter closed with an account of the long hiatus in pastoral production—only two pastorals were written in over fifty years. The tensions among ethnic and intellectual factions, competing ideologies, and Vatican pressures had caused the American Church to withdraw from public attention. With the commencement of the First World War, however, the bishops found themselves in the familiar position of being forced to make protestations of Catholic patriotism.

The alliances of the war made allegiance a difficult issue for immigrant Catholics. The many citizens of German extraction, the Eastern Europeans who had belonged to the Austro-Hungarian Empire, and the Irish with their anti-British bias—all had apparent reasons for conflict in their loyalties.[1] Thus the bishops had an urgent task in demonstrating the patriotism of their members. Public officials had solicited the hierarchy to encourage Catholic support for the war effort.[2] The bishops actively promoted various war drives.[3] The proliferation of efforts around the nation attested to the eagerness of Catholics to participate, and eventually a national umbrella agency was needed to serve as a clearinghouse for various Catholic resources.[4] It was proposed that a National Catholic War Council be established to coordinate war relief efforts. The bishops approved the idea in November 1917.[5] Twenty-seven societies and sixty-eight dioceses convened in Washington in 1917 to divide work among committees staffed by priests and lay people under an administrative committee of bishops. The organization was so successful that it became the accredited contact point with the government, dealing with canteen services, orphans, refugees, and bond drives.[6] According to Elizabeth McKeown, the national mobilization brought a "new degree of recognition to the Catholic population within the nation."[7]

Establishment of a national organization was significant for several reasons. First, the bishops had refrained from displaying a national presence in the past due to the persistence of nativist hostility, which made it preferable to avoid attracting public attention. Now, as a coordinating agency for war efforts, they had a legitimate reason for their presence in the nation's capital. Moreover, the existence of a bureaucracy created a unified Catholic presence that represented an American Church working with national purpose, overcoming the factionalism of previous decades.[8] The War Council "gave a new sense of Catholic strengths in the American political system. Their efforts were given much positive publicity; their representatives enjoyed unusual access to public officials in Washington."[9] Such publicity was a positive counterpoint to the public silence the Church had maintained in previous decades due to the nativist resurgence of the Ku Klux Klan and the admonishments from Rome about "Americanism" and "modernism," which condemned any movement to adapt the Church to contemporary culture.[10]

Those factors continued to create wariness in the bishops about bringing attention to themselves when the war ended shortly thereafter. However, a proposal to continue the National War Council's existence could be justified by the need to have a national forum to lobby for Catholic interests. Thus the idea of a making the National War Council a permanent bureaucracy rather than continuing the tradition of convening bishops at ad hoc national councils was vigorously debated. A permanent organization was an anomalous structure in Catholic ecclesiology. Under Church law, each bishop constitutes the highest authority of his own diocese and is under the direct jurisdiction of the Vatican. No other country had a national organization, because of the potential for infringing on the prerogatives of an individual bishop or the pope.[11] Supporters of the concept maintained that the Church "could not afford to be out of sympathy with American democratic instincts if Catholicism was to be of significant influence in the culture. The tone of this response indicates a new sense of corporate power among those who supported the Council."[12]

Recognizing that the Church's influence in American affairs was less than proportional to the number of Catholics constituting the population, the senior prelate, Cardinal Gibbons, supported the idea.[13] Therefore, at an annual meeting of bishops in September 1919, the decision was made to create a permanent episcopal organization that would provide a focal point for the nation's large body of bishops and coordinate their representation to the government and their responses to proposed legislation.[14] The word "War" in the title was changed, so the organization became the National Catholic Welfare Council (NCWC). The structure of the agency would continue as a series of committees overseen by a rotating central administrative board of five bishops, who would report to the entire body of bishops at their annual meeting in Washington.

THE NEW ORGANIZATION

The new organization began its existence precariously. The decision to ratify the proposal for a national council had not been unanimous. Those bishops opposed to the idea as an infringement on their own authority immediately petitioned Rome. McKeown points out that some American bishops feared that the combined strength of the bishops would decrease American loyalty to Rome.[15] John Tracy Ellis attributes their motives to fears that the council constituted an invasion of their jurisdictional authority.[16]

Although the reigning pontiff of the time, Benedict XV, had granted tentative approval in April 1919 to the idea of an annual national meeting of bishops, the intervention of the dissenting American bishops and their supporters in Rome persuaded him to withdraw his consent. However, he died in January 1922 before fulfilling that intention. In February his successor, Pope Pius XI, to comply with his predecessor's intent, put his signature on the decree that would dissolve the organization. When word reached the administrative board, they hurriedly dispatched the bishop of Cleveland, Joseph Schrembs, to Rome, where he successfully presented the supporting case. His petition pointed out that "the authoritative voice of a united episcopate" could become an effective voice with "public men."[17] Papal approval was finally granted in July 1922, with the proviso that the title change from "Council" (which conveyed a specific level of authority under Church law) to "Conference."[18]

The success in establishing the NCWC as a national organization signaled the Church's further adaptation to American ways. Richard Linkh calls it a force for assimilation: "After the war, with the organizational machinery of the NCWC at their command, Catholics became a major factor in immigration welfare work and in 'Americanization' programs designed to teach new arrivals the English language and the rudiments of American government."[19] Moreover, the organization was an innovation of the American Church that had a distinct effect on the frequency and scope of the pastoral letters. One reason was the delegation of responsibilities possible with standing committees. Another was the hiring of permanent staff who could provide continuity and follow-up to administrative assignments. Finally, the conference provided a central forum for bishops who had been beset by factionalism.

However, the change in the direction of American pastoral discourse would be affected by more than the structure of the organization. Its purpose was "welfare," a move that finally aligned the Church closer to the reform rhetoric of the Progressives. Not only was the new organization an innovation as an American Catholic institution, but it also demarcated a new era of involvement in public life. Joseph McShane attributes two significant impacts on the Church stemming from the war. The first, the creation of a central agency, fostered the ability of American Catholics to overcome their ethnic differences.[20] The second was "a heightened sense of Catholic identification with American ideals."[21] The merging of these forces sparked a new shift in discourse. "The social activists within the church, who had previously worked without portfolio, were able to capitalize on the church's new war-born unity with the reformist spirit."[22] These trends of unity, idealism, and public involvement in national issues, buttressed by the nation's validation of the Catholic war effort, emboldened the bishops to abandon their long public silence and embrace the Progressive rhetoric of reform.

Social Reform

The relationship of the American Church to social reform had been un-easy throughout the nineteenth century. The bishops had refrained from embracing the abolition of slavery for fear of fracturing their unity and alienating the substantial well-to-do Catholic populations in slaveholding areas such as Maryland, Louisiana, Kentucky, and South Carolina.[23] Mel Piehl also attributes the lack of Catholic support for abolition to the avoid-ance of politics and the assignment of responsibility for humane treatment to the individual.[24] Nor did the bishops address the issue of women's suf-frage. Similarly, while encouraging moderation in drinking and enforcement of liquor laws (see the pastoral letters of 1840 [1:135–137], 1843 [1:143–145], and 1884 [1:232]), the bishops did not officially support the temperance movement. Since wine was an integral part of the daily Eucharist, its exist-ence and use could not logically be condemned by the bishops. Moreover, because beer and wine were part of the culture of their German, Irish, and Italian congregations, making such alcoholic consumption illegal would have been contrary to the social customs of those ethnic groups. Catholic fears of socialism and government interference made moral persuasion and personal conversion the preferred Catholic solution.[25] The Church was too preoccupied with its own self-preservation and defense, leaving few re-sources to apply to concerns about "the wider social order."[26]

The same reasoning had applied to early efforts to ameliorate immi-grant poverty. In spite of court appeals, Catholic clergy were legally ex-cluded from entering public institutions to provide for the religious needs of orphans, hospital patients, or prisoners until 1879.[27] The pastoral of 1843 had complained that recipients of aid were required to attend Protes-tant worship services (1:141). Previous social outreach by the Church, therefore, had concentrated on establishing its own institutional struc-tures—hospitals, orphanages, schools, asylums.[28] A number of factors are cited by scholars for this separate system of assistance. Piehl describes Catholic sentiments about their treatment as a target of reformist leader-ship: "For many Protestant reformers, the Roman Catholic religion—no less than war or liquor or slavery—was one of the evils to be reformed out of American society."[29] The reasons for the wide network of Catholic schools, hospitals, and other institutions are summarized by Robert Cross: "Hostile to the Protestant majority, suspicious of governmental enterprise, and averse to the active, melioristic spirit of the times, these Catholics met secular culture so far as possible only on their own terms."[30]

Moreover, contact with secular society was to be minimized because the Church saw itself as a refuge from temporal concerns.[31] Rather than being organized advocates for public reform, Catholics tended to see opportunities to alleviate poverty as a personal spiritual benefit to the giver.[32] Jay Dolan points out that during the nineteenth century, most bishops leaned toward conservatism and a laissez-faire stance: "The vast majority were concerned more with charity than with justice, with parochial schools rather than labor unions."[33] However, as the new century unfolded, needs for change became pressingly evident in the urban ghettoes and the industrial workplaces that constituted life for the majority of Catholic immigrants.

Instead of joining Protestant efforts to pass new amendments as a legal route to improve living conditions, Catholics turned to the labor movement, which could allow workers to create their own social and economic progress. Unlike social reform efforts, labor reform had not become associated with Protestant endorsement.[34] Unions provided "in the ideologically safe American labor movement a religiously acceptable way to protect their interests."[35] The issuance of the papal encyclical *Rerum Novarum* elevated the Church's defense of labor from an expedient means of retaining worker loyalty to a matter of natural law and human rights.[36] In writing his encyclical, Pope Leo XIII legitimized for the Church the rights of labor to organize and the responsibility of the state to act for justice.[37] Bishops had come to realize that the labor movement formed the root from which economic progress could elevate their members.

At the turn of the century, more direct assistance to the poor began to be provided by individuals—priests, sisters, and lay persons—who founded settlement houses and soup kitchens and initiated home visits.[38] Lack of job security, unionization, and the threat of socialism "seemed to challenge the church to abandon her long-standing timidity with regard to social issues."[39] Dolan designates the labor movement as the catalyst for the Church's transformation from emphasizing charity to advocating social justice.[40] Much of this had to do with timing. The urbanization and industrialization of work in factories intersected with the peak of immigration. These new immigrants were those most affected by the appalling living conditions for those laboring in the mills, mines, and sweatshops.

Indeed, for many Catholics in the late nineteenth and early twentieth century, the phrase "social reform" simply meant labor and economic reform. The fact that American Catholicism could plausibly claim to be a defender of the rights of workers eventually came to be a proud index of its relevance to modern American society.[41]

This background explains the motives behind an extraordinary document that marks the bishops' entrance into the public arena in the twentieth century. Objectives for postwar social reconstruction were being proposed by a number of other institutions, and the bishops resolved to do likewise. While *The Bishops' Program for Social Reconstruction: A General Review of the Problems and Survey of Remedies,* described in the following section, was not itself a pastoral letter, it was a precursor to the pastoral that would follow in the same year. Its rhetorical management demonstrates a turn to a new style of public outreach and a new willingness to engage in public debate. The bishops' pride in the radical publication that resulted, and their desire to see to its promulgation, caused them to initiate a publicity campaign designed to enhance the Church's image in the public eye, a step that represented a remarkable departure from their previous reticence.

The Bishops' Program of Social Reconstruction

In an effort to address the needs of the new order of postwar life, the bishops assigned to a committee of their new organization the task of proposing a plan for reconstruction. In a move that would have repercussions for future pastoral statements, the committee created to formulate the statement invited lay representatives to participate: former government officials, professors of economics and political science. Staff for the committee also included members of various professions, labor, business, and women.[42]

The clear purpose was to educate the public mind, so that, as the chair of the committee, Msgr. Michael J. Splaine of Roxbury, Massachusetts, stated, "The legislator will reach a public opinion so crystallized that the public at large will not be satisfied with any system that is not fundamentally sound and capable of affecting good for the whole people."[43] This educational goal affected the format of the 1919 proposal and would have a marked influence on future pastorals, establishing the custom of providing a philosophical basis for Catholic social teaching as well as suggesting practical applications. But the document was also intended to be persuasive. Monsignor Splaine informed the bishops that its purpose "will be the influencing of the political, industrial and economic leaders of the country so that they may adopt all measures . . . safe and beneficial from a moral and religious standpoint."[44]

After the committee was unable to formulate any positive consensus (except to warn against radical agitation), the chair, under the pressure of a deadline, turned to another source. The final document was produced entirely by a single author, Monsignor John Ryan, based on a speech he was preparing.[45] However, Joseph McShane, who has provided a detailed historical account of these events, notes that Ryan, delighted by the opportunity to advance his agenda when the bishops of the administrative board placed their signatures on his work, consistently referred to the statement as the *Bishops' Program*.[46]

Ryan's document framed the principles evoked by Pope Leo XIII in *Rerum Novarum* but couched its proposals in Progressive rhetoric, thereby winning over both bishops and social activists.[47] His combination of philosophical reflection and specific objectives established a model that would be used in pastorals fifty years later. The dual rhetorical nature of the document contributed to the bishops' desire to make the value of the Church evident to the American public by establishing it as a source of moral guidance. Ryan's proposal "broke the long silence in social issues in a public and authoritative manner. . . . [I]t also helped remake the image of the church in industrial society."[48] The nature of the bishops' audience was mixed: church members, the government, and the American public as a whole.[49] Pastorals that followed the *Program* would follow its cue in addressing such multiple audiences.

To maximize knowledge of their recommendations, the bishops decided to disseminate their *Program* through an organized promotional campaign, utilizing aggressive public relations techniques. The bishops were persuaded by a prominent Catholic layman to hire a public relations firm.[50] An eight-part campaign included interviews and mailings to national publications, weekly magazines, foreign newspapers, agriculture, labor, and Catholic publications. The resulting coverage did not ensure a favorable reaction. As their publicist Larkin Mead predicted, "Knocks and Boosts are going to fly thick."[51]

Business interests viewed the *Program* as a radical departure from previous conservative Catholic positions and a betrayal of American principles. Industrialists questioned the bishops' competency and demanded a retraction.[52] The swift and vocal reaction of the business community raised the interest level in the bishops' statement, added to its publicity, and shook the public from its complacency in regarding the Church as guardian of the status quo. The reforms proposed represented a marked departure from the bishops' previous exhortations cautioning Catholic workers against labor unions and other radical notions. In contrast to nineteenth-century pastorals, this proposal was willing to challenge the existing American system. The *Program* "was rightly viewed as a forward looking document; it clearly and courageously called upon public authority to assume responsibility for social welfare, and for these reasons it had the power to encourage social thought and action."[53]

Moreover, for the first time the bishops deliberately broadened the circulation of their ideas to the general public, stirred public debate, and touched on issues of interest to the entire citizenry. Despite the anti-Catholicism that was still rampant, the bishops were willing to attract public attention, eliciting both criticism and praise. The publication of their views also garnered comment from academic circles. Pamphlets were sent to all the colleges and seminaries in the country to be discussed in class, and voluminous response resulted.[54] The result was that the *Bishops' Program* became more widely known than the sixty other proposals for postwar reconstruction then in circulation.[55]

The bishops' desire to emerge as the voice of moral authority in the public arena seemed fulfilled when publications such as *The Nation* acknowledged the bishops' leadership role: "The radical character of the pronouncements is in its treatment of the ethics of remuneration and industrial management, and the philosophy of its carefully worded statements marks the leaders of the church as among our advanced labor thinkers."[56] The *Program* advocated a legal minimum wage, as well as social insurances for illness, disability, old age, and unemployment.[57] Other innovations included proposals for government housing, a national employment agency, price controls, equal pay for women, and abolition of child labor. It also noted defects in the industrial system: waste in production and distribution, insufficient incomes for workers, and unnecessarily large incomes for a small minority of privileged capitalists.[58] Proposals were tiered for the near and distant futures. Aaron Abell comments that rather than being "radical," the proposed measures "were essentially remedial in character: they implied no radical change in the existing economic order, and they were attainable within a reasonable time. The 'more distant developments' . . . would permit and encourage the majority of workers to 'become owners, at least in part, of the instruments of production.'"[59]

The Pastoral Letter of 1919

The *Bishops' Program of Social Reconstruction*, despite its acclaim, had no legal or ecclesiastical authority. Moreover, the vituperative response from some Catholic sectors, particularly businessmen, concerned the bishops. The idea that the *Program* was perceived by the public as radical was worrisome to Cardinal Gibbons of Baltimore, the senior member of the hierarchy, who saw such reaction as a sign of the need for public education on Christian social principles.[60] Therefore, the status of the *Program*, which had been issued on February 12, 1919, was buttressed by the pastoral letter of 1919, which emerged from the NCWC's first annual meeting held in September of that year, the first plenary meeting since 1884.

Unlike the *Program,* the 1919 pastoral letter was a much more conservative document. Less specific than the sixteen-page reconstruction proposal (1:255–271), the sixty-one-page letter (1:272–333) provides a context of current social conditions through a lengthier, thorough explication of the state of the Church in America. According to Hugh Nolan, "In a departure from its predecessors, this Pastoral's theology shows a great concern for the alleviation of temporal problems, touching on practically every phase of human existence."[61]

This indication of a new phase of pastoral rhetoric as exercising public influence in a broader sphere set a precedent for the following decades. It established a new image and mission for the American Church, one in keeping with the new importance of the nation in world affairs. As of 1908, the missionary status of the Church in the United States had finally been lifted by Pope Pius X, so that it was no longer junior in rank to older, European Churches (1:275).[62] With the pastoral of 1919, the bishops no longer speak with a sense of subserviency, either as Catholic clergy or as American citizens.

The pastoral opens with a reminder of the thirty-five-year time span since the last letter. The ability to reconcile Catholicism with civic loyalty and the importance of the nation to the world are neatly underscored simultaneously: "In his name [Pope Benedict XV], and in our own, we greet you, dear brethren, as children of the Holy Catholic Church and as citizens of the republic on whose preservation the future of humanity so largely depends" (1:273). Note the usage of the direct salutation, emphasizing the epistolary nature of the document, a stylistic element which links the eighteenth- and nineteenth-century pastorals but which disappears after this. Documents issued in the following decades, although still categorized as joint pastoral letters, will be in the form of statements and essays.

The first section of the 1919 pastoral is devoted to internal matters: papal relations; the need for charity, for family prayer, and for those lost in the war; and attendance at services (1:273–284). The bishops warn of the danger of "shipwreck" to faith wrought by social ambition, by business or public career, or by the fallacy that "faith is hopelessly at variance with scientific truth" (1:278). The importance of Christian education at all levels, from the family home through university is extolled (1:283–286). An appeal for workers in Catholic charities and missions to persons of color, Indians, and foreign lands leads to an articulation of the need for vocations (1:287–292). This section echoes the familiar rhetoric of earlier pastorals in its exhortation toward devotion and support for Church activities.

The second section shifts to external affairs: "The temporal order, in the last thirty-five years has undergone radical changes" (1:294). In their rhetoric, a progressive notion of history manifests itself:

> During the first three decades of this period, the advance of civilization was more rapid and more general than in any earlier period. . . . The sound of progress, echoing beyond its traditional limits, aroused all the nations to a sense of their possibilities. . . . Toward this end the highest tendencies in the secular order were steadily converging. A wider diffusion of knowledge provided the basis for a mutual understanding of rights and obligations. Science, while attaining more completely to the mastery of nature, placed itself more effectually at the service of man. Through its practical application, it hastened material progress, facilitated the intercourse of nation with nation, and . . . made possible a fuller exchange of ideas, and thereby revealed to the various peoples of earth that . . . they had more in common than was generally supposed (1:294).

The importance of America as a beacon for others is stressed: "As this consciousness developed in mankind at large, the example of our own country grew in meaning and importance. For a century and more, it had taught the world that men could live and prosper under free institutions" (1:294).

It is in retrospect that we can better appreciate the letter's position as an intermediary between the multiple domestic issues written about in the pastoral of 1884 and the national and international issues that would concern subsequent letters. The bishops here reveal an early understanding of international effects and common cause among nations that would continue to be a theme in the following decades. While such thinking seems a matter of course at present, the isolationist mood of the nation then rampant makes their position in 1919 a prophetic anomaly.

The remainder of the letter focuses on all the tiers of society, in widening circles. The bishops begin with a justification of their role: "The state itself should be the first to appreciate the importance of religion for the preservation of the common weal. It can ill afford . . . to reject the assist-

ance which Christianity offers for the maintenance of peace and order"
(1:306). Social relations comprise a section, under which are addressed
marriage, home life, divorce, and a qualified endorsement of women's suf-
frage: "So far as she may purify and elevate political life, her use of franchise
will prove an advantage" (1:314).

After dealing with the home, the bishops turn to employment, the
rights of workers to organize, and the benefits of labor and trade unions
(1:314–319). The pastoral's endorsement of reconstruction reform is much
less specific than the objectives of the *Program*. For example, the *Program*
clearly asserts: "The general level of wages attained during the war should
not be lowered" (1:262), and "the majority of workers [must not] remain
mere wage earners [but] somehow become owners, or at least in part, of
the instruments of production" (1:269). The pastoral generalizes:

> The right to a living wage . . . is happily no longer denied by any consider-
> able number of persons. What is principally needed now is that its content
> be adequately defined. . . . In particular, it is to be kept in mind that a liv-
> ing wage includes not merely decent maintenance for the present, but also a
> reasonable provision for such future needs as sickness, invalidity, and old age
> (1:318).

The pastoral also reminds workers of mutual obligations, honest work,
openness to negotiation, and the rights of the public not to be inflicted with
unnecessary strikes (1:318–319).

Following comments on the nation's tasks, the importance of citizenship for immigrants, vigilance in politics, prudence in public office, and the
power of the press (1:319–323), the final section touches on the need for an
international peace organization and reiterates the critical interrelation-
ship between an educated populace and sound civil life (1:323–331).

The letter is sign by Cardinal Gibbons alone. McShane attributes to him
recognition of the need to disabuse the public of the notion that the *Program* was the work of a fringe element. "Gibbons was challenging his fellow
bishops to go on record as favoring the program. . . . Such an action
would buttress the document's claim to moral authority within the church
and solidify the church's new social image."[63] But the importance of the letter transcends its endorsement of the *Program*. Thomas McAvoy considers
it "the platform for Catholic activity during the next generation. . . . The
higher attainments of Catholics between the two wars were possible chiefly
because, for the most part, the leading Catholics followed this pastoral . . .
making good American citizens of Catholics."[64] Evoking the Church's role
in contributing a moral perspective to secular issues had begun.

BETWEEN THE WARS

In contrast to the plaudits received for Catholic efforts during and after war, the 1920s presented a series of setbacks for Catholic progress. A flare-up of nativist bias was spearheaded by the Ku Klux Klan.[65] Their success in obtaining enactment of the restrictive Johnson-Reed Immigration Act of 1924 closed the influx of newcomers to Ellis Island.[66] The campaign of Catholic Al Smith, governor of New York, for president in 1928 was met with a level of virulence that led Catholics to retreat from public life.[67] The accumulation of these events cast "a chill on American Catholic ambition."[68] Perhaps for these reasons, only one pastoral was produced in this decade.

Instead, the formats available to the bishops for their joint public utterances were expanded at this time. In lieu of lengthy pastoral letters, the administrative committee of the NCWC during this decade produced three concise position papers, all addressing issues outside the American Church. A brief statement in 1922 (1:334) deplores the growing bureaucracy of the federal system. In 1924 resolutions expressing sympathy were issued about the persecution of twenty million Catholics in Russia (1:335) and the expulsion of clergy in Guatemala (1:336).

The joint pastoral of the decade was written in 1926 about the suppression of the Church in Mexico (1:337–365).[69] The pastoral had two interesting facets. In the first section, in which the bishops establish their motives for protest, they emphasize their stance as speaking in support of both a Church and a State that are just. Based on overtly American as well as Christian principles, the letter is a treatise on rights and law that interweaves the Declaration of Independence and Thomas Aquinas. In the following section the bishops turn pragmatic, and in rebuttal to the massive Mexican confiscation of Church property, provide an account of the educational and social welfare benefits the Church had provided to the Mexican people (1:337–368). The pastoral elicited a letter of papal approval, endorsing the effectiveness of the NCWC.[70]

The 1930s provided ample opportunity for the bishops to comment on social disorder. In terms of action, however, American Catholic historians assign most of the responsibility for social justice and economic reform in this era primarily to individuals.[71] Piehl attributes to the "accumulated intellectual and institutional effects of the papal condemnation of Americanism and modernism" the difficulty "for official Catholicism to respond positively to the diverse social problems and forces in American culture."[72] In spite of the preponderance of lay and religious initiative in establishing social programs, the bishops were not remiss in speaking out in general terms.

The bishops' only statement in 1930, *On Unemployment* (1:366–368), confirms that they have moved beyond charity as a religious solution to the nation's economic position. In a strong foreshadowing of more developed pastorals, they here reveal their collective position regarding economic justice:

> More than temporary alms is necessary. Justice should be done. This unemployment returning again to plague us after so many repetitions during the century past is a sign of deep failure in our country. . . . Both in its cause and in the imprint it leaves upon those who inflict it, those who permit it, and those who are its victims, it is one of the great moral tragedies of our time (1:366).

An additional precursor of a pastoral on arms occurs in the *Statement on the Economic Crisis*, which appeared in 1931. Here the bishops prophetically blame the arms race for the waste of public wealth and stipulate their desire to provide not only spiritual sustenance but "the material food essential to life and well-being of the individual, of the family, of all society" (1:369).

The brief statements of 1932 confine themselves to the corruption of indecent literature ("Publishers repeatedly issue new books outdoing the old ones in obscenity"—1:371–372) and the proper use of time ("Government . . . does not protect its idle citizens; it leaves them to be the prey of the theater and movie house owner"—1:373).

The first major statement of the decade appeared in April 1933, entitled *The Present Crisis* (1:375–403). Here the bishops expand on the theme that would continue as a refrain throughout the pastorals—the interrelatedness of the world: "We have been witness of a great social and political catastrophe, the causes of which are not to be found in one place or in one nation, but in all places and among all peoples, and the effects of which are devastating and world-wide" (1:375). Even more striking, however, the bishops have begun to articulate the interconnectedness of social institutions and individual welfare, and the need for a moral compass to ensure the American ideal of justice for all. The cause for the current economic devastation, the bishops find, lies in the fact that

> in common with other nations, we have brought about our present unhappy conditions by divorcing education, industry, politics, business, and economics from morality and religion, and by ignoring for long decades the innate dignity of man, and trampling on his human rights. We have failed to realize that these rights are supreme so far as the purpose of human society is concerned; that they include . . . the means of a normal healthy life of mind and body . . . sufficient means to provide for himself. . . . And, when speaking of man as a social being, we mean men, women, and children . . . in a word, the human family (1:378).

The bishops go on to urge wider readership of economists, sociologists, and moralists who have studied the issues. They ask for fuller discussion by leagues, societies, and associations of the topics broached in the pastoral and provide for such discussion an array of possible social economic issues: security of bank deposits, remission of war debt, deceptive advertising, credit unions, gambling, probate of wills, farmers' cooperatives, dishonest stock promotion, mortgages, bribery, and price-fixing, to name a few. By encouraging readers to educate themselves, the bishops continue the trend begun in 1919 with their desire to contribute to a higher level of public participation through an understanding of social justice.

During the remainder of the decade, only brief statements were issued. However brief, the statements pull no punches. The *Statement on Family, Youth, and Business* of 1933 (1:404–407) blisters the "fraud, graft and corruption" of municipal government, the "extravagance" of state government, and the squandering of public money by Congress. However, the bishops do not hesitate to lay blame on the governed: "The people themselves are responsible for the kind of government they got." They reiterate their theme: "Before there can be any hope for a return to political liberty, social peace, or economic justice, the spiritual life of the nation must be renewed" (1:406).

In 1937 the bishops issued a *Statement on Social Problems* (1:422–425), which criticizes Communist propaganda and the struggle between the major labor unions, a theme echoed in their *Statement on Industrial and Social Peace* in 1938 (1:430–431). Over and over the bishops repeat the refrain: "Materialism excites greed. From greed stems hatred, rivalry, envy, the inviolable character of human war" (*Statement on Peace and War,* 1939, 1:434). To their colleagues abroad, the bishops extend expressions of support to the beleaguered bishops of Spain (1:416–418) and Germany (1:419–421) in 1937, and Poland (1:435) in 1939.

In 1940, in spite of international tensions, the bishops are still preoccupied with economic issues. A longer *Statement on Church and Social Order* (1:436–453) reiterates Church teaching on the moral aspects of trade and industry. Disclaiming involvement with technical business issues, the document contains sections about property and labor. Depicting the insecurity of those laborers who are reliant solely on uncertain wages, the bishops admonish: "This insecurity not only leads to the creation of a strong social tension expressing itself in social disorder, but is also contrary to the prescriptions of Christian morality" (1:443). McAvoy calls this statement of 1940 "one of the finest statements on social reconstruction published by the hierarchy of the United States but, coming as it did when the country was tending to be engrossed in the growing war, its fulfillment was delayed."[73] This issue of timing to gain public attention to their message was an aspect that would come to have increasing importance. Over time it became clear that the social context of the moment was responsible for the unevenness of the public's reception of the bishops' pronouncements. James Hennesey comments on the bishops' frustration after raising social issues between 1926 and the 1930s: "But public opinion did not change, and American Catholic criticism became more strident."[74] By 1940 the nation's attention had moved to events in Europe, and the Depression no longer took center stage.

WORLD WAR II AND ITS AFTERMATH

As social disorder mushroomed into global conflict, propelling the United States into the maelstrom of the Second World War, the bishops found more frequent need to voice their views on the moral concerns of the struggle. The pastoral letters began to appear with faithful regularity. Nolan points out that "from 1940 to the present there has been at least one pastoral letter or one general statement from the hierarchy annually, with the exception of 1965."[75] Henceforth the bishops, patriotically participating in both international and domestic issues, do not hesitate to address the ethical issues of governance.

Understandably, by 1941 peace is an overriding theme as war breaks out. That year the bishops justify their patriotic support at the same time as they call for peace by denouncing both Nazism and Communism in *Crisis of Christianity* (2:28–35). They justify this involvement in governance by referring to the necessity for freedom to exercise choice: "Our concern is the supreme interest of religion. . . . neither system understands nor permits freedom in its true Christian sense. Both systems usurp arbitrary power over the lives and destinies of men; their dictators assume a power which belongs to God alone" (2:31). The bishops thus desire a "just peace," which would allow for freedom of worship. In discussing the suffering peoples of invaded countries, the treatment of Jews is singled out for condemnation. The bishops go on to urge defense of the nation, respect for civil authority and the rights of others, and domestic sacrifice (2:33).

The bishops complete their statement with sections on labor, peace, and approval of labor unions. They recognize the difficulties of supporting a family and insist on the "inviolability of private property"; they condemn both unrestrained capitalism and Communism (2:34). Their final phrases again express concern about labor and workers' welfare and invoke the public weal with words such as "the common good of the country," "the general welfare," "national defense," "general public," and "unity among our citizens" (2:34–35). Aside from their pastoral, the bishops send a message that year to the President pledging their patriotic support of the war effort: "The historic position of the Catholic Church in the United States gives us a tradition of devoted attachment to the ideals and institutions of government" (2:36–37).

The letters issued during the war deal with philosophical observations on its contributing factors and the plight of human groups, both at home and abroad. The letters between 1942 and 1944 focus more on the internal injustices that jeopardize peaceful existence. The 1942 statement, *Victory and Peace* (2:38–43), justifies the necessity for the war but goes on to express grave concern for the moral welfare of working women and of young men in the military (2:39). Two sections are devoted to "the rights of our minorities," for whom the bishops ask respect, economic opportunities, and the ability to realize their hopes and ambitions (2:41). As more knowledge becomes available, they shift attention to persecuted groups outside the nation, with a longer and stronger section on the plight of Jews abroad than the previous year, expressing "a deep sense of revulsion" for deaths by reprisals and starvation, and sentencing to concentration camps (2:42).[76]

The letters of the mid-war years are surprisingly forward-looking, providing hope by attending to life after the war. Even in those dark days, with no assurance of victory, the bishops concentrate on future peace rather than present battle. *Essentials of a Good Peace*, the 1943 statement (2:44–49), focuses on philosophical doctrine rather than dwelling on the war. The bishops pinpoint the issues of civic life that can assist in maintaining peace. The letter opens by explaining their reasoning that the victors will be responsible for postwar reconstruction, but since the "sword cannot make peace," the basis for peace is the vision in the "minds and wills of the victors" (2:44). War has been caused by the lapse of moral law. The ideal of human brotherhood is from God; it does not mean surrender of individual nationhood but presents a "norm for the right ordering of the internal life of nations" (2:45–46). Sections follow on the lawlessness of youth, the importance of family, and "neopagan" views on marriage. The theme of justice and moral law culminates with another plea regarding the treatment of groups in our own country, for "fellow citizens of the Negro race," toward whom our history "imposes on us a special obligation of justice." The same generosity of spirit is asked "toward our fellow-citizens of Latin-American origin or descent"(2:48).[77] The bishops go on to establish the principal theme of the decade in the last sentence: "A first principle must be the recognition of the sovereignty of God and of the moral law in our national life and in the right ordering of a new world" (2:49).

By 1944 the bishops share the sense that the war is won, and their *Statement on International Order* already focuses on postwar conditions (2:56–61). Their demands anticipate both the Marshall Plan and the United Nations. Blaming "monstrous philosophies" that seek to distort the sense of the common good, the bishops urge economic assistance to avoid future grievances and the creation of new strife (2:57). Supporting the concept of an international organization, the bishops call for its members to guarantee innate human rights (2:58).

The immediate postwar years are spent drawing attention to the Soviet takeovers abroad and pointing out the polarization of ideologies that separate the Eastern and Western blocs. The statement of 1945, *Between War and Peace* (2:62–65), begins with an anguished claim, "The war is over, but there is no peace in the world." Lamenting the lack of a cohesive plan, the bishops protest Russian aggression in Eastern Europe. Their humanitarian focus during the early war years returns as they depict the dire need for relief efforts: "Millions will die from starvation and exposure this winter." They urge the United States, with its vast resources, to provide the major part of assistance. The bishops end by linking democracy to responsibility, "the heart and hand of America . . . vigorous champion of democratic freedom and the generous friend of the needy and oppressed throughout the world" (2:65). McAvoy points out that the difference between the 1945 and 1919 statements was that earlier the bishops had established the lead in proposing economic and social reforms, whereas at the end of the Second World War they offered only opposition—to Communism.[78]

The 1946 document, *Man and the Peace!* (2:67–73), returns to the themes of individual rights and civic society. The repudiation of basic human rights by the spread of Russian totalitarianism negates the whole reason for the recent war: "It persecutes the citizen who dares assert his native rights" (2:68). The bishops then address the massive postwar migrations of peoples by noting successive groups stranded by the war, prisoners of war, displaced persons and refugees, forced repatriations, and ethnic deportations. Again the bishops plead for continued relief efforts during the "hard, bitter winter" (2:69–71). They conclude that the public focus on the horrors of mechanized war, enemy brutality, and our use of atomic weapons should not overshadow

> the headlines in our daily press which even now tell of racial and religious persecution, of the transplantation of millions of people from one area to another and the seizure of political control by the liquidation of opposition. How can there be a beginning of a tolerable peace unless the peacemakers fully realize that human life is sacred and that all men have rights? (2:72).

Material Prosperity

By 1947, as national attention turns homeward, commentary by the bishops moves away from the war and international issues to concentrate on the domestic milieu and social mores. The postwar economic boom alarms the bishops as American society appears to turn away from its religious foundations to secular materialism. Both the *Statement on Secularism* of 1947 (2:74–81) and *The Christian in Action* of 1948 (2:82–89) broach similar themes. The former assesses the effects of a lack of God in the lives of the individual, in the family, in education, in work, and in the international community. The bishops point out the ways in which separation from God's natural law subverts respect for human rights. In 1948 they continue this theme by referring to secularism as the "most deadly menace to our Christian and American way of living." They go on: "We shall not successfully combat this evil merely by defining and condemning it. Constructive effort is called for to counteract this corrosive influence in every phase of life" (2:82). Sections follow on religion in the home, education, economic life, and citizenship. The 1947 statement, by articulating an ecumenical position with which other faiths could concur, gained the bishops' attention from other religious leaders.[79] This ability to point out the moral overtones of dismaying social trends would continue to win endorsements from other faiths in future pastorals, as the bishops assume a growing leadership in articulating moral concerns.

The baby boom is clearly reflected in statements of the next two years, *The Christian Family* in 1949 (2:90–96) and *The Child: Citizen of Two Worlds* in 1950 (2:97–105). In the 1949 letter the bishops see the family with strong religious values as essential to the state, as well as in shaping the individual and contributing to the Church. In 1950 they make the same case for children: "Striking advances have been made in meeting the child's physical, emotional, and social needs; but his moral and religious needs have not been met with the same solicitude and understanding" (2:97). Again the ground of their reasoning is the preservation of public life: "It is of primary importance for our people to realize that human freedom derives from the spiritual nature of man and can flourish only when things of the spirit are held in reverence" (2:97). In urging parents to impart a sense of God to their children, the statement is specific in citing forms of devotions and religious instruction (2:98–99). The bishops remind fathers that they also have obligations in this regard and not merely in providing material support. Acknowledging the growing public discussion about sexual matters, the bishops raise the issue themselves. Parents are urged to exercise their natural competence in sexual instruction: "Sex is one of God's endowments. It should not be ignored or treated as something bad. If sex education is properly carried on in the home, a deep reverence will be developed" (2:101).

The attention to both domestic and international affairs that characterized the letters of the war years does not wane. Instead, focus intensifies on both arenas as prosperity preoccupies the country at home and Communism engulfs Eastern Europe. During the 1950s the themes of statements can be summed up under two topics: the persecution of the Church behind the Iron Curtain and concern regarding lifestyles, including public service. Yet the letters of the period were alternately ignored and acclaimed by the press and the public, depending on the level of their abstraction and intellectual rigor. Acclaim by the laity, both Catholic and non-Catholic, appears to have corresponded to a pastoral's emphasis on religion versus an application of theology to the social order. When the bishops embedded their moral message in a material context, they were better able to elicit a popular response.

The decade of the 1950s began auspiciously. Nolan states: "The American Church was coming of age in many ways and its impact on even American secular thought was beginning to be felt in ever widening circles."[80] Mark Massa affirms: "Whatever the truth of that charge in 1899 [Americanism], the boundary markers between the Catholic community and American culture had shifted even more dramatically by 1945, when Catholics were laying claim to being a legitimate part of the cultural mainstream."[81] It is probable that Catholic confidence increased after the Second World War for the same reason as it had after the First World War: the accomplishments of Catholics on behalf of the war effort had reinforced their reputation as stalwart patriots. David O'Brien indicates that confidence also arose from significant Catholic population growth during the 1950s (66 percent growth, with a doubling of seminaries and priests).[82] Thus, when the bishops chose to criticize the behavior of politicians and bureaucrats, it was not taken amiss by the nation.

Indeed, the 1951 statement, *God's Law: The Measure of Man's Conduct* (2:138–145), on the morality required of public servants, received complete reprints in dailies of New York, St. Louis, and Washington. *Time* magazine covered it under "National Affairs," while *Newsweek* restricted it to the "Religion" section. The wire services promoted it as a feature story.[83] The news reports interpreted the statement as apt given current political scandals, including the Army-McCarthy hearings, and both Washington newspapers addressed complimentary editorials about the bishops' statement to their government employee readership. Here again, Protestant commentary felt able to support the bishops' stance.[84]

The publicity received by the 1951 letter contrasted sharply with that accorded the 1952 treatise on the philosophical and theological necessity for moral law, entitled *Religion: Our Most Vital National Asset* (2:148–157). The latter, which addressed national moral bankruptcy and the religious spirit of the nation, received little notice. But the 1953 statement, *Peter's Chains,* denouncing Communist persecution of the Church, had enormous popular appeal, necessitating one of the largest reprints to that time—half a million copies.[85] It is likely that the significance of Communist persecution resonated with the large population of Catholic families that had emigrated from Eastern Europe.

The 1954 pastoral, *Victory . . . Our Faith* (2:172–177), reiterates the theme of aesthetic materialism. Again, although the document received praise in restricted circles, the public did not pay attention. Nolan points out that a statement which was appended, *A Plea for Justice,* which was forwarded to the President and other high-ranking officials about the suffering in Vietnam, received far more notice, presumably due to its specific political intervention.[86]

The pendulum of public opinion swung again in 1955, when that year's pastoral captured the public eye. *Private and Church-Related Schools in American Education* (2:179–184) was widely distributed and received considerable press notice, especially in editorials. Because commentators could not distinguish between the case for aid for items such as textbooks and transportation, which the bishops were proposing, and outright tuition grants, lengthy diatribes followed about separation of Church and State. Protests from Protestants interpreting the statement as a pitch for government money created controversy and helped propel articles about the statement onto the front page of fifteen newspapers.[87]

The bishops' sensitivity to current events and their desire to respond to material conditions became evident by their willingness to orient their pastorals as appropriate. The intended statement for 1956 was *The Right of the Church to Teach,* but the international situation that year led the bishops to change their subject to *Peace and Unity: The Hope of Mankind* (2:186–189). That was the year of the Hungarian revolt and the Suez crisis. China, India, Vietnam, Korea, and all of Eastern Europe—Hungary, Czechoslovakia, Poland, Albania, Bulgaria, Estonia, Latvia, Lithuania, Romania, as well as the rest of the Soviet Union—had repressed Catholicism. Two hundred bishops had been killed, imprisoned, or exiled; sixty million Catholics were under Communist control.[88]

This letter of 1956 received prominent press notice because of its linkage with Hungary. European wire services circulated press releases to subscribers throughout the world. The lack of controversy limited the public response; no one could contest the bishops' view that the United Nations represented the best hope for peace.

The variety of topics covered in a series of statements in 1957 indicates the bishops' desire to influence myriad aspects of American life. That year the NCWC issued statements on *Persecuted Peoples* (2:199), on *Censorship* (2:192–198), and even on *Traffic Safety:* "In far too many situations where death and injury occurs in automobile accidents the driver is at fault" (2:200).

When the bishops decided to address *Discrimination and the Christian Conscience* (2:201–206) in their statement of 1958, they were again in tune with the shift in the nation's principles, again providing teaching on social justice, and again commenting on American civic life. The Supreme Court had ruled against school segregation in 1954 in the case of *Brown v. Board of Education.* Yet the bishops were not mere followers, nor was the pastoral their opening salvo on the subject. In 1943 they had mounted a campaign against segregation in Catholic institutions. By 1947 the Archdiocese of St. Louis ended segregation in parochial schools, followed by San Antonio, Washington, New York, and North Carolina.[89] However, to avoid inflaming public sentiment, bishops such as Archbishop Patrick A. O'Boyle of Washington specifically asked the press to refrain from reporting on actions to integrate churches and schools, and the local press complied.[90] In contrast, coverage of the 1958 joint pastoral by the wire services, Associated Press and United Press International, led to many stories. The topic was featured on the covers of *Time* and *Newsweek,* and *U.S. News and World Report* reprinted the full text. Favorable reaction was reported in the black press, and Methodist and Episcopal bishops also issued statements at that time. In the forefront of national opinion, the bishops anticipated the high point of the civil rights movement by several years. Seven hundred thousand copies of the pastoral were printed (compared with previous "best-sellers" *Peter's Chains* and *On International Order,* of which a half million copies were distributed).[91]

The bishops' second statement in 1958, *The Teaching Mission of the Catholic Church,* applied to the American community the thrust of Pope Pius XII's 1954 speech "Teaching Authority of the Church." Their statement emphasizes that the Church must have the right to teach, that those teachings are a necessary bulwark against secularism and materialism, and that it is the teaching function of the Church most often challenged in the United States, especially regarding divorce and birth control. The bishops would face this issue repeatedly in coming decades.

The proliferation of statements continued into 1959, with mixed public reaction. *Freedom and Peace* (2:214–220) was seen as a restatement of Christian views rather than a Catholic stand on a controversial topic.[92] Its critique of Communism was linked with the threat that materialism and laxity presented to American greatness. Such confidence in critiquing American ambition for material success underscored the new assurance felt by the Catholic community. "By the late 1950's, Catholic intellectuals like John Courtney Murray could proclaim not only the congruency of Catholic and American democratic principles, but the mutual dependence of those principles if American democratic culture were to survive."[93]

Public attention focused instead on the bishops' other publication of that year. *Explosion or Backfire?* (2:221–225) was a proposal of specific countermeasures against the public campaign for birth prevention, which was being promoted in the interests of restricting population growth. Rather than being an exegesis of Catholic teaching, the statement focused on practical measures, soliciting Catholic opposition to public funding to promote birth control. Such specificity had not been seen since 1919 and presaged the philosophical/pragmatic mix of future pastorals. Newspaper editorials debated whether it was government's business to tamper with population control by imposing stipulations when issuing foreign aid.[94] Some criticized the pastoral's effect on John Kennedy's presidential nomination, claiming it would harm his chances. Kennedy responded with an address to the Greater Houston Ministerial Association on September 12, 1960: "I do not speak for my church on public matters—and the church does not speak for me."[95]

Coverage of the pastorals was uneven. Fifty-six editorials had been written on *Discrimination* in 1958; fifty-four addressed *Explosion* in 1959, but only four commented on 1960's *Personal Responsibility*.[96] The press created publicity only for those pastorals with public social themes and expressed no interest in the bishops' proclamations about private morality.

The Activist 1960s

Recognizing the link between public reception of their message and its applicability to material conditions, the bishops, in their statement of 1961, again cast their criticism in a nationalistic light, alleging that America's survival as a moral people rests on the soundness of its society. *Unchanging Duty in a Changing World* (2:241–250) depicts the moral decline of society as evidenced by crime, violence, sexuality, greed, racial prejudice, dissolution of family, and disregard for human life, issues on which all could agree. "In an American Catholicism that was beginning to split widely into the so-called progressive and conservative camps, the Statement was well received by both groups."[97]

Catholicism during the 1960s was dominated by the Second Vatican Council, a rare, worldwide convocation of Catholic bishops in Rome. Pope John XXIII's decision to modernize the Church by convening the council was for purposes of *aggiornamento* ("bringing up to date"), or as he described it, opening the windows of the Church to let in fresh air.[98] In 1962 the American bishops held their annual meeting in Rome and issued a *Statement on the Ecumenical Council* (3:11–16), informing people about the upcoming council. In their statement they portray the American Church as

> grown to maturity in an atmosphere not always friendly . . . [whose] people spring from ancestors . . . [who] a few generations ago came to this country unlettered and in great poverty. It has had to struggle with excessive preoccupation with material things . . . and against a public philosophy strongly affected by a special kind of secularism. The marks of our origin and history are certainly upon us (3:13).

The bishops state that the nation's religious and political freedoms are the Church's strengths and contribute to its vitality. They approve of the new level of active lay participation, which has been fostered by the nation's extensive educational system, and acknowledge that in contrast to the divisions that marred the past, there finally exists a sense of a "national Catholic life" (3:14).

Even during the years 1962 to 1964, while the Second Vatican Council was in progress, the American bishops did not fail to issue their annual pastoral, and, interestingly, it did not deal with events of the global Church but with the civil rights movement at home. Nolan calls the 1963 statement *On Racial Harmony* (3:17–19) "one of the strongest Statements ever made by the American hierarchy."[99] The bishops remind their readers of earlier statements on the topic of racism issued in 1943 and 1958. They again articulate the moral principles involved in the light of public responsibility. "Respect for personal rights is not only a matter of individual moral duty; it is also a matter for civic action," due to the need for "a well-ordered human society" and "civic order" (3:17–18). Yet the bishops do not neglect the personal element: "Go beyond slogans and generalizations about color and realize . . . all shar[e] the same human nature and dignity, with the same desires, hopes and feelings. We should try to know and understand one another" (3:18). They suggest communication as action, advocating open and sincere talk where one's profession or workplace provides a common meeting ground. Knowledge and an exchange of ideas represent a prelude to the removal of legal barriers to voting, jobs, housing, education, and use of facilities. The bishops pose even the most essential commandment in terms of national ardor: "Love one another, for this is the law of God," the bishops admonish, so that "our nation will reflect its true greatness, a greatness founded on the moral principle that all men are free and equal under God" (3:19).

The statement on racial harmony did not receive the notice or praise accorded *Discrimination and Christian Conscience* in 1958, perhaps, Nolan speculates, because it was issued from abroad (the bishops had convened again in Rome) or because the press also was preoccupied with the Second Vatican Council. *On Racial Harmony* is dated August 23, 1963, and refers to "the present crisis" (3:17). It seems likely that the statement was formulated in response to the events that had occurred in May, when federal troops were sent to Birmingham, Alabama, after Martin Luther King, Jr.'s home was bombed, and the nation watched as "Bull" Connor directed firehoses and police dogs on children, and in June, when Alabama governor George Wallace defied federal school integration and Medgar Evers was assassinated in Mississippi.[100] Certainly, the bishops' reaction to an ongoing news event constituted a distinct change from the detached, philosophical, summarizing treatises of previous statements, and the speed of their response was unprecedented.

The statement issued in November 1963, the usual time for issuance of a pastoral, was *Bonds of Unity* (3:20–27).[101] It is a *tour de force* of American invocations. The bishops note: "We address ourselves . . . to our people in the United States . . . in regard to those national bonds of union that we as Americans respect and cherish. Recent events in the community have severely tested these bonds" (3:20). The Lincolnesque reference is to the rupture in social unity caused by the events of that summer of 1963. Citing forefathers, mutual rights, and reciprocal duties, the rhetoric of Lincoln is strongly evoked in their language: "The aspirations of all peoples center about their altars and their firesides," and "A more perfect union is . . . impeded by the sad controversy over civil rights" (3:25). Their language emphasizes a vocabulary of the collective, using words such as "common," "national," "shared," "consensus," "cohesive." Their metaphors are vivid: "to clothe with the living flesh and blood of morality the otherwise stark skeleton of legal justice" (3:26). Credit is given to those Old World peoples who influenced our national character and civil traditions. The bishops cite Cicero, natural law, the American compact, the Declaration of Independence, even an inscription on the wall of the House of Representatives. The bishops consider nation, government, traditional law, family, society, equality, right of conscience, private property, all of which create shared bonds of union. "Thus, a major element of our heritage has been the translation of the rights of man, conferred by God, into civil rights, guaranteed by the state." They go on to articulate the moral grounding of social problems that creates the justification for imposing their views on the public: "This shared heritage . . . is not, of course, narrowly American. . . . But, as a nation, the United States faces certain problems of its own that are ours to solve. While many of these problems have social, political, and economic aspects, they are, at the core, human, and therefore moral" (3:22).

Continuity is expressed when the bishops reiterate the themes they have emphasized throughout the decades: "A national examination of conscience would reveal that we are in danger today of becoming a people weakened by *secularism* in our social philosophy, *materialism* in our concept of the good life, and *expediency* in our moral code" (3:23). The bishops articulate a brilliant point that becomes a rationale for their future writings, defining the lack of a moral imperative as constituting the contemporary challenge to democracy:

> When the common defense was first spelled out, it meant hardly more than that which a disciplined military and vigilant police could provide. In an age of aggressive ideologies, not less perilous to the commonweal than invading armies or marauding pirates, the national defense is increasingly a matter of intellectual education and spiritual formation. We face a deadly menace to the truths by which we are made and kept free (3:26).

The bishops close with a commitment: " . . . we pledge the religious, educational and moral resources at our command. We do so motivated by the piety and patriotism that we and our Catholic people are privileged to share with millions of our fellow citizens" (3:27).

In spite of the bishops' plea for civic harmony, they failed to divert the attention of their primary audience. For lay Catholics, the changes in worship mandated by the Second Vatican Council seemed to raise more compelling interest and alarm than the nation's situation did. Services held in Latin and exclusive use of traditional music were ended, to the great consternation of many. The 1964 document *Use of the Vernacular at Mass* (3:35–46) seemed to be addressed to the clergy. "The widespread interest in the Council . . . has prepared the people for changes," changes that ask them to deepen their participation beyond their formerly passive role: "Beyond the use of the language which the people understand, there must be developed an understanding of the 'language' of the liturgy in a deeper sense" (3:35). The bishops encourage compliance, knowing there will be resistance to change among the clergy as well as the laity: "Since . . . it is now a primary pastoral duty to enable the people to take their full internal and external part in the liturgy, it is clearly our duty to equip ourselves at once to carry out this task" (3:36).

No pastoral letter was written in 1965, a singular exception, because the sixteen major documents produced by the Second Vatican Council had been issued by then. Given the volume and complexity of the conciliar documents, the bishops preferred to let people read and study those. Among the most significant was the Pastoral Constitution on the Church in the Modern World *(Gaudium et Spes)*, which answered the question of the Church's relationship to the external world: "The Church . . . believes that through each of its members and its community as a whole it can help to make the human family and its history more human."[102] The repercussions of the council in the contemporary Church have been considerable. Among these, the scope and pace of joint pastoral texts speeded up notably after the council endorsed the concept of the Church at work in the world in 1965.

A NEW MISSION

After the council had formally encouraged the formation of national organizations of bishops, the American bishops reorganized as the National Conference of Catholic Bishops (NCCB) at their meeting of November 14–18, 1966, with Archbishop John Dearden of Detroit as its first president. The old Welfare Conference became a parallel lobbying arm, the United States Catholic Conference (USCC).[103] A new but limited openness to the press resulted: "An innovation at the 1966 meeting was the arrangement for three news conferences. . . . The bishops' meetings itself, however, remained closed to the media."[104]

The number of statements issued in 1966 reflects the freedom and responsiveness to engage social issues that the Vatican Council had endorsed. American bishops had been claiming all along that their faith and their nation were compatible and linked in mutual benefit. The council legitimized that position. Timothy Byrnes articulates the new distinction:

> We have seen how the insular, defensive style of the past lost relevance as Catholics assimilated into the mainstream. In these new circumstances, when parochial defense was no longer needed, Vatican II authorized the bishops to turn their attention to the whole range of social problems facing the American people. . . . [T]he bishops were also encouraged to expand their potential audience to include all Americans and to move away from a style of authoritative pronouncement toward one of dialogue and persua-

sion. The bishops were no longer to view American culture as a force against which the church had to defend itself. Rather, they were to view that culture as the very arena in which the church would pursue its mission.[105]

Thus Church was envisioned as "a challenger and critic of modern culture."[106] The council's Pastoral Constitution charged the bishops with "reading the signs of the times and of interpreting them in the light of the Gospel."[107] This phrase would be reiterated regarding future pastorals as the bishops address what are seen to be increasingly secular issues. Thus the American bishops received overt encouragement from the universal Church to continue and expand along the rhetorical trajectory they had already shaped.

The bishops lost no time in putting their new directive into effect. Several statements were issued in 1966. The *Statement on Government and Birth Control* urges government to be a neutral institution that "neither penalizes nor promotes birth control" and separates the issue from welfare (3:71). The bishops warn that requiring birth control in order to receive foreign aid will create resentment and violate the intimate mores of other cultures (3:72).

Although the bishops had faithfully endorsed peace throughout both World Wars, they had never opposed government policy but declared its military actions to be justified. They did the same in 1966 with *Peace and Vietnam* (3:73–77). The justification they provide is that "we, the Catholic Bishops of the United States, consider it our duty to help magnify the moral voice of our nation," and to distinguish between true and false patriotism, "citizens . . . must always look simultaneously to the welfare of the whole human family, which is tied together by the manifold bonds linking races, peoples and nations" (3:74). The bishops conclude: " . . . in the light of the facts as they are known to us, it is reasonable to argue that our presence in Vietnam is justified" (3:76). They do, however, warn of the danger that the war in Vietnam could "diminish our moral sensitivity to its evils" (3:77). In this statement also, the bishops, while not advocating unilateral disarmament, do commend the Treaty Against Nuclear Proliferation (3:76).

Ironically, among Catholics in 1966, it was the *Pastoral Statement on Penance and Abstinence* (3:78–83) that received the most attention. Because the council's removal of an ancient and scrupulously observed ban regarding eating meat on Friday was widely misunderstood (it was not abolished, but its status changed from Church law to voluntary observance), it attracted the attention of the majority of lay Catholics.[108] A *Pastoral Statement on Race Relations and Poverty*, the fourth in two decades regarding black, Hispanic, and American Indian peoples, half of whom lived in poverty, also came out that year, addressing not only Catholics but all citizens of the United States. "Slogans have at times taken the place of reasonable dialogue. We ask that dialogue replace slogans" (3:85). The theme of rational communication ("dialogue and discourse" versus "slogans and epithets") augments the personal interaction endorsed in 1963.

The changing order of modern society is reflected in the inner life of the Church and the exodus of many in religious life. A *Resolution on Clerical Celibacy* affirms the council's adherence to Church law and negates hope for any change in policy regarding marriage for clergy, even though the bishops acknowledge, "We know the loneliness that at times accompanies the life of the priest" (3:92). A statement on Catholic schools reflects the problems and expense caused by the attrition of unpaid teaching sisters.[109]

By November 1967 the bishops had begun to flex some political muscle, sending a resolution to the House of Representatives in support of the War on Poverty legislation. Since the massive protests against the Vietnam conflict had become the overriding public issue of the time, the bishops also implore the nation for rational debate: "In the longing for peace we ought not forget our moral and civic responsibilities," but make clear their support for the intervention: "We are not pleading for peace at any price" (3:90).

For their the major statement of 1967, the bishops turned away from the pragmatic problems of Church life and of public issues. "In 1967, the American hierarchy for the first time in its history issued a completely doctrinal pastoral, *The Church in Our Day.* . . . This major didactic Statement developed more completely the Church and its mission than all previous Pastorals or Statements."[110] The premises set forth in this pastoral establish the future direction for the bishops' pastoral production.

The foreword of the letter focuses on the present, the "needs of the hour." There is a reference to its distinct nature: "The format for this collective Pastoral Letter is a departure from the customary Statements of the American Hierarchy. Specifically, it is to be a doctrinal exposition on the life and development of the American Church in the light of Vatican Council II" (3:98). Throughout the text there are several references to "this first collective Pastoral Letter," (3:98–154), which indicates that the bishops had something in mind for a special series of substantive documents. This fifty-two page pastoral breaks the custom of statements limited to several pages in length that had characterized the bishops' recent writings (since 1933, when *Present Crisis* was issued in twenty-eight pages).

The American bishops of the previous century, such as Archbishops Ireland and Spalding, would have been thrilled to see their views of the Church as embedded in culture finally acknowledged: "The Church emerges not only from the grace of God but from mankind and its history" (3:104). The social as well as the spiritual realm is recognized: "We seek Christ not only in the Scriptures but in the signs of the times . . . in all human cultures, in the human condition itself" (3:111). The universality of the Church is understood not merely as geographical but temporal: "In no essential sense can the Church be constricted within a contemporary Church, a futuristic Church, a traditionalist Church, or a Church of the past. A Church monopolized by any group or reserved to any one period or comfortable in any single culture would run counter to the pluralities recognized and demanded by Vatican II and would, in effect, become that monolithic, uncatholic institution" (3:116).

The bishops present their teaching office as bridging the divide between the individual and the institution: "One of the most vexing problems of our day is the proper relationship between conscience and authority" (3:141). The acute polarization caused by conflicting loyalties and plural ideologies makes the bishops' task "that of formulating the Catholic faith in terms which speak to modern mentalities" (3:153). This task supersedes their tradition of governance: "The structures for teaching the faith are doubtless more important in the total work of the Church than are those of governing" (3:117).

In view of their ministry to interpret the gospel for modern times, the bishops emphasize collegiality and continuity. However, in an unprecedented approach, they extend an overture for participation by the laity, where between "the silence of the past and the occasionally strident confusion of the present must be heard the authentic voice of the layman" (3:117). A specific invitation is extended: "We welcome, not avoid, the consultation of the laity in every manner consistent with the mission of the Church. . . . Thus, it is not a rhetorical concession to the mood of the hour, but an exercise of the pastoral office . . . to say . . . 'Recognize, O Christian, your dignity!'" (3:121). The bishops here establish a basis for lay participation and expression through consultation, a move that they would in fact activate in future pastorals.

In spite of the importance of the 1967 document to Catholic understanding of Church structure, *The Church in Our Day* was of interest only to its members, and even that was limited. By contrast, the reception to the writings of 1968 reflected the public nature of their selected issues.

Social unrest is the theme of the bishops' *Statement on the National Race Crisis* in April 1968, by which they established an Urban Task Force regarding education, jobs, welfare, and housing. They issued an endorsement of President Johnson's intention to limit bombing in North Vietnam (*Resolution on Peace*, 3:161), expressing sympathy for the war's burden on the spirit of young people. They also express their intent that their pastoral letter of that year would be on war and peace. In September of that year the bishops asked for aid to the starving, since the government seemed oblivious to the human suffering in Africa: "We are forced to express our profound horror at the deplorable impasse to which negotiations about humanitarian relief have come" (*Statement on Human Suffering in Nigeria-Biafra*, 3:162–163).

In July 1968 Pope Paul VI released his encyclical on human reproduction, *Humanae Vitae*, reaffirming the Church's stance against artificial contraception. The bishops of many nations issued pastoral letters in response to the encyclical. The collective pastoral of the American bishops was called *Human Life in Our Day* (3:164–194). They appear to have followed their recommendation of broader consultation of the previous year. Nolan describes the process: "The final text took into consideration several hundred recommendations, oral and written, submitted before and during the conference."[111] The bishops' purpose was to explain that the encyclical was not intended to replace individual conscience regarding birth control and other reproductive issues, but to set forth the Church's interpretation of divine law to which conscience must conform. They addressed not just procreation but human life in a number of facets, including war in general, Vietnam in particular, and the growing issue of conscientious objection.

The document was divided into two chapters, the first of which, "The Christian Family" (3:165–182), discusses the procreative nature of conjugal love and responsible parenthood, the question of individual conscience and the basis for decision-making, and the changing nature of the family. As in 1950, they express the need to educate children about sexuality and applaud more egalitarian marriage patterns that expand the roles of men and women (3:177). Chapter 2, "The Family of Nations" (3:182–194), expands its consideration of life by addressing arms control, the draft, Vietnam and conscience. The bishops explain the Second Vatican Council's decision to condemn the use of nuclear weapons, but not their possession for purposes of deterrence (3:185). This section raises the building of an international community (3:187–190) and poses a series of questions about the issue of proportionality regarding the conflict in Vietnam (3:190–191). The development of a holistic view of life is one that would grow more explicit for the bishops, a view not articulated in the secular press. Although highlighted in the public eye, comments on abortion actually occupied only a limited portion of the first section.

Because of the controversy regarding birth control, and the conflict of the Church's position with contemporary social trends, a media blitz resulted.

Newspaper and television media misrepresented the lengthy statement as a simple prohibition of birth control. Press coverage grew even greater when several bishops held press conferences complaining of distortion and misrepresentation. Yet an editorial in a Catholic publication reported that the bishops had difficulty articulating a clear, non-technical explanation of their views and countered by closing their sessions to the press.[112]

The press's selection of a single portion of a comprehensive statement, so striking in the case of *Human Life in Our Day,* was one that would have important ramifications for future messages. By ignoring the full context in which a point was embedded, the press distorted the intention of the bishops' teaching and diluted its influence with the public. Headlines would prove to be the only acquaintance many would have with the full text of the pastorals.

Although Nolan claims that joint pastoral letters were issued every year since 1960, no major statement was issued between 1968 and 1972. Whether because their previous remarks were taken out of context, or they were preoccupied with implementation of the Vatican II decrees, or were overwhelmed by the pace of events during that time, the bishops confined themselves to a brief statement on abortion again in 1969, calling for equal protection of the Fourteenth Amendment toward the unborn and empowerment of the poor. The episcopal statements between 1966 and 1971 regarding Vietnam follow a path of growing skepticism on the morality of U.S. intervention. In 1966 the bishops had declared that the military action of war must be accompanied by support for peace and that the government must be honest about the progress of the war. In turn, people must protest if moral limits are exceeded. By 1968 the bishops conclude that U.S. escalation of the war had caused devastation that exceeded any potential benefits that might be derived from the conflict, and thus violated one of the conditions by which the Catholic Church deems a war to be "just."[113] In 1969, in *Prisoners of War in Southeast Asia,* they commend the government for its efforts but specify further objectives: release of names, exchange of the sick and wounded, and inspection of facilities. By 1971 the bishops conclude that any moral good is being outweighed by the increasing destruction: "It is significant for understanding the bishops' stated perspective that their final rejection of the war was based on the principle of proportionality and not on any judgment of the justice of America's role in Indochina."[114]

On the domestic front, a 1968 *Statement on Farm Labor* acknowledges the problems of both growers and migrants but points out that the while government assists owners, similar assistance is not rendered to field workers. The bishops urge Congress to legislate protection for field workers and urge settlement of the ongoing grape boycott.

When the bishops again produced a pastoral statement of substance, they moved from civic life to deal with the inner life of the Church. The major statement issued in 1972, *To Teach as Jesus Did,* a pastoral letter about Catholic education (3:306–340), was followed by one on Mary, *Behold Your Mother: Woman of Faith,* in 1973 (4:408–452). A document issued in 1975, *The Right to a Decent Home: A Pastoral Response to the Crisis in Housing* (4:99–119), reflected the nation's preoccupation with deteriorating urban and rural conditions.

To Live in Christ Jesus: A Pastoral Reflection on the Moral Life in 1976 (4:170–195) explicitly addressed moral issues involving the family, the community, the nation, and the world. It was directed not just to Catholics but to "fellow Christians" and those who "may wish to know our vision of the moral life and our perception of many of the critical issues of our day" (4:170). The first part focuses on elements of the spiritual life, such as conversion, conscience, and Scripture, and the second explains the Vatican II's Pastoral Constitution on the Church in the Modern World (4:178–183). This section addresses special groups—the vulnerable, children, the aged and dying, and homosexuals—who are owed a "special degree of pastoral understanding" (4:182). Under "nation" (4:184–189) are mentioned the unborn, women ("There is much to be done in the Church in identifying appropriate ways of recognizing women's equality and dignity"—4:185), racial and ethnic respect, housing, employment, and crime. The final, international section discusses development, peace, and human rights (4:189–193).

Focused on reaffirming traditional values, the document did not receive much attention. Archbishop Joseph Bernardin, who was NCCB president for the 1974–1977 term, acknowledged the bishops' failure to implement their teaching: "We develop a good document on a good topic, and then we say, 'Well, now we've done our job, now it's up to somebody else to do something about it.' Then nothing happens."[115]

The 1970s ended with a brief statements in 1978 entitled *To Do the Work of Justice* (4:243–254), which sought to implement ministries at the diocesan, parish, and family levels suggested in a bicentennial project on economic justice. "Our episcopal conference will continue to speak out for full employment, adequate income, the rights of workers to organize, and defense of the poor. . . . We shall seek to make our voice heard more effectively in our own Catholic community and where public policy is made" (4:250). Another pastoral on discrimination, *Brothers and Sisters to Us* (4:342–455), in 1979, bluntly states, "Racism is a sin," and makes several recommendations for recruiting minority vocations, leadership training, and inner city parochial schools. *Marxist Communism* (4:380–400) in 1980 was a political/economic examination of its "contempt for human rights" (4:395) and its differences from Christian philosophy. However, the bishops explicitly remind readers that Western capitalistic structures should not be equated with Christianity either: "Catholics should remain aware of the very severe judgment which the Roman pontiffs and various European hierarchies have passed on unrestricted economic liberalism" (4:399).

Historian Mel Piehl identifies several strands of Catholic reform efforts in the nation during this period: the Catholic left, which was primarily anti-war; social justice activism among women religious; and urban and race initiatives in inner-city parishes. However, of these,

> the most nationally visible strand of Catholic social reform was the official one centered in the National Conference of Catholic Bishops. . . . Continuing the long North American tradition of official Catholic social statements and action . . . the bishops made social concerns of far greater importance within the American church, and brought Catholic social perspectives before the wider American audience in unprecedented ways. Throughout the 1970s and 1980s, a stream of hearings, studies, drafts and official pronouncements . . . [gained] varying degrees of public attention. . . . Most of their statements went unnoticed outside narrow ecclesiastical circles, but others became touchstones of wider debate in the ideologically charged environment of contemporary American politics.[116]

The emphasis on civil allegiance and the apologia for Catholic patriotism, the need for conformity, and the aloofness toward public controversy had all dissipated with the turn of the century. The shift from a silent, inner-directed Church to an outspoken public critic began early in the twentieth century and progressed in intensity. The growing political importance of the United States, coupled with the increasing integration of Catholics into civic life throughout the century, emboldened the bishops to consider the nation's actions in a global context. With their organization and their pronouncements on public life legitimized by the Second Vatican Council, the bishops were further spurred in expanding the scope of their commentary by the social activism prevalent throughout the nation. The pastorals of the twentieth century were marked by a new willingness to comment on public policy, to make recommendations to the government, an openness to consultation with the laity, and uneven attention from the press.

The bishops' role as moral teachers to individual Catholic members interacting with secular life in the nineteenth century had become, in the twentieth century, an exercise in public leadership seeking to intervene in shaping secular life. They sought to influence the public in the areas of civic reform and social justice through the presentation of Catholic social thought. All these hallmarks would be highlighted with the production of the next pastoral letters.

Chapter Three
The Challenge of Peace ════════════════

THE PRECEDING EXAMINATION OF THE RHETORICAL PATH of joint pastoral letters from 1792 to 1980 has demonstrated the changes in their purpose and scope, which paralleled the Church's evolution as it sought to establish a footing within the developing nation. In the nineteenth-century letters, the bishops defended their patriotism and sought to preserve religious differentiation while advocating civic assimilation. The expansion of the United States' involvement in international affairs in the twentieth century was accompanied by the Church's expansion of interest in social reform. In the process of articulating a role for its American citizens, the bishops broadened their own role beyond that of advocating appropriate civic behavior.

Twentieth-century pastorals were forthright in providing commentary on specific contemporary issues that were considered primarily as part of the political, governmental, and civic domains. Although this move may have seemed radical to onlookers, it was, in fact, a fulfillment of the bishops' persistent belief that the Church offered a perspective beneficial to the nation and that its moral grounding contributed valuable insight in coping with public problems. From their previous confidence that Catholic Americans could constitute a substantial asset to the nation's citizenry, the bishops had, through the turn of the century, deepened their certainty that Church teaching likewise offered a public contribution. Underlying all the pastorals was a conviction that the theological and philosophical traditions of an ancient faith could remind the nation of its founding principles. The bishops never wavered in their sense that the ideals which the founders regarded as natural rights were consonant with God's law and that the nation's destiny should be to seek the realization of those ideals.[1] Thus the bishops sought to deepen American commitment to a sense of moral as well as material advancement. Yet, although previous statements and resolutions expressed their opinions on various matters confronting public consciousness, the bishops had limited effectiveness in effecting change.

Therefore, the development of joint pastoral letters entered yet another new phase. The bishops sought to apply their influence in a more fundamental way, combining the moral authority of the Church with the molding of individual conscience. Their desire to influence secular affairs penetrated the Church/State divide primarily through the education of individuals regarding the Church's social teachings. The pastoral letters were the means of interpreting and promulgating those teachings in a context of public dialogue. Moreover, the bishops could maintain their posture of good citizenship even in their new mode of criticizing public policy by framing their censure as a desire to reform American institutions.[2] The topic they chose to analyze in 1980 was a reexamination of the Church's traditional doctrine on war and peace in light of the danger posed by the potential of nuclear annihilation. In testimony before a U.S. Senate hearing of the Foreign Relations Committee, Archbishop John Quinn articulated this goal: "The Church enters the arms debate in her capacity as a teacher of morality and a shaper of conscience." He added that the aim was to build "a psychology of peace," which would, in turn, affect public policy.[3]

The pastoral on nuclear arms, entitled *The Challenge of Peace*, in laying out concerns with human existence itself, became a contested rhetorical battle over the bishops' trespass into the public arena. The topic itself seemed radical to many, but it was also the approach to producing the pastoral that would heighten the sense of novelty. During creation of the pastoral, elements introduced in the previous chapter regarding public involvement, attention from the media, and vociferous controversy reached new levels.

This chapter presents the public nature of this pastoral letter on nuclear arms and how it came to introduce innovations in the process of production and reception that were unparalleled in American pastoral history. Based on the following analyses, five reasons are proposed to account for the greatly different reception of this pastoral from preceding letters. First, the bishops' openness about releasing drafts and seeking input created a new level of responsiveness. Second, the publicity received by a succession of drafts kept the matter before the public for a prolonged period. Third, the letter represented a change from previous patriotic positions, establishing a sense of opposition that made news. Fourth, the letter intentionally addressed a wider audience that responded, including governmental agencies, scholars, other religions, and other nations. Finally, it has been suggested that by framing an established government policy as a moral issue, the bishops created a space for civic discussion about national assumptions that had been missing from the public square.

As each of these issues is addressed, it will become clear that, intentionally or not, the circumstances surrounding the pastoral contributed to its placement before the public eye. The repercussions of these processes led to important, and at times unintended, consequences for future pastoral statements. After tracing the inception of the pastoral on nuclear arms, this chapter will present the consultative process that distinguished the letter and made it precedent-setting. That section will be followed by a discussion of the factors and forces that joined to raise the letter to a new level of pastoral discourse in terms of addressing national policy in a highly publicized forum.

INCEPTION

The idea of addressing a militaristic, political, and technical topic such as nuclear arms might, at first glance, have seemed inappropriate for a group of churchmen. Catholic activists had participated in the Ban the Bomb movement of the 1950s, had protested the Vietnam War in the 1960s and early 1970s, and had joined the nuclear freeze movement of the early 1980s, but a major peace movement affiliated with the Church had not materialized.[4] Although the bishops had been writing about peace since 1919, they had not articulated specific opposition to the government on a major foreign policy issue until their 1971 resolution against the Vietnam War.[5]

Traditional Church teaching regarding war was based on a framework developed over the centuries and known as *ius belli,* or "just war" theory. Its hypothesis rested on the concept that the waging of war could be justified if certain conditions were met.[6] The Second Vatican Council had called attention to the dangers of nuclear war but had failed to pass judgment on the morality of building an arsenal for purposes of deterrence.[7] The bishops had raised the specter of using nuclear weapons in their 1968 pastoral letter *Human Life in Our Day,* which condemned the threat of human annihilation posed by nuclear arms (3:186). Nuclear war was raised again in the 1976 pastoral letter on morality, *To Live in Christ Jesus:*

> With respect to nuclear weapons, at least those with massive destructive capacity, the first imperative is to prevent their use. As possessors of a vast nuclear arsenal, we must also be aware that not only is it wrong to attack civilian populations, but it is also wrong to threaten to attack them as part of a strategy of deterrence (4:192).

Although such a censure of deterrence moved Church teaching even further along pacifist lines than just war theory, it received little discussion in either the press or among the bishops themselves.[8] In the 1978 pastoral letter *The Gospel of Peace and the Danger of War,* the bishops began to synthesize pacifist and just war principles.[9]

In September 1979, Cardinal John Krol of Philadelphia testified at the hearings of the Senate Foreign Relations Committee in support of SALT II, asserting that immorality is not limited to the *use* of nuclear weapons, but that even the *threat* of such use is immoral, condemning people to live in fear.[10] He added that possession of nuclear weapons as a deterrent is tolerable *only* as long as progress continues toward their limitation, reduction, and eventual abolition.[11] This testimony moved the American Church further toward the pacifist position.[12]

Other bishops also gained public attention by their stand on the issue. Bishop Raymond G. Hunthausen of Seattle urged Catholics to refuse to pay part of their income tax to protest the Trident nuclear submarine based there;[13] Bishop Leroy Matthiessen of Amarillo called on workers on the neutron warhead at the Pantex plant to resign; Bishops Walter Sullivan of Richmond (an area replete with military bases and personnel), Philip F. Straling of San Bernardino, and Roger Mahony of Stockton led a chorus of what came to be forty bishops who wrote individual pastoral letters or newspaper columns protesting the possibility of nuclear war.[14] The condemnation of nuclear weapons by Archbishop John Quinn in his address to the Catholics of San Francisco was typical: "The moral problem arises, however, when the effects of our defensive weapons are no longer fully predictable or within our control."[15] The *San Francisco Examiner,* which reprinted the speech on the following day, reported expressions of support from the diocese as well as from Protestant and Jewish leaders: "Thank God for such a strong leadership voice."[16] Bishop Mahony's diocesan pastoral was even more explicit:

> Recently, we have heard public officials speak foolishly, and imprudently, of "limited" and "winnable" nuclear wars, as if to prepare us to accept and accustom ourselves to such moral monstrosity. . . . Any level of loss is apparently acceptable as long as our side "wins." In the face of such arrogance, such aridity of feeling and moral bankruptcy, we must not remain silent.[17]

The suggestion for a joint pastoral on nuclear war, therefore, was not surprising. Several bishops had supported the idea of educating Americans about the Church's teachings on conflict. P. Francis Murphy, auxiliary bishop of Baltimore, is credited with suggesting a concise summary of

Church teaching on war and peace as a topic for consideration.[18] The emphasis on focusing the pastoral on the moral aspects of war is attributed to Thomas J. Gumbleton, auxiliary bishop of Detroit and president of Pax Christi-USA.[19] Other bishops on both sides of the ideological spectrum supported the idea from their own vantage points.[20]

The bishops' resolve to address the issue collectively received a timely boost from Pope John Paul II's words at Hiroshima in February 1981: "In the past it was possible to destroy a village, a town, a region, even a country. Now it is the whole planet that has come under threat. . . . From now on, it is only through a conscious choice and through a deliberate policy that humanity can survive."[21] Thus the bishops were encouraged in their new endeavor in two ways: first by the public response to earlier, individual actions, and by the Pope's call for a new policy. Within a year the *San Francisco Chronicle* was reporting that 133 Catholic bishops in the nation had endorsed a bilateral nuclear weapons freeze, based on the belief that there could be no justification for the existence of the equivalent of twelve tons of TNT for every person on earth.[22]

PREPARATION

The NCCB president in 1981, Archbishop John Roach of St. Paul and Minneapolis, appointed a noted consensus-builder, Archbishop Joseph Bernardin, then of Cincinnati, as chair of the ad hoc committee that was to prepare a draft report on the pastoral for the bishops' November 1982 meeting. Bernardin in turn selected a committee of bishops who spanned a spectrum from liberal Thomas Gumbleton of Detroit to hawkish John O'Connor, who held the rank of rear admiral as chief Navy chaplain, buttressed by moderates Daniel Reilly of Norwich, Connecticut, and George Fulcher of Columbus, Ohio.[23]

Secular Consultation

One of the innovations launched in the creation of *The Challenge of Peace* was extensive consultation with experts in a variety of disciplines. The concept had been escalating gradually. In the preparation of *To Teach as Jesus Did,* the 1972 pastoral on campus ministry, it was suggested that the bishops consult with those working in the field, and five hundred pages of comments on the first draft were collected within two months.[24] The 1981 pastoral statement *Reflections on the Energy Crisis* introduced technical consultations when invitations to offer input into a draft document were extended to the laity as well as theologians.[25] In the case of *The Challenge of Peace,* the process seems to have arisen spontaneously. Philip Hannan, pro-defense bishop of New Orleans, urged the bishops to consult a military expert when the topic was first proposed.[26] Bishop Edward O' Rourke of Peoria, concerned about unrealistic proposals by the bishops, suggested the need for expert assistance in understanding the technology of weapons.[27] At their first meeting, on July 26, 1981, Archbishop Bernardin asked committee members to suggest the names of people from whom they wanted to hear. Bishop O'Connor, who recommended a long list of experts, would say later, "We hadn't thought of the process as unique. It just seemed the natural thing to do."[28] The staff also, at that initial meeting, presented a list of "suggested specialists in government, arms control, the military and weapon systems, political science and moral theology for the committee to call on as needed."[29]

High-ranking experts accepted invitations to attend the bishops' panels, which provided a forum for expression of their concerns: former Defense Secretaries James Schlesinger and Harold Brown; SALT I negotiator Gerard Smith; Reagan officials Defense Secretary Caspar Weinberg, Arms Control and Disarmament Agency director Eugene Rostow, and Under Secretary of State Lawrence Eagleburger.[30] Bruce Russett, political science professor at Yale, was invited to serve as author and principal consultant.[31] Over the course of twelve months, the bishops held at least fourteen meetings, at which they heard from thirty-six witnesses, including military experts, theologians, physicians, biblical scholars, and peace activists.[32] The *Boston Globe* was among those that commented on the "unusually broad consultation" that provided the bishops the "sober and perplexing experience of talking to specialists."[33]

In November 1981, Archbishop Bernardin provided a progress report to the full body of bishops at their annual NCCB meeting. The first draft, completed ahead of schedule, was to be distributed at the NCCB's 1982 summer assembly in Collegeville, Minnesota. Its advocacy of arms control and nuclear disarmament and its revisionist consideration of the concepts of deterrence and "just war" were clear even in that initial draft.

Although the pastoral had not yet been made public and was still provisional, the *Washington Post* broke a story describing its orientation, which captured the attention of the wire services. The emergence of this rough first draft is generally described as "leaked" to the press.[34] Jim Castelli, who has written a detailed account of the creation of what came to be known as the "peace pastoral," ascribes its premature unveiling to one of the committee members, Bishop Thomas Gumbleton, whose speech to the Catholic Theological Society in early June highlighted the draft's goal to be the Church's nuclear-age version of traditional "just war" guidelines. Marjorie Heyer, the reporter from the *Washington Post* who had covered the meeting, recognized in the bishop's remarks a significant departure from previous pro-defense Catholic postures.[35] When her article was picked up by the wire services, it quickly became national news. Accordingly, the bishops read about the draft's contents in the newspaper before they even received the text.[36] Although Bishop Gumbleton was chagrined about the slip, two precedents were established that resulted in significantly widening the public scope and press coverage of the pastoral letters. First, the releasing of drafts to the public came to be seen as an innovative opening of the Church's discursive process. Second, the press's response to what was considered the draft's "liberal" stance garnered immediate headlines and generated tremendous publicity for the Church, the bishops, and public policy on nuclear arms.

Four Versions

The first draft, a sixty-six page document entitled "God's Hope in a Time of Fear," was completed in time for distribution to the bishops' summer meeting in July 1982, but by then many of the bishops already knew about its thrust from newspaper reports.

The introduction to the first draft acknowledges the complexity of maintaining peace, and the differences of opinion that could be justifiably held to accomplish that. In the first seven pages the bishops focus on pacifism, a focus that some would claim gave the impression that it formed an obligatory position for Catholics.[37] The bishops trace New Testament examples and identify nonviolent practitioners, such as Francis of Assisi, Dorothy Day, Mahatma Gandhi, and Martin Luther King, Jr.

The document then addresses the Church's just war tradition and its intended application as a presumption for peace.[38] The bishops confront the paradox of deterrence, by which possession of nuclear weapons, meant to deter attack and maintain peace, constitutes the gravest danger of war. Next, six substantive recommendations are provided regarding the prohibition of use on civilian and non-combatant populations and initiation of attack. The document cites Cardinal Krol's 1979 testimony and concludes, "We find ourselves at odds with elements of current deterrent policy."[39] The draft closes with a section on spiritual actions to be taken by bishops, educators, parents, and politicians.[40] Although the words "freeze" (agreement not to add new weapons to the existing nuclear arsenal) and "no first strike" (a commitment not to initiate a nuclear attack) are avoided because of their political implications, the thrust of the document is clearly toward initiating disarmament.[41]

The release of the draft outside the NCCB created so much public response by September 1982 that the committee asked for more time to process the volume of commentary.[42] Seventy bishops provided written comments, and over twenty of those had held hearings in their own dioceses. Although no papal reaction on the draft was directly received, the Vatican Peace and Justice Commission praised the document's fidelity to Catholic intellectual tradition. The resulting input forwarded to the committee, as well as critiques by experts and laypeople, came to more than seven hundred pages.[43]

In October 1982 the second draft, exceeding one hundred pages, was sent to the bishops, incorporating many of the ideas that had been received.[44] This time, in acknowledgment of the tremendous public and press interest in its development, the draft was released to the press simultaneously. Renamed *The Challenge of Peace: God's Promise and Our Response*, the bishops offer their dual role as pastoral teachers and concerned Americans as justification for their purpose of shaping Catholic conscience and contributing toward public debate on national policy.[45] In expanding its scriptural basis by including more Old Testament citations, the bishops attempt to erect a foundation for articulating a theology of peace (308–310). The pastoral goes on to explicate the choices available as a response to the disruption of peace, from nonviolence to just war (311–312).

The second section, "War and Peace in the Modern World: Problems and Principles," moves from the first draft's theoretical approach to a more realistic appraisal of the possibilities of waging limited nuclear war by posing a series of questions about the ability of leaders to be discriminate in targeting and to exchange information, and long-term effects on survivors. The bishops call for an alert and wary citizenry: "There should be a clear public resistance to the rhetoric of 'winnable' nuclear wars. . . . We seek to encourage a public attitude which sets stringent limits on the kinds of actions our government will take on nuclear policy in our name" (314).

The concept of deterrence as "evil" or "sinful" came up for debate, as well as whether it was morally "tolerable" or "acceptable."[46] The draft supports a freeze on adding new weapons to the existing arsenal. The language of this draft is deliberately ambiguous and nuanced in an attempt to mollify critics who had read the bishops' hedged statements in the first draft as a blessing on limited nuclear war. Thus, while the draft avoids saying that nuclear weapon use can never be justified, the intent of the bishops' repudiation is clear.[47] A new addition from the first draft is the development of a third section proposing alternatives to waging war. "The Promotion of Peace: Proposals and Policies" contains seven specific recommendations that advocate opposing the MX missile, immediately halting the development and testing of new armaments, not seeking to achieve superiority of weapons strength, and forgoing deterrence as policy (318–322).

Vatican Intervention

Because the drafting committee was so balanced in representing a spectrum of opinion, the consensus they were able to reach generally reflected views acceptable to the majority of the assembled bishops. Nevertheless, the bishops spent half of their time at the November 1982 annual meeting discussing the document. Moreover, it was not only the public and American bishops whose views merited consideration; the drafting committee had been requested to meet with the Vatican and to attend a special meeting of European conferences of bishops in January 1983. Given the potential effects of the proposed letter on NATO defense capabilities, the Vatican had invited representatives of other bishops' conferences to review and comment on the American pastoral.

Representatives from the European hierarchies of France, West Germany, Great Britain, Netherlands, Belgium, and Italy convened to review the second pastoral draft on January 18–19, 1983.[48] Vatican concerns centered on the ecclesiastical authority of the letter. The specific policy recommendations made by the Americans were new in pastoral discourse. Vatican officials claimed that national conferences had limited authority and could not propose views at odds with those of the bishops of other nations, but could present only binding universal Church principles.[49] The Americans were told to resolve the dilemma by rewriting the pastoral so as to distinguish between those scriptural and philosophical portions of the pastoral that had the authority of binding Church teaching, while the bishops' recommendations were made provisional, a matter of "prudential judgment" for Catholics to accept or reject.[50] In spite of the fact that a number of theologians had concluded that just war theory was invalidated by the potential for nuclear planetary annihilation, Vatican officials informed the bishops that it was to be clearly affirmed as established Church policy, while pacifism was to be identified as a stance that could be held only by individuals, not governments.[51]

Not only were the pastoral recommendations more specific and concrete than the universal Church would endorse, but the fact that NATO relied on deterrence as a strategy created tension between European and American national hierarchies.[52] Bishops of European nations geographically located between the superpowers had reservations about conceding rights to self-defense; French and West German bishops responded with their own joint pastorals.[53] Both of these held that nuclear deterrence was a legitimate form of maintaining stability.[54]

These factors were addressed by several changes made for the third draft.[55] Roman concerns about unity were reflected when the concept of Church as a community of conscience and its acceptance of pluralistic ideas were dropped.[56] The ratio of verbiage in the second draft addressing just war versus pacifism had been less than two to one; by the third draft it increases by five to one.[57] The bishops accede to Rome in reaffirming just war as the primary policy of the Church.[58] Support for a freeze on additional nuclear weapons is removed in the third draft, which asks only for a "curb" on the arms race.[59] Nevertheless, while the bishops refrain from contravening Vatican or conciliar teaching, they are willing to go beyond it by opposing specific dimensions of government policy.[60]

The draft's introduction addresses the issue of the bishops' authority and the distinction among statements: "At times we state universally binding moral principles as well as formal church teaching; at other times we make specific applications, observations and recommendations which allow for a diversity of opinion on the part of those who assess the factual data of the situation differently than we do" (698). The introduction shifts from a focus on pacifism to emphasize the right of nations to self-defense (706–709). Discussion of the realistic impossibility of a "limited nuclear war" is strengthened (699, 712), and the unacceptable consequences to civilians of any attack are raised (711). The bishops discuss the huge amount of money spent on weapons as deterrence and the "contagion of conflict" by which a state of war-preparedness becomes the norm (712–716). The newest draft removes mention of specific weapons, such as the MX and Pershing missiles, from the text to footnotes.[61] The pastoral proposes six "Steps to Reduce the Danger of War" (716) and closes with "Shaping a Peaceful World" (719–722). Although the wording becomes more "realistic," the substance does not radically change.[62]

The greatest debate among committee members involved the concept of a "freeze" on the status quo. Pro-military Bishop O'Connor insisted on the use of the word "curb" in testing, producing, and deploying strategic weapons, while other members preferred the more definitive "halt."[63]

By April 1983 the 150-page third draft was sent out, and again the press was included in the initial distribution. On May 3, 1983, a special NCCB meeting to adopt the pastoral convened in Chicago. As the bishops gathered, so did the interest of others. Triple the usual number of journalists pre-registered to attend what was considered to be a historic event.[64] During the course of the meeting, Catholics for Peace, wanting an even more stringent document, paraded in protest along Michigan Avenue, as did those opposing the pastoral.[65]

The meeting itself was highly structured, with both proponents and opponents limited to one or two minutes on the 515 proposed amendments under review. Because most of these were not supported by the drafting committee, many were withdrawn.[66] After two days of spirited discussion on the "curb" or "halt" issue, eventually "halt" was chosen. However, the bishops, urged by committee chair Archbishop Bernardin, who recognized the conflict it would create with Church policy, refrained from an outright moral condemnation of deterrence in the final version.[67] Additional refinements strengthening the letter's anti-nuclear thrust were incorporated, and softened language that had hedged the bishops' position in the second draft was reversed.[68] In the final analysis, the bishops had managed to accede to papal and conciliar teaching while retaining specific references to American culture. Moreover, in providing a statement of principle that was in the process of development, the bishops initiated an original contribution that extended rather than reiterated Church teaching.[69] When the NCCB adopted *The Challenge of Peace,* the assembled bishops accorded it the highest number of affirmative votes in recent pastoral history, an amazing achievement given its length, complexity, and controversy.[70]

This fourth and final version is almost 110 pages long, including an 18-page summary. The pastoral is divided into four sections. Part One covers the biblical, ecclesiastical, and moral components of Catholic tradition and provides explanations of just-war and nonviolent principles (200–225).[71] Part Two looks at the concepts of initiating, limiting, and deterring nuclear war (227–244). The bishops cite their research:

> Former public officials have testified that it is improbable that any nuclear war could actually be kept limited. Their testimony and the consequences involved in this problem lead us to conclude that the danger of escalation is so great that it would be morally unjustifiable to initiate nuclear war in any form (233).

Part Three presents six specific recommendations, such as accelerating efforts at arms control and developing means of alternate conflict resolution (245–261). The fourth and final portion presents spiritual forms of response, involving prayer, penance, and educating the conscience (262–267). The bishops conclude by addressing specific sectors of the Catholic community: religious, educators, parents, youth, military, defense workers, scientists, media, and public officials (267–273).

THE PUBLIC RESPONDS

The issuance of a series of drafts succeeded in keeping the pastoral letter before the public eye and in the forefront of media attention. Pope John XXIII's 1963 encyclical on nuclear arms and the Cold War, *Pacem in Terris (Peace on Earth)*, which, like the peace pastoral, was addressed not only to Catholics but to "all men of good will," drew from Catholic sources but had broad appeal in imparting a sense of urgency to the thoughtful outside the faith.[72] That document had set the previous standard for public visibility, but it was eclipsed by the wave of publicity that accompanied the American pastoral letter.[73] The peace pastoral was considered the most significant religion story in the country in 1983, and its process as well as its content was key to its impact on the entry of the Church into the public sphere.[74]

Certainly, the public response to the pastoral exceeded that accorded to any previous pastoral letter. Aside from the general public, consisting of Catholic and non-Catholic respondents who reacted to the contents of the letter and the policies proposed by the bishops, more specific aspects of "public" can be segregated into three categories. The first sense of public was concerns aroused in authoritative institutions seeking to safeguard the status quo, in this case the Reagan Administration and the Vatican. Ideological responses from those who disagreed with the bishops' conclusions presented a series of objections to the intrusion of the bishops into public policy. Finally, the catalyst that both provoked and recorded responses from the first two groups was the press, through the extensive coverage it afforded the pastoral.

Government Protest

The White House reaction to the first draft established an early sense of opposition and invested it with an importance that was unusual for a Church document. Reagan Administration officials had belatedly begun to respond to the first draft, criticizing its inclination toward "freeze" and "no first-use" recommendations. Thus the strengthened second draft, a clear confrontation by the bishops with current government policy, resulted in front-page news coverage in major newspapers throughout the country.[75] The *Boston Globe* reported: "The draft letter is being taken very seriously, not only within the Catholic Church but also in the Administration itself."[76]

Part of the seriousness may have had to do with the perception of Catholic clout. The size of the potential audience for the pastoral letter was impressive, prompting John Chancellor on "NBC Nightly News" to point out that the pastoral would go to fifty million American Catholics and that 75 percent of the American population supported a freeze on adding nuclear weapons to the existing arsenal.[77] John Bennett pointed out that the bishops had unusual visibility and influence because of their huge constituency.[78]

The *Boston Globe* reported that a task force from the State Department and Arms Control and Disarmament Agency and the National Security Council was convening to rebut the bishops' argument. The significance of the bishops' position and the influence that it might come to have was indicated in the Administration's efforts to "short-circuit" the pastoral by appealing over the bishops' heads to Rome.[79] Vernon Walters was sent as an envoy on a papal visit shortly after the first draft appeared, which was seen as a White House move to forestall the pastoral.[80] Later the U.S. Ambassador to the Vatican visited Cardinal Agostino Casaroli, Vatican Secretary of State, to emphasize the government's disagreement with the pastoral's thrust.[81] White House response continued to be indirect, reacting to news headlines rather than analysis of the texts.[82] For instance, Navy Secretary John F. Lehman, Jr., did not address his comments on the pastoral to the bishops but went directly to the press, where he conceded that while the bishops' "points on moral paradox are logical and well-founded in moral philosophy," their recommendations were "neither well-informed or logical."[83]

In reaction to the "dovish" first draft, the White House responded by writing letters requesting support from influential American Catholics. Conservative Catholics within the Reagan Administration were importuned to use their influence on the bishops.[84] Two Democrats and twenty-two Republicans signed an eight-page, single-spaced letter opposing the second draft of the pastoral, citing three popes, John F. Kennedy, Solzhenitsyn, and John Courtney Murray to bolster their argument.[85] The move may have been prompted to match a letter expressing support and defense of the bishops' right to speak signed by former CIA director William E. Colby, chief arms negotiator Gerard Smith, Senator Mark Hatfield, and retired Admiral John Marshall Lee.[86]

The antagonism between the bishops and the government reached a climax when National Security Advisor William Clark, in response to the second draft, sent a letter to committee chair Archbishop Bernardin, which was published in the *New York Times* before it was received by the archbishop. The letter contended that the Administration's deterrence policy fulfilled the moral guidelines of the Church, and that since the bishops supported the draft letter by a margin of two to one, the Administration felt it had to make its case directly to the public, over the heads of the bishops.[87] Archbishop Bernardin civilly called Clark's message "another link in the dialogue," although he expressed that he was "somewhat surprised" to read it in the *Times* first. Other bishops reacted with gratification that "their views were being taken so seriously by the White House."[88] Charles Curran claimed, "There can be no doubt that by their opposition to the second draft, [the Administration] gave more importance and significance to the bishops' document." [89]

The White House attempted to salvage victory by attempting to pass off changes to the draft as concessions by the bishops. State Department spokesman John Hughes proclaimed that the third draft "endorsed the objectives which the administration seeks." Michael Novak also sought to claim victory, saying, "the bishops really . . . did listen" to criticisms of earlier drafts. Some of these claims stemmed from the ambiguity and nuance with which the bishops invested their document.[90] In turn, Archbishop Bernardin and NCCB president Archbishop Roach rejected that spin effort, issuing a press statement on April 10 that refuted such an interpretation, saying the pastoral was still "explicitly critical."[91] Such denials in turn spawned additional headlines about the bishops' "unusual step of denying that they had yielded to White House pressure."[92]

By the time they issued the third draft, Archbishops Bernardin and Roach sought to focus attention on the document rather than on their differences with the Administration.[93] They attributed the changes made to the final version not only to dialogue with their colleagues and a stack of written comments but as a response to their "exchange of views" with representatives of the Holy See and European episcopal conferences.[94] Thus, while the bishops did adjust their position regarding pacifism and deterrence, their motivation was provided not by the President but by the Vatican.

The Vatican

In January 1983 the American committee was called to Rome to consult on the draft pastoral. Cardinal Casaroli, the Vatican Secretary of State, and Cardinal Joseph Ratzinger, the Prefect for the Congregation of the Doctrine of the Faith, had been designated to deal with the Americans. The Catholic News Service reported that the assignment of "two of the most powerful positions in the Vatican after the Pope" represented an "indication of the importance which the Vatican attached to the topic."[95]

These officials may have been anxious about the example being set by the American Church when they expressed concerns about the innovation of a democratic process of commentary and response, the more radical theological interpretation of peace, and the conferral of unwarranted theological authority by a national conference.[96] Nevertheless, observers noted that two committee members received new appointments from the Vatican. Military Vicar John O'Connor, who had opposed a number of points in the pastoral, nevertheless voted for the document. "Two months later he was made Archbishop of New York."[97] Others considered the elevation of Archbishop Bernardin to the rank of Cardinal of Chicago during this period to be a sign of implicit approval of his work as committee chairman.[98]

The bishops had accepted Roman injunctions to emphasize papal and conciliar pronouncements and reversed their emphasis to highlight just war doctrine rather than pacifism in the third draft.[99] However, the bishops did not accede to Cardinal Ratzinger's desire for a generalized theological statement. Archbishop Roach, NCCB president, responded, "Our position in the United States is that if we were to issue a document that outlines only the moral principles and not the application, no one would listen to us."[100] By agreeing to differentiate between levels of authority, thus making their specific recommendations matters for prudent consideration by Catholics rather than binding, the bishops were able to incorporate policy objectives. In spite of Vatican concerns, the bishops' aim to be concrete, active, and progressive conformed with American cultural values and demonstrated the Church's experience of assimilation in the U.S. The process they initiated and the innovation of articulating policy objectives contributed to the development of a new sense of the American Church.[101]

The bishops had steered between the conservative wing and the American liberals, who wanted a document condemning all nuclear arms and calling for unilateral disarmament.[102] Their stance was described as a moral and intelligent understanding of the planet's predicament, "not diagnostic radicals but prescriptive moderates."[103] By fostering a sense of a philosophy under development rather than presentation of a *fait accompli,* the bishops opened discourse to non-Catholic Americans and generated needed public debate. There were commentators who recognized the distinctive forum for public discussion that the bishops were providing. Sebastian Moore pointed out that since the White House had no public hearings, the bishops themselves were contributing to "the process of spontaneous democracy." He found it ironic that in spite of diatribes regarding the sanctity of Church and State separation, the bishops' committee "finds itself a sort of *ad hoc* lower house where voices not acceptable to the monarch may be heard."[104] Despite this desire to have many voices heard, many of those who captured public attention had a very narrow focus, and ideological debate came to dominate much of the discourse swirling around the pastoral.

Ideologies Polarize Debate

The factions that emerged to contest the pastoral were broader and more divisive than past Protestant-versus-Catholic divides; now the split was between Catholic against Catholic, conservative against liberal. This factionalism was played out in the press, where, in editorials and columns, ideological differences tended to contravene both civility and rationality. The ideological debate surrounding the peace pastoral emanated from, and contributed to, public reaction to the letter. The press coverage spun an eddy of public opinion that created its own momentum as columnists attacked the bishops, letters to the editors attacked the columnists, cartoons attacked both camps, headlines were made, and both the general and Catholic public became swept up in the publicity surrounding the letter. Initial dissent would grow and distort the dialogue that the bishops had hoped to encourage. The extensive press coverage may have fueled the initial divisiveness, since conservative interests were quick to react.

The serious press coverage given to the peace pastoral prompted conservative Catholics to counteract the effects of its public appeal. Philip Lawler from the Heritage Foundation, Ernest Lefever, head of the newly created Catholic Center for Renewal, and Michael Novak, a spokesman for corporate conservatives and author of a number of articles opposing the bishops, held their own conference in imitation of the bishops' nuclear fact-finding but failed to gain public credibility.[105] A parallel document entitled "Moral Clarity in the Nuclear Age" was published as an open letter in a special edition of *National Review*.[106]

> A highly vocal group of Catholic lay . . . dissidents sought to elicit signatures to an alternative pastoral letter drawing diametrically opposed conclusions. Among the signers to this letter, which had anticipated the endorsement of high government officials who would repudiate in advance the moral teaching of the bishops, was not a single recognized authoritative or responsible (civil or military) official concerned with defense questions.[107]

The absence of signatures by policymakers indicated recognition of the fact that a war must be winnable to be rational. "Nuclear war does not meet this simple and commonsense criterion."[108] In an op-ed piece, Roland Evans and Robert Novak called the bishops a "heretical hierarchy" that "threatened a schism," because their position on nuclear arms was equivalent to fourth-century heresies, and they claimed that it was also "undermining the U.S. government moral stature in its own country."[109] Such extreme reactions from those dissenting with the pacifist approach attest to the perceived significance of the letter.

More effectively, simultaneously articles appeared making many of the same points against the bishops, giving credence to reports that a public opinion campaign had recruited conservative editorial writers and columnists to oppose the bishops' position.[110] The concerted reactions of conservative columnists to the bishops' stance, such as William F. Buckley Jr., James Kirkpatrick, and George Will, editorial writers, and other media pundits generated a level of controversy that had not occurred before.[111]

One repeated element of contention by the critics was the entrance of the bishops into the realm of public discourse. Certainly the charges against them seemed to stem from their increasing presence and influence in the public arena. The criticisms fell into four categories, all commenting less on the content of the letter than on the bishops' right to write it. Critics tended to raise one or more of the following points: first, the violation of Church and State relations; second, the competence of the bishops to comment on matters beyond their scope of knowledge; third, the staff of the United States Catholic Conference, which was accused of imposing a "liberal" position; and fourth, the secularization of the bishops' focus, which, by addressing social issues, would diminish their call to spirituality.[112]

The responses to the first of these charges came from Americans who pointed out that every religious denomination had entered politics on some issue and that the First Amendment did not necessitate a separation of the Church from society. The bishops' defenders also pointed out that these issues had not arisen as long as the bishops had been supporting the government's agenda. On the issue of competence, Archbishop Bernardin noted that newspaper editorialists were not competent in every field, but their views were published. He pointed out that the bishops were not positioning themselves as experts but were sharing their reasoning.[113] On the issue of staff, the bishops did not respond to the presentation of themselves as meek followers being manipulated by an agenda-driven staff. The very diverse views existing among the highly educated bishops would have precluded any such passivity. Archbishop Bernardin did respond to the multiple criticisms of secularization made by pundits unaware of recent pastoral history. He linked the bishops' moral competence (which some critics reluctantly conceded) to their responsibility to address the moral dimensions of social issues and depicted their goal not as issuance of an authoritarian fiat but as an invitation to dialogue.[114]

From the beginning, many of the criticisms of the bishops in the daily press were marked by rhetorical exaggeration and a lack of civility. Ignoring, or ignorant of, the bishops' 1980 pastoral critiquing Marxism and their long history of patriotism, much was made of the bishops' being Communistic. Phyllis Schlafly spoke of the bishops "loving the Russians" and making the Kremlin happy.[115] One priest published a book accusing the bishops of being moles planted by the KGB years before as a long-term strategy to defeat the

U.S.[116] Larry McDonald, a Georgia congressman, called the bishops "Marxist-loving" and had entered into the *Congressional Record* an article from *Washington Dateline* that referred to the "bombastic bolshevist bishops."[117] A letter from a group of Massachusetts citizens was also entered, stating, "It is pure myth to hold that civilization would be terminated in its aftermath," because the effects of nuclear war have been "grossly exaggerated."[118]

Idealism was another category for denigrating the bishops' competence. R. Emmett Tyrrell, Jr., scoffed, "The pope's agents here have always been somewhat quaint" in propagating their "trinity of bosh—persuasion, moral example and high-minded negotiations."[119] In one of many articles entitled "The Bishops and the Bomb," the director of research for the Hudson Institute wrote in the *New York Times* that the bishops were subject to "some abstract or emotional judgment" rather than being "exponents of objective analyses," because there was "no evidence" that nuclear war would "threaten created order."[120] Erik von Kuehnelt-Leddihn also chided, "The bishops' letter breathes idealism," and averred that "moral imperialism, the attempt to inject theology into politics, ought to be avoided except in extreme cases, of which abolition and slavery are examples."[121] Presumably nuclear holocaust did not satisfy his criteria. A *Milwaukee Journal* editorial called the pastoral letter "almost facile at avoiding the claims of the real world."[122]

Past bishops had been accustomed to countering attacks on their loyalty because of anti-Catholic sentiment. However, the contemporary pastoral letters gave the bishops the novel experience of having their patriotism questioned from *within* the Church.[123] Even within their own ranks, Archbishop Philip M. Hannan of New Orleans publicly claimed that the drafters of the pastoral had exceeded both their authority and expertise and stepped beyond their positions as moral teachers and pastors.[124] Catholic William F. Buckley assured readers that the pastoral would be ignored, since the bishops lost credibility by addressing subjects other than religion.[125] Thus the bishops found themselves facing opposition in many directions, all of which fueled continual public interest and attention. Instead of reasoned discourse, diatribe replaced civil debate, impeding the bishops' ability to promulgate their message about creating a new attitude toward peace. The divisiveness created by the pastoral itself became a focus of attention.

Accounting for Press Coverage

A number of factors contributed to the press reaction to the letter: intrigue with a divided Catholic stance on public policy; the unusual openness of the process; a sense of controversy created by the rhetoric of conservative opposition; opposition to the sitting Administration's pro-defense policies; press access to the bishops' meetings; and the movement of stories over time from the "Religion" section to the front page.

Initial speculation by the press as to the bishops' reasons for the about-face in their public policy stance framed a number of early articles. Early press reports continually highlighted what seemed to be a surprising deviation for the patriotic, establishment-supporting hierarchy. Typical was a *Des Moines Register* editorial commenting that the document was remarkable because since World War I, the clergy had supported every U.S. military effort.[126] Joseph Berger in *Newsday* called the pastoral "a remarkable departure from their moderate image."[127] He went on to call their new image a "radical conversion," spurred by the new bellicosity of the Reagan Administration.[128] *Time* magazine articulated the paradox, "[M]any people both inside and outside the church are wondering how it is that the bishops, who only a few years ago praised the Lord and passed the ammunition are now backing . . . a pacifist-tinged cause."[129] The shift in the bishops' position took the public by surprise, but it was the change in the process of producing the pastoral, so different from the universal Church's secretive way of operating, that generated a great deal of commentary. "Some bishops point out, with a bit of exasperation, that they have in fact taken provocative positions on major policy issues in the past, although without catching the public eye as they have on nuclear arms."[130]

Public Outreach

As if the novelty of inviting secular experts to provide testimony was not enough of a radical innovation, the bishops followed up this process of input by offering a similar opportunity to the public. Once the *Washington Post,* followed by the wire services, revealed the thrust of the initial draft and the pastoral letter became news, bishops actively solicited input from their dioceses and publicized the pastoral by issuing their own letters, giving speeches, writing newspaper columns or articles, and granting interviews in local Catholic and secular publications.[131]

Venues for reaching the public were varied. Press reports increased during the time of the NCCB's annual November meeting. *Time,* in its "Nation" section, and *Newsweek* covered the bishops' efforts.[132] Morning shows aired interviews with Archbishop Bernardin[133] and NCCB president Archbishop Roach;[134] both appeared on November 16, 1982. The McLaughlin Group televised a half-hour debate of diverse opinions.[135] Radio interviews with bishops and Administration officials offered other opportunities for varied views.[136] Later St. Peter's Church in Washington was selected as the location for a nationally televised debate among Rev. Brian Hehir, staff to the bishops; Senator Patrick Leahy; William Colby; congressman Dan Lundgren of California; and Lt. Gen. Daniel O. Graham, former head of the Defense Intelligence Agency.[137]

Over the course of the letter's production, the bishops received as much attention as the letter's content. Authorship of previous pastorals had been unpublicized; now the bishops themselves were in the limelight. The committee chair, Archbishop Bernardin, who by then had been named head of the Chicago diocese, was depicted on the cover of *Time* (November 29, 1982). The *New York Times Magazine*'s cover story was titled "America's Activist Bishops."[138] Lampoons in "Doonesbury," on "Saturday Night Live,"[139] and in cartoons appeared.[140]

While the bishops' objections to nuclear deterrence elicited much critical commentary, no such negativity was directed at the process they used. On the contrary, their new openness attracted a great deal of notice and provided an important innovation in pastoral creation.

OPENING RHETORICAL DIALOGUE

Commentators made much of the dramatic change in the process of producing this pastoral. Americans were intrigued not only by the bishops' expressing policy views but by the spectacle of the bishops listening and giving voice to a diversity of opinions out in public. "In another age the meeting would have been held in seclusion and secrecy," said *Time* in describing press access to the bishops' conference in 1982.[141] The fact that Catholics were being asked not to "read and obey" but to "weigh and consider" also constituted a significant change in the usual way of doing things.[142]

That such deviation from the norm would alarm Vatican officials was predictable. The *New York Times* reported Cardinal Casaroli's worry that the expectations created by the U.S. bishops would affect the bishops in the rest of the world.[143] Not only did other nations' conferences hold different views on bilateral disarmament and nuclear deterrence, but the open process used by the Americans represented a distinct contrast to the usual Church practice of maintaining secretive guard over projects until the finished document was released. A French prelate, referring to the U.S. bishops' decision to develop their pastoral in the full glare of public debate and to allow successive drafts into the public realm, remarked, "In France that would be unimaginable."[144] This democratic mode extended not only to the process used to create the pastoral but to its rhetorical style.

Public Argument

It was the very "American" style of the process adopted in the U.S. Church that signaled for some observers a final step of merged identities. "The revolution in communications signified by the pastoral letters is more than a net gain in public relations skills, as if the focus of concern lay with the successful dissemination of church documents. The focus is instead upon . . . equality of access to public moral argument."[145] Dennis McCann described the consultations as reminiscent of American town meetings, and the resulting series of drafts as meeting a standard of American reasonableness, because they revealed an ability to revise ideas and accommodate the legitimate concerns of opposing viewpoints.[146] *Time* also noted the pastoral's prompting of dialogue, so that what was issued was not "an authoritarian fiat" but an invitation for Americans to participate, marveling at the novelty: " It is the openness, the tentative quality of the pastoral, that appeals." [147] The Philadelphia *Catholic Standard and Times* wondered if so much attention to the process was detracting from the pastoral's message but concluded that the bishops' moral leadership was effective precisely because they had facilitated the involvement of so many in a process of reflection rather than relying on a final product.[148]

The bishops had explicitly articulated as their goal the desire to mold public opinion regarding the use of nuclear weapons. In contrast to their accustomed reticence about controversial public issues like slavery, these bishops wanted to contribute the wisdom of the Church to the debate: "For too many our teaching is an undiscovered or ignored resource."[149] Charles Curran acknowledged, "Many Roman Catholics today are very surprised to learn about the existence of the body of teachings which the American bishops have issued on social questions in the last fifteen years."[150] Aside from this presentation of teaching, the bishops hoped to make people think and debate with "civility and charity": "This pastoral letter is more an invitation to continue the new appraisal of war and peace than a final synthesis of the results of such an appraisal."[151]

The process of listening and responding represented a very different stance from the traditional dictum of "pray, pay, and obey." The bishops did not want to issue a dictatorial proclamation but sought to convince their audiences through rhetorical means that strongly echo classical tradition: "The voice of the peacemaking church must reflect the facts, rest on competent analysis, and demonstrate good will. It cannot just proclaim positions; it must argue its case understanding the complexity as well as the urgency of the issues."[152] One editor praised the fact that the pastoral did not pontificate or dictate what readers were required to think, but established arguments that asked people to think for themselves.[153] Observers recognized that the bishops' attempt to influence others outside their membership required a different approach: "They can persuade people outside that constituency because they did not issue an ecclesiastical edict, which would depend for its authority on their role as bishops. They came to their post by a process that non-Catholics, both religious and secular, can appreciate."[154] A *Boston Globe* editorial claimed that the pastoral " will stand as a tribute, not just to Catholic theology . . . but to the intelligence and openness of the American people."[155] Evangelical Christians acknowledged that "because of the nature of the document itself, the letter has become the focal point of the national debate surrounding nuclear weapons; indeed, with the pastoral letter the bishops have in many ways defined the parameters of the debate—certainly in its moral dimensions."[156]

The public process that was instituted with the peace pastoral contributed to the bishops' ambitions of appealing to a wider audience and establishing a dialogic approach.

> The process itself greatly helped and abetted the purpose of making Catholics and the general public much more aware of the moral issues involved in this question. The best teaching device is no longer merely a letter coming from on high which will probably be read and studied by very few. The public and participatory process thus enhanced the teaching aspect and the influence of the letter, to say nothing about the internal strength of the document itself.[157]

Referring to the peace pastoral, NCCB president Bishop James Malone declared, "The national attention paid to the letter was due to what we said, but also the way we said it."[158]

The sessions of listening to experts on all sides, the succession of drafts, and the bishops' appearances in public discussions were all novel elements that created a democratic process of reaching their position. Archbishop Bernardin himself revealed his understanding that the model established by the peace pastoral process would become a standard for future efforts, telling the assembled bishops in November 1982, "The process of discussion, writing and witness which has already been generated by the statements of the bishops and particularly the pastoral may be the most important long-range consequence of our efforts."[159] While the original motives for the open consultation and multiple drafts may have been happenstance, both the process and the publicity it incurred contributed significantly to the bishops' original purpose in preparing the pastoral.

The Technical Sphere

A rhetorical focus for contention between factions centered on the authority or ability of the bishops to question matters reserved to technical experts. The basis for denigrating the bishops' competence to comment on nuclear arms stemmed from the assumption that the right to comment on public policy questions was reserved to qualified professionals. Although this would deny the masses of people to reach their own judgment on matters affecting the national welfare, the bishops were attacked for presuming to interfere in the technical sphere. Typical was the accusation by Phyllis Schlafly: "Religious leaders do not have the expertise to make technical judgments."[160] Conrad Komorowski pointed out that the *New Republic* or *National Review* "arrogates to itself the competence to hold views on nuclear war policy but denies it to the bishops."[161] This column was one of the very few commentaries on the duplicity of the press in freely criticizing the bishops' participation in making public policy without noticing their own infringement on the bishops' right to make a statement to their own members.

As their detractors made their case in the press, proponents defended the rights of the bishops to speak. Among the signatories of a defense of the bishops' stand were Secretary of Commerce Philip M. Klutznick; former CIA Director William E. Colby; Gerard Smith, chief negotiator on arms talks; Senator Mark Hatfield; retired Admiral John Marshall Lee; retired Brigadier General Robert M. Montgomery; and a number of professors.[162] Not only did they assert that silence on the part of the bishops would be indefensible, they went further, "We cannot rely on government to act on this matter in a timely fashion," and defended their competence in being "better informed technically than most of their critics."[163] An editorial in the *Los Angeles Times* reminded readers that the nuclear issue was not only a scientific and technical question but a validly moral one, and that the Church's constructive contribution consisted of "its willingness to engage the world as it is."[164] A *Philadelphia Inquirer* editorial pointed out that the bishops represented a valid counter-voice: "Public opinion needs to be sustained against the hawkish policies of the Reagan administration and the Soviet regime. The Bishops' pastoral letter . . . meets that challenge head-on."[165]

The *Boston Globe,* editorializing on the first draft, called it "compelling reading for non-Catholics as well as Catholics. In its impact on American attention, the pastoral letter seems destined to become the most important public document in more than a decade." It attributed this status not only to its contents but to its aims of urging ordinary citizens to apply their intelligence and conscience to policy issues, and thereby "defrock the 'nuclear priesthood'" of national security specialists who undergo little public scrutiny.[166] Jonathan Schell, among others, concurred with the bishops that ultimately no one could delegate the responsibility: "Once the citizen has gone to the scientists and received the information that they have available, he must, without further professional help, take counsel with himself."[167]

Thus the core of the bishops' pastoral magisterium required civil enlightenment of their communities. In the case of this pastoral, their warrant was a pragmatic one, prompted by the crisis of nuclear proliferation.[168] In his first-year update to the NCCB, Archbishop Bernardin had been very explicit about the bishops' acting on their civic responsibilities. He listed some of the problems with U.S. policy, namely, the intention of fighting "limited " nuclear wars, which few believed could be controlled, the readiness to revert to such weapons, and the creation of automatic systems that limited human intervention. He then explicated the committee's desire for effective persuasion: "As teachers we must always be concerned about the quality of the public debate. The Church should bring to this debate the best arguments which reason can muster." The bishops, he said, were acting not only in a pastoral capacity but a civic one: "The duty of responsible moral action falls equally on both superpowers. But if we direct our attention particularly to the United States, it is for the simple reason that we are American citizens and have a right and duty to address our government."[169]

Broadening the Audience

In a U.S. Catholic Conference press release,[170] two distinct and overlapping audiences for the pastoral were identified, along with dual purposes for the letter: first was a Catholic audience, for whom the letter was to be an aid in forming their consciences by articulating Gospel values and Catholic moral tradition; second, the letter was addressed to a wider civic community, a more pluralistic audience, of whom Catholics were also members, in order to contribute to the public policy debate regarding the morality of war.

In this regard, William Murnion attributed to the bishops an achievement beyond pluralism, writing that they "convoked a homogeneous audience, without distinction of religion and perhaps not of nationality, to hear what they [had] to advise."[171] Timothy Byrnes categorized the letter thus:

> *The Challenge of Peace* was a forceful, unapologetic analysis and critique of American defense policy that the Bishops offered the whole country in terms that the whole country could understand. Traditionally, the Bishops had supported American foreign and defense policy for the purpose of defending the patriotic credentials of an immigrant people. The tone and content of the pas-

toral letter, however, suggested that the bishops of the 1980s were very confident of their own voice and of their church's place in American society.[172]

Harvey Cox, Catholic theologian, explained why the involvement of mainstream Churches was so critical, "[N]o other single element can offer the base and legitimacy that religious leadership can provide. None other can reach so many people so intimately. And none is so uniquely positioned to change attitudes toward warfare or to articulate a new moral vision."[173] A *Des Moines Register* editorial concurred with the weight provided by collegiality, saying of the Church's voice, "From the pandemonium of public discourse, a single, clear statement emerges."[174] Joe Holland of the Center of Concern, a Catholic think tank in Washington, had called the movement against nuclear threat the "Third Great Awakening in America," after the revolution and abolition.[175] Schell agreed, writing that the spiritual process of the pastoral "might be described as an awakening rather than a movement" that could "alter the psychological and spiritual map of the world."[176]

Many did not understand the depth of change that the pastoral was attempting to bring about. It was not idealism that the bishops were espousing, but conversion away from instinctive reliance on military means. *The Challenge of Peace* was clear on this:

> Today the possibilities for placing political and moral limits on nuclear war are so infinitesimal that the moral task, like the medical, is prevention: As a people we must refuse to legitimate the idea of nuclear war. Such a refusal will require not only new ideas and new vision, but what the Gospel calls conversion of heart.[177]

One of the committee members, Bishop Daniel P. Reilly of Norwich, Connecticut, made the distinction that the pastoral was not political but spiritual: "Peace is more than just the absence of war. It embraces a quest for social justice."[178] Some were taken aback by such positivist rhetoric in an age of negativity: "The U.S. has wasted a generation of moral and intellectual resources since World War II defining itself—and us—by what it is against rather than what it is for."[179]

Many who narrowly criticized the bishops' specific policies failed to recognize the scope of their vision.

> We see with increasing clarity the political folly of a system which threatens mutual suicide, the psychological damage this does to ordinary people, especially the young, the economic distortion of priorities. . . . Today military preparations are undertaken on a vast and sophisticated scale, but the declared purpose is not to use the weapons produced.[180]

The explicit rhetorical purpose of the peace pastoral was to bring attention to a new evaluation of existing conditions and to arouse public opinion about these conditions, not by fiat but by creating an opening in public discourse. The bishops succeeded in gaining public attention, but the opposition they faced distorted their ability to provoke thoughtful dialogue. However, other forums beside the press were successful in disseminating the pastoral's teachings.

AFTER THE PASTORAL

The desire of the bishops to penetrate the public consciousness through more thorough means was not limited to preparation of a summary for those unwilling to read the entire document. The sincerity of their desire to shift passive public acceptance of defense policy is indicated by multiple efforts to disseminate, explain, and examine the contents of *The Challenge of Peace.*

Education

The desire of the bishops to effect change and to educate listeners of their message did not stop with the publication of the pastoral. Reminded by Bishop Thomas Gumbleton of Detroit that "other pastoral letters have just flitted off into space," a number of local efforts were made to ward off a similar fate for the peace pastoral.[181] These endeavors took place in several venues, on campuses and in parishes, aided by the production of varied media aids. Archbishop James A. Hickey of Washington, D.C., declared, "Thousands of people in more than half our parishes have participated in discussion and educational events on this issue."[182]

Bishop Maurice J. Dingman of Des Moines promised that the pastoral would not gather dust. On a diocesan level, homilies, classrooms, and conferences were all to be used as instruments for analysis by the laity. Programs of prayer, study, reflection, and discussion were aimed at shaping what Archbishop Hickey called a "constituency of conscience," with critical policy not left to technicians or a few leaders. Adult education programs and parochial school curricula allowed the pastoral to reach all age groups.[183]

Peace workshops, task forces, and special Masses were joined by the formulation of peace and justice groups in many parishes and schools. Across the nation, regions devised their own methods of keeping the pastoral alive. Milwaukee established January as a month of reflection. On Long Island, parish bells rang daily for five minutes as a reminder to pray for peace. Kits and visual aids were prepared for groups that wanted to discuss the pastoral. Aside from many reprints in newspapers and magazines, 365,000 copies of

The Challenge of Peace were sold. The pastoral was made available in Braille and on cassette. Various groups prepared their own materials geared toward their memberships' needs; for example, the National Catholic Educational Association provided a program for teachers. Two-thirds of Catholic colleges devoted a specific period for focus on the pastoral, and twenty campuses provided credit courses with the pastoral as the major text.[184]

The bishops established a follow-up committee and an office for implementation of the pastoral, which functioned as a clearinghouse for resources and programs.[185] In some parishes, teams were established to help promulgate the pastoral; others held discussions and lectures, aided by "A Call to Peacemaking," a national conference held in Washington to educate parish leaders and teachers. Interfaith groups were formed to study the pastoral.[186] Pax Christi and Benedictines for Peace produced written and visual materials and held educational workshops. Chaplains and military colleges used the pastoral to discuss the ethical aspects of modern warfare. Manhattan and St. Bonaventure Colleges established interdisciplinary peace programs as courses of study. High school and elementary grade children brought the issues raised in the classroom home to their parents.[187]

After adoption of the pastoral, NBC TV-News broadcast a one-hour special on "The Bishops and the Bomb" on Sunday afternoon, May 15, 1983, which consisted of interviews and analysis of the pastoral by correspondent Edwin Newman. Afterward an announcement offered transcripts and study guides on request.[188] Other materials that were produced included a one-hour videotape with a study guide, "A Call to Peacemaking: What Does the Peace Pastoral Say?" by Peter J. Henriot;[189] tapes containing two lectures by the lead staff person to the bishops' committee, Rev. Bryan J. Hehir, "Peace Pastoral Seminar"[190] and "The Challenge of Peacemaking," a fifty-minute videotape discussing the pastoral.[191] One of the committee members, Bishop John J. O'Connor, televised four half-hour segments covering the basic texts, "An Introduction to the Bishops' Pastoral Letter: The Challenge of Peace."[192]

Another member, Bishop Thomas Gumbleton, narrated "The Peace Pastoral and Christian Conscience,"[193] a one-hour audio recording. Another audiocassette produced was John J. Egan's "The Bishops' Pastoral Letter on War and Peace."[194] Other publications sought to give the pastoral immediacy, such as "Education and Action Guide: For Implementing the Peace Pastoral of the U.S. Catholic Bishops,"[195] and "Pastorals on Sundays: A Week by Week Resource from *The Challenge of Peace and Economic Justice for All*."[196]

Such a variety of media provided those wishing to teach the pastoral a wide range of options for many types of audience. It was clear from these productions that the bishops were serious in their intention to "lift up the moral dimensions of the choices before our world and nation."[197]

Effects

Catholics did not simply sit and talk about the pastoral. One report, acknowledging that the pastoral letter had weathered attacks by both right and left and was generally considered a thoughtful, realistic assessment, questioned whether it had penetrated Catholic consciousness. It went on to describe Connecticut Catholic protest of General Electric's involvement with development of MX and Trident missiles, the B-1 bomber, and the Trident submarine as a rare case of suburbanites picketing corporate headquarters, a result attributed to parish education programs.[198] According to a poll conducted by the National Opinion Research Center, the number of Catholics who thought that too much money was being spent on weapons rose from 22 percent in 1983 to 54 percent in 1984.[199]

Positive responses to the pastoral were not limited to Catholic communities. Commentaries by a number of faiths, mostly favorable, created an opportunity for ecumenical dialogue. A press release by the Synagogue Council of America called for sensitizing the Jewish community to the indifference on the nuclear arms race and noted that "the pronouncement of the American Catholic Bishops represents an extraordinary opportunity for major religious groups to join together in cooperative efforts."[200] The *Congressional Record* reported, "Both Protestant and Jewish leaders have already warmly welcomed the pastoral letter and have begun a dialogue with Catholic leaders."[201] The Union of American Hebrew Congregations awarded their Einstein prize to the NCCB "for moral leadership in rousing the conscience of America" in Houston on November 10, 1983. The commendation praised the way in which the pastoral letter sought to "open space in the policy debate for the explicit analysis of the moral dimensions of policy." In his acceptance, Archbishop Bernardin warned, "When apathy prevails, policy lacks both the discipline and the support afforded by public opinion."[202] The $50,000 grant was to be used for six media projects such as radio spots, a video of a pastoral letter symposium, visuals for presentations on the pastoral by the bishops, and children's materials, such as a comic book.[203]

The acknowledgment made by Protestant and Jewish organizations of the bishops' leadership emphasized the extent to which the Church's outreach had changed. The pastoral effort offered a significant contrast to the previous century's lag of Catholic contributions to social reform. Ironically, the credit was given to the strength created by a hierarchy that allowed the bishops to speak authoritatively as a single voice. Other faiths had not conducted such a complex and exhaustive examination by exploring a variety of views.[204] Eighteen organizations represented by 1,400 Evangelical Christians gathered in Pasadena at the end of May 1983 for a conference, "The Church and Peacemaking in the Nuclear Age." "Inspired by the thought-provoking and carefully crafted work of the American Catholic bishops . . . [a]fter many years of silence on this issue, Evangelicals are now entering the national debate on this important policy issue."[205] Crediting the Catholic bishops with "inspiration and energy" and expressing a similar desire to mobilize the Jewish community, the Union of American Hebrew Congregations, representing over 700 Reform synagogues, produced a 300-page educational manual entitled "Preventing the Nuclear Holocaust—A Jewish Response."[206] Thus the bishops were acknowledged for the leadership they had demonstrated with the pastoral. "Their appointment of a follow-up committee to develop diocesan educational materials was an action followed by other religions."[207]

The ecumenical effect of the pastoral was impressive in its ability to gain the approbation of national associations. The Synagogue Council of America proclaimed that the "pronouncement of American Catholic Bishops represents an extraordinary opportunity for major religions to join together in cooperative efforts."[208] The pastoral was endorsed by other organizations of faith, such as the American Academy of Religion and the Council of Methodist Bishops.[209] The Southern Baptist Theological Seminary produced an informative videotape.[210] The National Council of Churches endorsed the pastoral for study by Protestant, Anglican, and Orthodox denominations.[211] The success of the pastoral's dissemination program may be judged by the concern of the pastoral's critics. *Betraying the Bishops: How the Pastoral Letter on War and Peace Is Being Taught* took issue with the peace orientation of educational efforts that, according to its author, failed to emphasize the carefully crafted nuances of the pastoral.[212] *The Ultimate Weapon* also sought to dampen a widespread tendency to interpret the pastoral from a pacifist perspective.[213]

The Challenge of Peace represented a pinnacle of pastoral achievement on several levels. The visibility it received acquainted many, both Catholics and non-Catholics, with a new source of leadership for input on the moral aspects of public issues. The open process created by the bishops provided a sense of dialogue encompassing the inclusion of lay voices, the distribution of drafts, and listening to comments, and imbued the pastoral's production with a democratic sense of participation that gratified Americans and Catholic laity. The praise from intellectual, academic, journalistic, and ecumenical circles, the manifold attempts to discredit the bishops' authority, and the attention of the White House and the Vatican all attested to the pastoral's significance for, and impact on, the public. In laying down theological foundations for consideration of a policy issue, the bishops' careful wording to accommodate interpretation and conscience, and the innovation of providing both philosophical and specific guidelines distinguished by differing levels of acceptance, established a precedent for their right and ability to speak on public issues. They received credit not only for creating a space for their own voice but for providing a fulcrum for general public debate.

The publicity that brought so much attention to the bishops' message also diluted its scope and sophistication. Their desire to generate public dialogue had succeeded, although the dissension at times seemed closer to cacophony than civic conversation. Nevertheless, the bishops' legacy was to provide a forum for scholars, commentators, politicians, and the public to revisit and reconsider a national reliance on global annihilation as a legitimate form of self-defense. Their success in raising the nation's consciousness created a momentum that quite naturally spilled over to the next pastoral, the letter on economics.

Chapter Four
Economic Justice for All

THE DECADE OF GREED THAT CAME TO CHARACTERIZE THE 1980S was as yet un-
knowable and unnamed when the bishops made the decision to address
morality issues surrounding capitalism during their November 1980 meeting. This was the same meeting that gave rise to the suggestion for a pastoral
on war and peace. It was also the same meeting at which the joint pastoral
letter of 1980, a critique of Marxist Communism, was adopted by a vote of
236 to 17. The dissenting votes had occurred because of the perception on
the part of some that the pastoral's denunciation of Marxist doctrine was
too severe.

Although the pastoral managed to avoid the typical vocabulary of anti-
Communist rhetoric, its ultimate condemnation of the system appeared to
bestow tacit approval on its counterpart, capitalism.[1] Therefore, Peter
Rosazza, auxiliary bishop of Hartford, suggested a pastoral to complement
the study on Marxism, one that would examine the ethical dimensions of
capitalism.[2] However, because the process to produce what came to be
known as the economic pastoral took six years, it appeared to be a consequence of the publicity surrounding the peace pastoral. In spite of asser-
tions by critics who accused the bishops of instigating an attack on
President Reagan or capitalizing on the successful publicity achieved by the
peace pastoral, in fact, the economic pastoral, initiated at the same time as
the peace pastoral, was not motivated by it.[3]

This chapter demonstrates that the process of producing the economic
pastoral followed that of the peace pastoral and that the delay in the process, while not deliberate, enabled the bishops to maximize the breadth of the
debate on American capitalism. The economic pastoral benefited from the
creation of its predecessor's model of participation, review, successive drafts,
and press attention. These elements were expanded as they were formally

implemented as part of the pastoral process. Thus the time lag between the peace and economic pastorals, although proposed at the same meeting, created a momentum that emphasized a sense of the development of a new mode of pastoral discourse. The effect was enhanced by the public's recent awareness of the bishops' aims, thus bestowing an instant spotlight on their next effort. The increase in the perceived influence of the bishops' discourse aroused a parallel reaction in their opponents, resulting in a lay alternative statement and amplifying vituperative rhetoric to an unprecedented level. The economic pastoral represented the apogee in the new array of pastoral elements that enabled the bishops to extend the influence of Church teachings to the larger community but exposed them to the controversy of divisive ideology.

PRECEDENTS

Critics, who would again accuse the bishops of unwarranted trespass into an arena of technical policy, seemed to be unaware that the Church had been addressing economic issues prior to the pastoral. A series of late nineteenth- and twentieth-century papal encyclicals had emerged in the wake of the Industrial Revolution, beginning with Pope Leo XIII's 1891 statement *Rerum Novarum*, which addressed the rights of workers, humane working conditions, the inequitable concentration of wealth, and the responsibility of the state to serve the common good.

Pope Pius XI's 1931 encyclical *Quadragesimo Anno* emphasized similar themes, criticizing economic greed and the excessive concentration of wealth, and supporting the rights of workers to collective bargaining and just wages.[4] In this country, the Bishops' Program of 1919 had systematically critiqued the work and wage structure of the industrialized United States. The Depression galvanized Church leaders to support New Deal efforts to implement the reforms they had proposed.[5] Thus the American Church, unlike its European counterparts, had a publicly supportive posture toward the working class.[6] The industrialized nature of work in which urban immigrants were engaged had impelled the American bishops to support labor rights for their constituents.

As the century progressed, the bishops turned the nation's attention to recognizing the growing interdependence of nations, a prominent theme in postwar Church documents. "By 1940, the Catholic Church had permanently modified its reputation for conservatism; liberal and Protestant leaders expressed their admiration for the progressive position of the Church's leadership on issues of economic reform."[7] In that year, in their *Statement on*

Church and Social Order, the bishops' denunciation of secularism resulting from the divorce of social life from religion included the concentration of capital and called for state action (1:440). However, their opposition to Communism and its persecution of religion kept them quiet during the 1950s.

Pope John XXIII, in *Mater et Magistra* (1961), points out the complexity and interrelatedness of global economic relations created by scientific and technological progress, and repeats the role of government in promoting the common good and protecting the basic rights of the poor, so that prosperity is measured not by the total sum of wealth but by its equitable distribution.[8] After the Second Vatican Council, when pastoral statements became more topically specific, much of the bishops' commentary on economic conditions was embedded in statements focused on welfare reform (1970), world famine (1974), the elderly and new immigrants (1976), Native Americans (1977), the handicapped (1978), and housing (1972, 1975). *The Economy: Human Dimensions* in 1975 followed up on their 1930 response to the unemployment of the Depression.[9]

Pope John Paul II issued *Laborem Exercens* ("On Human Work") in 1981, emphasizing the role of work, unions, adequate wages, and participation in decision making. In it he establishes a theme that the American bishops would later stress, namely, that workers are not mere cogs or tools, another element in the material system of production: "However true it may be that man is destined for work and called to it, in the first place work is 'for man' and not 'man for work.'"[10] His premise that both the idle rich and the idle poor are deprived is based on the concept that work represents an activity of self-realization.[11]

The American bishops had addressed the concept of employment in statements issued in 1919 and during the 1930s. Their latest document on economic issues, the 1980 pastoral critiquing the systemic structure of Marxist Communism, was ignored by both the press and the public.[12]

As with the issue of the peace pastoral, the economic issue was informed by the experiences of individual bishops, who had seen in their own regions the human affliction resulting from corporate decisions to maximize profits by reducing employment. The worsening economic climate for agriculture, especially family farms, took an enormous personal and cultural toll throughout the Midwest. Huge plants in industrialized cities closed, demoralizing entire regions. Reporting on the plight of nine states in the Midwest, the *Chicago Tribune* recounted the human costs of joblessness created by triple the national average unemployment rate, resulting in child and spousal abuse, suicide, marital separation, ill health, and higher mortality rates.[13] Without sufficient resources to assist these blue-collar families, individual bishops, such as Bishop James W. Malone of Youngstown, Ohio, himself the son of a steelworker, were left struggling to combat the corporate abandonment of the Rust Belt.[14]

The united stance of the bishops to conduct an inquiry into the morality of capitalism may have evolved from their recognition that "in 1982 the richest 20% of Americans received more income than the bottom 70% combined."[15] It may have also come from the continual strain on their resources created by the consequences of dismantling social services for the hungry, the jobless, and the homeless.[16] While the President and the press celebrated economic prosperity, the bishops were besieged for soup kitchens and homeless shelters.[17] Such close exposure to the plight of many made them see that "poverty is creating a mass of voiceless and powerless citizens."[18]

Thus, prior to releasing the first draft, although the bishops argued about the tone and emphasis of certain sections, the subject of the pastoral itself appeared to receive no internal dissent. Their accord on the topic of economic injustice resulted from the fact that "the bishops deal first-hand with poverty and despair," and the recognition that "wealth can come at the expense of much suffering among people who labor in mines, factories or shops, or whose skills are no longer needed by the economy."[19]

Nevertheless, the bishops' position evoked surprise, because early pastorals had generally encouraged individual economic prosperity through education and immersion in the American work ethic. In their search to explain this seemingly new position, some in the press made comments similar to those prompted by the peace pastoral, namely, that such a controversy would have been unthinkable twenty years ago. "American bishops . . . used to bless the American economic system in the same way that they blessed battleships."[20]

However, other public commentators recognized the unfolding direction of the bishops' discourse. CNN reported that poverty was just one of several policy issues the bishops had addressed in recent years.[21] The *Los Angeles Times* pointed out that the topic was not unprecedented, being a direct descendant of the pastoral letter of 1919.[22] Archbishop William Borders of Baltimore noted simply that the bishops needed to remind Catholics of their great prosperity as a group in recent decades: "We've used up the economic and education ladder but we've not lived up to sharing the world's goods."[23] Moving out of poverty and away from blue-collar existence seemed to make Catholics less mindful of the less fortunate.[24]

UNDERTAKING THE PASTORAL

NCCB president Archbishop John Roach of Minneapolis/St. Paul appointed Archbishop Rembert Weakland of Milwaukee to head the ad hoc committee of bishops who would create a draft pastoral on economics. Other bishops selected for the committee were Bishops Joseph Daley of Harrisburg, George Speltz of St. Cloud, William Weigand of Salt Lake City, and Peter Rosazza, auxiliary bishop of Hartford. When Bishop Daley resigned due to illness, he was replaced by Archbishop Thomas Donnellan of Atlanta, who had been an outspoken opponent of the peace pastoral.[25]

In contrast to the theoretical analysis used in the letter on Marxism, the bishops needed to find an approach that could enable them to deal with a system that was not associated with an identifiable philosophy. Moreover, capitalism existed in differing modes, so the decision was made to focus on the phenomenological form of free enterprise found within the United States by explaining Catholic social teaching in four areas: creation of jobs, adequate living wage, interdependency of trade, and economic planning and policy.[26] After two years of consultation with experts from a variety of sectors, the first draft was issued in November 1984, followed by the second in October 1985, and approved in November 1986.

Consultations

The process of creating the economic pastoral followed the model that had been provided by the peace pastoral. The bishops activated their investigative process by listening to the testimony of credentialed sources. In February 1982, President Carter's economic advisor Charles Schultze and Nixon-Ford advisor Herbert Stein were consulted.[27] William Norris, chair of Control Data, and Alice Rivlin, director of the Congressional Budget Office, spoke to the bishops in April 1982. The bishops also heard from private-sector businessmen, including several executives from General Motors and labor representatives, including Thomas R. Donahue, officer of the AFL-CIO. A number of academics in the fields of economics, law, ethics, religion, as well theologians from other faiths and administrators of institutional services, came before the bishops in August 1982. Sociologist Robert Bellah spoke about the need to examine an amoral economic system that considered itself immune from ethical considerations.[28] A three-day symposium held at Notre Dame in December 1983 allowed the bishops to hear a wide range of views from former Cabinet members and other public figures.[29] The vociferous debate generated among knowledgeable participants presaged the controversy the pastoral would arouse and alerted the bishops to the strong divergence of views they would confront. When he presented the first draft to the NCCB, committee chair Archbishop Weakland reported that the testimony came from 125 persons.[30]

The First Draft

The first draft of the economic pastoral was ready for unveiling by early November 1984 and was distributed to the press two days before the NCCB meeting. The committee embargoed its release date until after the election so as not to be accused of trying to influence its results.[31] Entitled *Catholic Social Teaching and the U.S. Economy,* the first draft consisted of 48 pages, two sections divided among 333 paragraphs, and ended with 12 columns of footnotes and an appendix noting the experts who had been consulted between November 1981 and August 1982.[32] Part One, divided into two chapters, addresses "Biblical and Theological Foundations," discussing the concepts of community, justice, wealth, and poverty. This section also discusses ethical norms for economic life, with sections on human rights, distribution of economic resources, and participants in the economic system (workers and unions, managers, investors, business owners, banks, citizens and government, international trade, consumers, and the Church). Part Two is composed of policy applications in five areas. Chapter Three, covering employment and causes and cures for its lack, heads the list, followed by Chapter Four on poverty; its racial, ethnic, and feminine discrimination; distribution of wealth and income; and welfare reform. The sixth chapter, titled "The New American Experiment," deals with the importance of economic cooperation as a contrast to the cultural values of independence and individualism. The final chapter examines the interdependence of this nation with the world economy, the relevance of Catholic social teachings to the issue, and critiques U.S. policies on international development choices regarding trade relations, Third World debt, and foreign investments.

A middle section on food and agriculture had not been written by the time the first draft was released but appeared several months later. It calls for protecting the viability of smaller farms, expresses concern regarding the concentration of land ownership, and protests the exclusion of minorities from participation in anything more than the lowest-paid work. The bishops conclude by praising the intrinsic value of rural life.[33]

In his presentation to the assembled bishops at their annual meeting, Archbishop Weakland emphasized three points: the need for balance in a society that prizes rugged individualism by promoting the concept of solidarity; the need to push for economic rights, as had been done with civil rights; and the need for new modes of handling economic issues to promote justice.[34] In a debate open to the press, thirteen bishops presented mostly favorable reactions, among which were recommendations for a stronger note of hope and a more inspired writing style. The session was followed by a news conference.[35]

However, a few weeks *before* the bishops released their first draft, it was supplanted by the appearance of another statement on the economy. This version originated with a group of wealthy Catholics who feared the bishops' position and wanted to preempt the hierarchy in forming public opinion.

THE LAY LETTER

Before any draft was released, the news that a new pastoral was underway was in itself sufficient basis for considerable news coverage. The reaction of the press prior to the issuance of the first draft of the economic pastoral was predicated on the controversy that had been generated by the peace pastoral. A number of headlines anticipated the controversial nature of the bishops' positions, and so stirred conservative reaction without any real knowledge of the stance the bishops might take. The framing of the pastoral as confrontational rhetoric was already present in press reports as early as 1983, when the *Washington Post* warned that the pastoral was "expected to be highly controversial."[36] *Forbes* predicted, "Nobody thinks the bishops intend to praise capitalism."[37] The title of an article announcing the impending pastoral, "The Bishops Start a New Controversy," clearly blames the authors rather than the critics for fomenting the controversy.[38]

The concern conveyed so early in the process by conservative and business interests signified their perception of the NCCB's influence. A column entitled "Behind the Headlines" expressed a common sentiment: "One has to marvel at the new-found power of the bishops to send shivers of apprehension through the business community when they just PLAN to issue a pastoral, and that not until 1985 or later."[39] The *Los Angeles Times* called the NCCB a new national political force.[40] The *Miami Herald* commented on the activism of a Church willing to criticize public policy, a Church with the nation's largest single religious voting bloc, and contrasted its new visibility with its low profile in the past.[41] Journalists noted the defensive stance of conservative opinion: "Even before it has seen the light of day, the anticipation . . . has generated criticism."[42] The *Daily News* predicted: "The unthinking cheerleaders of capitalism will not like what the bishops say. They will probably be attacked as a case of meddling by clergymen in something that is none of their business. One clergyman saw civil rights as his business and left America a fairer place."[43] *America,* which devoted its entire May 4, 1985, issue to the pastoral, attributed the concerted attack to the raw nerve touched by the bishops' refutation of facile conservative slogans in raising the specter of 35 million poor amid American affluence.[44]

Whether or not it was a case of self-fulfilling prophecy, the anticipation of conservative opposition turned out to be both correct and insightful, for before any portion of the bishops' statement even reached the public, they were preempted by a rival document in defense of capitalism. The marked public course of the pastorals seemed to guarantee a corresponding intensity of opposition. The attempt at an alternative statement in the case of the peace pastoral had been late and inadequate. Therefore, the increasing momentum of commentary, response, and praise accorded the pastorals seemed to call for greater efforts by those who opposed the bishops' positions.

What came to be referred to as the "Lay Commission," a self-selected group of conservative big business interests, attempted to diminish the effect of the bishops' recommendations with their own refutation of what they expected the bishops to say. The maneuver quickly affirmed the polemic nature of the economic pastoral and garnered the bishops far more publicity than had been accorded even the peace pastoral. While the actual contents of the lay letter may not have affected the public's acceptance of the bishops' message about capitalism, the antagonistic stance of a ready-made opposition and the press focus on ideology did dilute the complex and ambiguous discourse toward which the bishops were striving.

Preempting the Bishops

The origins of the Lay Commission and its letter to the laity seem to have been prompted by the expectations aroused by the peace pastoral. The wealthy conservatives who created a "Lay Commission on Catholic Social Teaching and the U.S. Economy" anticipated that, as with the peace pastoral, the bishops' position on the American economy would be critical, not favorable. These individuals had reason to believe that the bishops would take seriously the words used by Pope John Paul II during his September 1984 visit to Toronto: "The needs of poor must take priority over the desires of the rich and the rights of workers over maximizing profits."[45] The bishops' message about workers as dispensable elements in a corporate economy driven by profit, without regard for the human lives affected, was certain to be influenced by the notable failures of factories and farms throughout the country.

Even without knowing what the bishops might want to say, the businessmen who joined forces could anticipate rebuke. In fact, the bishops' message would center not merely on wages but on quality of life. Central to their pastoral thrust was the issue of equitable distribution of both power and money, on the need for workers to share in decision making as well as profits. More than dollars, the bishops' concern targeted the "replaceable-cog" mentality toward human labor that made jobs insecure and workers another form of equipment.

BusinessWeek credits William Simon with forming the Lay Commission, because he was concerned that the bishops would issue a report "not consistent with our deep beliefs in the market system."[46] The commission members claimed for themselves no special status as wealthy, prominent Catholics, declaring that, as concerned Americans, they had a responsibility to express their views. Michael Novak of the American Enterprise Institute, vice chair of the group, justified the unusual maneuver: "Nobody appointed us. We did the typically American thing: we saw a need and organized ourselves to meet it. We didn't pretend to any special authority."[47] The American Enterprise Institute was described as a $12 million dollar a year conservative think-tank, funded by a consortium of six hundred corporations, which had produced a document in 1981 titled "Toward a Theology of the Corporation."[48]

Among the members of the Lay Committee who commissioned and paid for the counter-statement were: William Simon, former Secretary of Treasury; Alexander Haig, former Secretary of State and former president of United Technology; J. Peter Grace, head of conglomerate W. R. Grace; Joseph Alibrani, chair of conglomerate Whitaker Corp.; Robert Buckley, chair of Allegheny International; William Ellinghaus, vice chair of the New York Stock Exchange; Frank Shakespeare, vice chair of RKO; Steven Rothmeier, president of Northwest Airlines; Peter Flanigan, managing director of Dillon, Read & Co.; Clare Booth Luce, writer, diplomat; George Gillespie III, of the Wall Street firm of Cravath, Swaine and Moore.[49]

Simon's intent was to anticipate the bishops' probable critiques of economic inequity and to produce a report that would refute their claims. The committee imitated the bishops' process of holding hearings by calling on a dozen poverty and policy analysts.[50] Unlike the bishops, however, they provided no opportunities for comment and revision.[51] Michael Novak, who had also produced the alternate statement on nuclear defense, wrote the brief report (30 pages) titled "Toward the Future."[52] The press reported that production of the letter had cost $100,000 and took six months. On November 7, 1984, two days before the bishops released their draft to the press, the Lay Commission mailed 19,000 copies to Catholic parishes, setting out their version of the position they felt the bishops "should be taking about the U.S. economy."[53]

The motives for the timing were not lost on observers. The *New York City Tribune* reported, "One way to undercut a report . . . is to get your own out first." The article continued, "Using all the artifacts of corporate public relations, the lay group put their statement into the hands of the media well in advance of the release date and provoked a controversy before the bishops could even come to bat."[54] Another item commented, "Some observers in the media have flatly declared that the lay commission has 'won' simply by virtue of getting equal billing. . . ."[55] The decision to compete with the bishops revealed the deep concern of the committee, whose reaction to the very *idea* of an economic pastoral elicited editorial remarks in San Francisco's *Examiner-Chronicle:* "The committee of contrary opinion on the policy options act as if they must mount the ramparts against a monolithic Church in full charge under a socialist banner."[56] Others also noticed this response: "The fact that the bishops' letter has drawn so much resistance from the rich, even before it is written, is good evidence that it is on the right track."[57] "Chicago News at Five" pointed out that "so much trouble to offset and minimize the impact the bishops might have . . . indicates that there may be something very real to fear from the bishops' analysis."[58] The *New York Times* noted: "Nobody is likely to make the mistake of dismissing the potential influence on U.S. economic policy of the recent pastoral letter."[59] The *Minneapolis Star Tribune* said that Simon and Novak had "honored" the pastoral by issuing warnings before its publication.[60]

Novak, a former Catholic liberal who had become a "leading neoconservative critic of progressive churchmen," was appointed spokesperson and thus became the point man for press reports.[61] He claimed his reason for writing the letter was to advance Catholic social doctrine, pointing out that rather than the Church seeking to influence America, the nation could lead the Church to improve its "underdeveloped" social teaching.[62] He had importuned the bishops early in the process about their assumed position, meeting with them as early as November 1981 and returning twice more, the only witness to do so.[63] Conservatives feared that there would be a return to a New Deal economy, that the free market would be declared evil, and that the Church's concern for the poor would lead the pastoral to condemn capitalism. The bishops had listened patiently but were not deterred.[64]

The rhetoric of the lay letter reveals a proclivity for Social Darwinism, in which the poor are proclaimed responsible for their own poverty. The Lay Commission's belief that virtue is its own reward and vice its own punishment is underscored by their juxtaposition of the 55 percent black illegitimacy rate with their 62 percent poverty rate.[65] Their justification of American capitalism is not to be debated by the bishops, who are instead focused on questioning a system in which those who do the hardest work are the poor, and who reject the idea that poverty is punishment for vice.

Ironically, Novak condemns the bishops' "ideological use of poverty," while himself equating poverty and moral ineptitude.[66]

Like competitive advertising, the attention brought to the pastoral by the lay group's alternative document outweighed any negative publicity it might have provoked. In seeking to offset the spotlight the bishops wished to shine on current inequities, the lay letter failed in its mission, because the result was a sharp focus on the presence of the invisible poor and even greater dialogue: "The Catholic bishops are eloquently asking not only Catholics, but all other Americans as well, to pray, think and talk about the phenomenon of poverty amid plenty."[67] A *Denver Post* editorial expressed shock that poverty was not viewed as a problem but as a natural condition reflecting the nation's fabric and reminded readers that Christians may not acquiesce in accepting hunger and homelessness.[68] One analysis noted that the bishops would be seen as spoilsports in reminding Americans that amid the buoyant economy the number of poor, invisible except at soup kitchens, had gone up, not down.[69] Rebutting points in a Simon article entitled "Bishops' Pastoral Is Santa Claus Wish List," Jay T. Harris retorted that the bishops' greatest service had been to call attention to invisible poverty. Commenting on the dominance of "right-wing rhetoric" that denigrated compassion, he disputed the idea that poverty was a problem of minority urban deadbeats, pointing out that 40 percent of the poor held jobs, that defense, not welfare, was the largest item in the federal budget, that two-thirds of the poor were white, and that the poorest counties in the nation were rural.[70]

Father George Higgins, one of the contributors to the pastoral effort, emphasized the skewed view of the lay production: "The Simon-Novak letter mistakenly assumes the approach to fighting poverty must be either all government or all private business. . . . It has to be both"; and he emphasized that the pastoral was intended to be a "long range teaching document, not . . . an essay on technical economics."[71] Sociologist Michael Harrington called the lay letter "thin," saying it was "very standard . . . stuff that could have been written any time in the last forty years.[72] Lawrence Rasmussen noted that the letter's use of Scripture, in contrast to the bishops' profuse references, was limited to Matthew 25 (parables about investing rather than hoarding and the need for acts of charity).[73] Harvard professor Donald Warwick complained that the committee's interviews with thirty people did not constitute a broad-based consultation, and the resulting lay letter smacked of "complacency," reflecting no urgency about change. He contrasted its endorsement of a single system with the bishops' emphasis on performance and outcomes.[74] Others commented on the lack of civility; the *Sacramento Union* editorialized, "When the Roman Catholic bishops speak, people listen," and reminded readers that agreement with their views was not necessary to acknowledge their right to speak: "We can at least be polite."[75] Robert McAfee Brown wrote, "The 'value' of the Will-Haig-Luce-Novak posture can be encapsulated in a single observation: they have shown us how *not* to respond."[76] Steve Bell, anchor of ABC's "This Morning," remarked that while the bishops had avoided partisan criticism, it was disappointing that their critics had not.[77]

Reminding his audience that the peace letter had sparked a national debate on nuclear arms policy, one writer contended that by raising the questions, the bishops made the plight of the poor a priority item for debate on the country's agenda.[78] The Reagan White House modified its opposition to this pastoral; David Gergen, chief communications advisor, spoke admiringly: "This nation still has a conscience toward the poor and the bishops did well to stir it."[79] CBS's "Nightwatch" called the pastoral a "bill of rights for the poor and jobless."[80]

More than any generalizations about the potential influence of American pastoral messages, the existence of the lay letter and its publicity campaign constituted a general acknowledgment of the increasing attention and influence attributed to the bishops' pastoral statements. The worry of these businessmen about the bishops' statement and their need to counter its message with a defense of the status quo speaks eloquently of the prestige and power they ascribed to the forthcoming pastoral.

The bishops did not criticize the lay letter nor respond to its contention that the free market represented the most effective economic system. They explained that their purpose was to study, to listen, to raise questions, always in a spirit of charity.[81] Such civility was in striking contrast to the antagonistic rhetoric of the conservatives.

CONSERVATIVE CONCERNS

The apprehension of the Lay Commission regarding the potential effectiveness of the economic pastoral led conservatives to expand their rhetorical repertoire beyond the lay letter. Having issued that document before the bishops' first draft was released, they used other tactics during the remainder of the process. Charges leveled during the process of the peace pastoral, such as castigating the bishops' technical expertise and impugning their patriotism, returned during the process of the economic pastoral. Another factor that attested to the perceived impact and influence of the bishops' statement was the language used by conservative commentators. The reasoned and civil public argument the bishops were seeking to generate was missing from conservative commentary. Rather than refuting the content of the pastoral, pundits instead attacked the presumption of the bishops in even approaching the subject. These commentators sought to suppress acceptance of the pastoral by denigrating its source. In an editorial, the *San Diego Union* opined that the acrimonious debate was likely to exceed even that of the peace pastoral, and that the bishops' letters constituted an "unprecedented intrusion of the church in U.S. public and government affairs."[82] The intensity of *ad hominem* charges regarding the intelligence and lifestyle of the bishops raised the specter of nativist hostility to the Church and caused even non-Catholics to protest in the bishops' defense.

In the peace pastoral, the bishops had been labeled as communists. The label of choice in the economic process was socialist, a member of the bishops' staff noting that "socialism" was bandied as a code word by those fearful of government intervention.[83] One critic interpreted the pastoral as forced collectivization: "The property of one is forcibly seized, and . . . handed to another. Coercion precludes compassion. It assumes the worst—that people are not Christian enough to take care of their less fortunate neighbors voluntarily." He charged: "The Bishops go to some lengths to disguise their advocacy of force. . . . The words *collaboration* and *cooperation* really mean submission." He even attacked the bishops' phrasing of a request: "Notice the moral confusion in *enjoining* us to cooperate. It is a disguised appeal for submission to government force."[84]

The attacks on the bishops were intended to disparage their authority on the subject by diminishing their credibility. Brian Halleth categorized critics' objections as "Economic affairs are not the affairs of priests" (Go back to the confessional and organize raffles); "Capitalism is fine" (world's greatest producer of wealth, stay out of its way); and "Real experts exist" (to gather data, do more studies).[85] While many ripostes against the pastoral were similar in their refrains, the tactics used ranged from offering countering data to denigrating the bishops' competency.

First, conservatives attempted to combat the research done by the bishops with their own set of facts. The data in the lay report was occasionally augmented by articles from the American Enterprise Institute, the organization to which Simon and Novak belonged. One such author, Ben Wattenberg, played the numbers game, commenting on a decreasing poverty rate, which for 1984 was a mere 8 to 9 percent, down from 12 percent in 1969. He also defended the status quo: "It may sound terrible to say that the richest fifth of families make about nine times as much money as the poorest fifth," but claimed that the differential between a doctor's salary and that of a busboy should be neither a surprise nor a scandal. He proved the bishops' very point about inequities of income distribution by stating, "Furthermore, there hasn't been much change in the proportion of who gets what over the years," admitting that since World War II, a 4½ percent share of total national income is allocated among the poorest fifth of the population and over a 40 percent share for the wealthiest fifth.[86] Don Feder called his article in the *Boston Herald* "Welcome to Bishonomics 101," with the subtitle "Forgive them, they know not what they are talking about."[87]

However, such a stance resulted in notable witnesses attesting to the bishops' contributions. A congressional hearing was convened to discuss the pastoral, at which James Tobin, professor of economics at Yale and 1981 Nobel Laureate, stated: "The bishops are doing our nation a great service by raising moral and ethical questions about our economic institutions and policies. . . . I, a non-Catholic and indeed an unrepentant 'secular humanist,' find them of universal appeal, striking responsive chords among persons of all religious faiths and of none. The ethics of equity and equality are very American."[88] Fellow Nobel Laureate, 1980 winner Lawrence R. Klein from the University of Pennsylvania, concurred: "Theirs is a careful, scholarly assessment and deserves equally careful consideration."[89] Eventually, editorials like "Politics and Moral Dimensions" would emphasize, "Supply-siders would have you believe the NCCB was walking blind when it approved the pastoral letter. Don't buy it. . . . The bishops do have facts on their side."[90] In the bishops' defense, Lester Thurow, economics professor at MIT, acknowledged that "economists have been able to cow the public, press, policy makers and politicians in ways not usually open to academics and technical people."[91]

The release of the first draft sparked a flurry of articles during the weeks of November 13 and 20, 1984. Some of these delighted in imaginative vituperation that focused on dismissal rather than analysis. William F. Buckley, Jr., provided his rhetorical take on the draft as "an accumulation of lumpen cliches," with a "puree of same vapidity."[92] Charles Krauthammer repudiated it as "no great contribution to American political discourse."[93] George Will charged that the bishops' "comic sense of moral bravery" convicted themselves of "child-like innocence . . . or vanity."[94] Vanity was also the motive attributed in *Policy Review,* which called the bishops "punch-drunk" from having discovered the pleasure of receiving accolades from the networks and the press.[95]

Another series of responses denied the bishops any right to speak, based on their lack of contact with the realities of finance due to their sheltered existence. James Kilpatrick sniggered that the bishops had the greatest job security on earth and never had to work like others.[96] He raised the same point a week later: "The Bishops know the working of the marketplace by hearsay; they themselves, living well fed and protected lives, are as innocent as kittens of economic risk and insecurity."[97] Bill Reel claimed that bishops have "practically unlimited personal funds."[98] By contrast, *USA Today* covered the impoverished background of committee chair, Archbishop Rembert Weakland, who recalled being taunted by other children during his welfare childhood as his widowed mother struggled to raise six children."[99] *Time*, in its "Economic and Business" section, cited his sale of the bishop's mansion and his invitation to Milwaukee's poor to attend the banquet for his installation as archbishop.[100]

Right up the adoption of the pastoral, critics continued the refrain. "What do clergymen know about economics in everyday life?" asked a *Boston Herald* editorial.[101] Simon said Weakland should "stick to subjects he knows something about," adding, "His comments are ridiculous. But they are also tragic in that this nonsense is going to be taught."[102] On National Public Radio's "Morning Edition," Michael Harrington referred to the fury of neo-conservatives piqued by the bishops' failure to "render homage to free enterprise" and "repeat the secular myths of the rich," explaining that the pastoral looked at economics from the vantage of a soup kitchen, not a boardroom.[103] The *Detroit Free Press* also described a different scenario: "The bishops' suggestion arose out of their experience as pastors, as administrators of hospitals and social service programs, and as supervisors of parish priests who minister to all sorts and conditions of people—their message is worth hearing and considering seriously."[104]

To the Bishops' Defense

The deliberate misreading of the pastoral and the blind bias of commentators in the press sparked a flurry of response by readers. Letters to the editors brought up the "specious arguments" and "strange attempt to discredit the bishops personally,"[105] "sloppy writing that reflects the minds of persons who . . . confuse exhortation with argument,"[106] and commented on the "patronizing scorn and sarcasm" from conservative commentators, noting that continual references to "poor blacks" implied a dearth of poverty among whites.[107]

Readers pointed out that the voluntary charity which conservatives so ardently touted might work "in a less acquisitive civilization." Others noted that socialism consists of government ownership of the means of production, not the desire to help the needy, elderly, and infirm. It was pointed out that conservative references to Adam Smith neglected to mention that he himself had been a clergyman and that his form of free enterprise also meant no special tax breaks for large corporations, low-interest loans, export aid, protectionism, import controls, and outright government grants.[108] A British journal pointed out that American management competed poorly even with the government protection provided by land grants, cash subsidies, and infrastructure development provided at public expense and turned over to private enterprises, making the "rhetoric about the pristine virginity of the free market . . . only that: rhetoric."[109]

David Broder surmised that conservative outrage might be attributed to "unease at the shaky moral foundations" of its own beliefs, in which "growth" had become a rhetorical talisman preferable to "greed."[110] *Newsweek*'s "Religion" section reported that there was no anti-capitalist document, that the pastoral never attacked private property or capitalism, and that it was hard to find fault with its underlying premise of more attention to "us" than "me."[111]

Most bishops did not defend themselves and refused to enter the acrimonious debate.[112] Walter Sullivan, bishop of Richmond, did express disappointment but not surprise over coverage given to patronizing cartoons and angry denunciations by right-wing pundits.[113] NCCB president Archbishop Roach also said he was not surprised by the harsh criticisms, because comments were "influenced by their convictions, which was as it should be." While some conservative views were more agitated about abortion than poverty, the archbishop reminded reporters that the bishops' concern was for the quality of life from "womb to tomb."[114]

PERMEATING THE PUBLIC

In mid-May 1985, NCCB president Archbishop Weakland sent a report to all bishops, indicating the volume of responses to the first draft of the economic pastoral from individuals and organizations. The report was not a compilation of responses but contained positive and critical categories from 109 dioceses (reports from consultations, hearings, and individual bishops), 88 Catholic organizations and institutions, 32 religious orders, 38 secular organizations, 44 academicians, 30 international sources, 14 interfaith and ecumenical groups, and more than 1000 individuals.[115] From a single Midwestern coalition of laity, religious, and clergy alone, commentary and response to the first draft covered over 100 pages of testimony as well as a 32-page report of recommendations.[116]

The Second Draft

An interim report regarding the progress on the second draft appeared in the NCCB publication *Origins,* revealing that the authors were seeking to reduce the 60,000 words of the original draft by one-third.[117] By the time the copious commentary responding to the first draft was tabulated and considered, spring and summer had passed. It was October 1985 when the second draft of *Economic Justice for All* was released. In spite of the editing effort, the 341 paragraphs composing the second draft exceeded its predecessor.[118]

This second version contained generally the same sections, but its change in style revealed a responsiveness to comments about "the harsh, provocative rhetoric in the first draft."[119] In terms of form, while the first draft had used a didactic style of asserting a conclusion or principle, followed by supporting arguments, writers recognized that Americans were more familiar with a deductive form in which the problem and facts were presented, drawing the reader to concur with the conclusion.

Moreover, some of the criticisms of the first draft were its reliance on government programs as solutions, making blunt political demands rather than stating ethical principles, examining only the negative aspects of the economy, and polarizing the middle class and the poor.[120] Extensive rewriting resulted in a new version with more nuanced statements. Regarding daycare, the first draft had said, " . . . all levels of government should help to assure provision of adequate care for children whose parents must work. The current level of federal and state subsidies for day care is inadequate." By contrast, the second draft is more inclusive in assigning responsibility, asking for societal change so that economic necessity does not force mothers to work away from home and suggesting that "employers, governments and private agencies need to improve both the availability and the quality of child-care services."

Rather than focusing only on the needs of the poor, the second draft acknowledges the threat of poverty in the middle class's vulnerability to economic disaster. Statements are put in a more positive vein, so that rather than "we challenge our Catholic schools to remain in poor areas," the second draft affirms, "Our Catholic schools have the well-merited reputation of providing excellent education for the poor." The Catholic News Service noted that the danger in acceding to criticisms was the potential to blunt the challenging principles proposed by the bishops, a factor that had weakened the peace pastoral until it was reconstructed in various drafts.[121]

In spite of easing the harshness of its rhetoric, the literary style of the pastoral did not attract the average reader. Some criticized the pastoral while was it clear that they were unfamiliar with its contents. Jerry Falwell labeled the pastoral "socialism," while freely admitting he had not read the document.[122] Despite the massive media coverage, "only a few indicated they knew that good pastoral letters, like good detective stories, are meant to be read from the beginning to the end."[123] Prominent Catholic business-men and women in Baltimore were criticized for denigrating the pastoral without having read it.[124] One banker called it a "knee-jerk reaction in the business press, but that lessened as businessmen took the time to read what was in the letter."[125] The *New Oxford Review* pointed out that even for Catholics, the pastoral tended to be filtered through news reports or the oc-casional conversation or sermon and stressed that reading commentaries of the draft was no substitute for reading the letter itself, which was available for a nominal sum from the NCCB.[126] The bishops found interested audi-ences for their work, however, in other venues.

Ecumenical Support

The ecumenical support for the peace letter that had surfaced after its publication came at a much earlier point when the economic letter was being composed. In May 1984, four senior rabbis and Nathan Dershowitz of the American Jewish Congress testified before the bishops, and religious spokespersons from the National Council of Churches also appeared. By July 1984, Jewish and Protestant leaders had joined in affirmation of the letter's thrust. Rabbi Alexander M. Schindler, president of the Union of American Hebrew Congregations declared: "All Americans owe the Na-tional Conference of Catholic Bishops a tremendous debt of gratitude for the moral vision that permeates the Bishops' pastoral letter. . . . Catholics and Jews share a common concern for the powerless derived from Sacred Scripture. We share a common experience as penniless immigrants."[127]

The broad nature of the letter's principles allowed many faiths to accept its premises. "Are you a Catholic, Protestant or Jew? Then you should read the Catholic Bishops' Pastoral Letter 'Economic Justice for All.' No docu-ment I have ever read does a better job of looking at the U.S. economy from a Judeo-Christian perspective."[128] The pastoral's early endorsement by leaders of other religious faiths was not highly publicized, but it affirmed the appropriateness of a clergy venturing to make a statement about eco-nomic life and would later result in an ecumenical participation in the commentary that followed.

The Bishops Move to Center Stage

Coverage of the economic pastoral began in the religion pages of metro-politan newspapers. An early report in the religion section of a St. Louis daily identified the pastoral as being only the bishops' third, along with their 1919 statement and the peace pastoral.[129] The *New York Times* and the *Washington Post* covered the three-day conference at the University of Notre

Dame, which elicited fifteen papers from a broad spectrum to help the committee apply social doctrine to the areas of employment and its absence, poverty and welfare, Third World trade, and principles for cooperation.[130]

The long hearing process that this pastoral had undergone did not match the relatively rapid pace that had characterized the peace pastoral, and there was little news to report except that consultations were underway. However, as business columns began to reference the effort, the project attracted more notice and moved into the news sections. *BusinessWeek* covered the pastoral in an article in its "Economy" section,[131] but a year later it had become a cover story.[132] *USA Today* placed two pairs of pro and con op-ed columns on the front page.[133] Reinforcing the importance of the bishops' debate in generating a fresh vision of the American experiment, Harvey Cox summed up the new view of the bishops: "They are an intellectual force to be taken with the utmost seriousness."[134] The *Minneapolis Star Tribune,* noting coverage of the pastorals by leading press organs such as the *New York Times,* the *Wall Street Journal,* the *Chicago Tribune,* and TV networks, contrasted it with the usual publicity: "The media often classifies church news as non-news."[135] Even NBC television covered the topic on "Bishops and the Economy."[136]

The headlines of various publications quickly established the tone of the publicity accorded to the economic letter. A scan of headlines and leads from publications throughout the nation announcing release of the first draft of the economic pastoral in November 1984 demonstrated the immediately confrontative stance with which the press treated the document. Around the country the press emphasized dispute rather than content. Typical examples are: "All Things Considered": ". . . once again their work is likely to provoke controversy"; CNN: "bishops' letter sure to reignite controversy";[137] *U.S. News and World Report:* "U.S. Bishops vs. Reagonomics: A Growing Furor";[138] and the *Miami Herald:* "The bishops' controversial letter."[139] Since Americans were alerted to expect a struggle over the document, in fact, it arrived.

Because the peace pastoral had demonstrated that the public found the bishops' documents newsworthy, by the time the first draft of the economic pastoral was released the bishops were catapulted directly to page one. As indicated above, the anticipation of contention and the presumption of a lay group attempting to correct the bishops' interpretation of doctrine provided ample material for the secular press. In *America,* Brien Hallett observed: "Even before the first draft of the pastoral was out, the media were ready with instant analyses and instant answers. . . . It missed the point."[140] No one waited to discover that the bishops were less interested in reorganizing the distribution of income and more interested in the process of productive work as the essence of human dignity.

The Vatican and International Reaction

Although no comment had been aroused by the bishops' release of their pastoral on Marxism, the economic pastoral on capitalism created "Vatican misgivings about American self-confident independence about dealing with subtle controversial issues."[141] The report goes on: "In Rome, Curia officials have expressed concern about the public and widely consultative manner in which the bishops have been preparing their pastoral letters."[142] Committee chair Archbishop Weakland countered that American bishops were not so hierarchical and that their listening process allowed for discernment. Eugene Kennedy characterized central Church officials as uncomfortable with American mores: "The Europeans are nettled by the American temperamental commitment to open discussion and debate— the habits of their lives in a pluralistic society, on questions of ecclesiastical policy."[143] In fact, he reported, although confident of Vatican support for the pastoral, which echoed papal themes on the topic, the NCCB was contemplating opening a lobbying office in Rome for the purpose of deepening Vatican understanding of the American mentality.[144]

The Third Draft

The release of the final draft in June 1986 generated a media blitz.[145] Major newspapers—*USA Today,* the *Wall Street Journal,* the *Boston Globe,* the *Miami News*—announced the release of the draft. The bishops had expanded the theological basis for their recommendations, but specific objectives were unchanged. Minor changes were made to some sections, such as specifically countering Social Darwinism arguments that the poor are morally weak or irresponsible (51). A section on leisure and worship from the first draft, which had been dropped in the second, was brought back in abbreviated form (64–65). Stronger condemnation is made of racism, "a sin that divides the human family" (50). The bishops relate the economic situation to their peace pastoral by lamenting the expenditure of funds and research spent on arms (48). They discuss the nation's attention, the "brain drain," and the budget devoted to the defense industry as misguided use of resources (58). Significant changes in the third draft are a more systematic treatment of global economic issues, reflecting meetings with Latin American bishops and Third World economists. Therefore, additions include recommendations for the reform of the World Bank, the International Monetary Fund, and the General Agreement on Tariffs and Trade (58). A section on family life was added (66). The eight thousand words of foot-notes remained in all the drafts.[146]

A few months later *Economic Justice for All: Catholic Social Teaching and the U.S. Economy* was adopted by the assembled bishops at their November 1986 meeting. In affirmation of the public's interest, the passage of the let-ter was announced in the center column of the front page of the *New York Times,* as well as in other dailies.[147]

Arguments for the Public Square

The issue of debate in a pluralistic society was a significant source of difference with the hierarchical, authoritarian Vatican. The American bish-ops were candid about their desire to appeal to national sensibilities. Their desire to broaden the acceptance of their message and influence general opinion meant that they could not be restricted to arguments understood only by Catholics. This strategy had worked well with the peace pastoral, and there seemed to be no reason to change that now. It was also validated by the ecclesiastical leadership.

In his first formal address as newly elected president of the NCCB, Bishop James W. Malone of Youngstown, Ohio, told the bishops that they had a special responsibility to speak out because the Church had "access to a major sector of the public" and because the Catholic vision was integrally social and holistic. He acknowledged that public engagement in a broad spectrum of issues required religious leaders to give an accounting of their rationale and accept responsibility for the quality and tone of the debate.[148] A few days later he elaborated that the Church could speak "corporately in a way few other institutions can match."[149] Archbishop John Quinn of San Francisco had stipulated that "religious organizations must earn their way into the public debate by the quality of their positions."[150] The bishops rea-soned that those who would influence the public must meet the standards of public argument: "One sign of the integrity of the pastoral process . . . is that so far the bishops have insisted that representatives of both groups meet standards of public argument that transcend the claims of accus-tomed privilege."[151]

The central moral and ethical argument of the economic letter focused not on market forces but on human activity, community, and cooperation. David Hollenbach, a major contributor to the letter, pointed out that each of the recent economic recoveries had left a higher rate of unemployment than the preceding one. The letter's emphasis on work as "co-creation," by which people are bonded to the community and meaning is created, was ignored by the press. The costs of unemployment to which the bishops referred were as much about isolation and loss of social participation as about income.[152] While Michael Novak expressed problems with the pastoral's footnotes, picking out individual words and sentences,[153] Simon's response was to quibble about the unemployment statistic: "Most experts today define full employment as 6%, not 4%."[154] The bishops pointed to the gradual toleration of increasing levels of joblessness, where once three or four percent was considered "intolerable," seven percent had become "normal."[155]

The purposes of economics were also an area of contention. George Will claimed that "American capitalism is the most efficient anti-poverty machine in the world,"[156] while Bishop Anthony Pilla of Cleveland said that the immense human and social tragedy created by unemployment indicated that economics must be governed not only by goals of efficiency and profit but by justice and dignity.[157] The same newspaper protested: "To dismiss the bishops' anguish, so eloquently expressed . . . as thinly disguised socialism is to do the authors an injustice. They have proposed a set of moral principles that, applied to political thought and action, could revolutionize the way American government serves its citizens."[158] Archbishop Weakland pointed out that the poor could not be served by a rhetoric focusing on the glories of capitalism, which has been greatly tempered by the nation's strong labor movement.[159] As a guest columnist for *USA Today,* he identified the bishops' pastoral goal as perfecting national values: "The justice and character of a nation is tested by how the poor are treated. . . . There is unfinished work in our experiment of liberty and justice for all."[160]

The poignancy of actual human experience was not an element that enlivened conservative discourse. Factory closings, large-scale layoffs, and the effects of mergers and acquisitions were not addressed. Bishop Victor Balke of Crookston, Minnesota, in contrast to Simon, called for fewer statistics and numbers: "We should have stories and illustrations to highlight the truth behind the figures."[161] The *Milwaukee Sentinel* echoed the lack of the "human side of the story of poverty and need," explaining the Catholic community's witness of families at suburban food banks, of selling blood to pay for tuition, of children whose first meal of the day was the school lunch.[162] Archbishop John O'Connor went to Wall Street to meet with three hundred people from the New York Stock Exchange. Instead of their usual profit-and-loss talk, they heard about the three thousand families put up by the city and about the almost one million homeless lodged by New York State.[163]

Some critiques of the pastoral complained about the lack of presence of the poor themselves at the bishops' hearings. Consultants on the economic letter noted to the bishops that while experts ("a roster of the positioned, the powerful, and the credentialed") were called to contribute, "no poor actually speak in these pages. No workers . . . ." Instead, persons from academia, government, industry, and religious life speak for them, "but there is no direct testimony *from* them."[164] The incorporation of personal accounts by persons living in poverty was touched on only peripherally in this pastoral effort, but this absence was remembered and would grow to become a major element in preparing the pastoral to follow.

The economic pastoral continued the advances made in magnifying the public aspect of hierarchical statements. While *The Challenge of Peace* established innovations such as consultation with secular experts, the release of drafts, opening debates to the press, the creation of education materials, and international attention, *Economic Justice for All* extended and intensified these elements. Publicity for, and press participation in, the economic letter matched that of the peace pastoral, but criticisms anticipating an attack on inequities in the U.S. economic system came earlier in the process, as did ecumenical endorsements of the bishops' leadership. The press continued to dilute and simplify the pastoral's complex message and ignored crucial aspects of the statement but did not fail to report on the bishops' various actions with each draft.

The bishops' increase of power and influence could be seen in accolades published in numerous volumes of academic commentary that cited their contributions to the common welfare, the public square, and the pastoral process. In the other direction, the aggravation they caused to conservative critics and anti-clerical pundits signified the emergence of pastorals that were no longer ignored. The level of organized resistance to their message, even prior to its appearance, represented a tribute to the clout and effectiveness they wielded.

The sense of progress in pastoral production since the peace pastoral had resulted in increased press attention, the expectation of controversy, dialogue with lay members, and a willingness to incorporate comments. Many of these innovations would come to characterize and eventually to haunt the bishops' next project—a pastoral letter on women.

Chapter Five
The Pastoral That Wasn't ═══════════

THE BISHOPS' SUCCESS IN RAISING PUBLIC AWARENESS with the peace and economic pastorals emboldened them to venture further into uncharted territory. The women's movement was then being avidly discussed, and the bishops recognized that sexism, no less than racism and ageism, was a recurring source of social injustice. Tackling a commentary on the unequal status of women in several spheres would again put the bishops in the vanguard of other national episcopal conferences and would fill a void that had been apparent for several years. They could salvage themselves and their Church from a stance that seemed glaringly out of step with modern sensibilities, and lend their moral authority to the inequities in women's lives. Moreover, the processes used in the previous pastorals provided a model of methodology that gave the bishops confidence in planning for maximal participation.

The bishops were very aware of the irony of attempting such a pastoral. These celibate men had far less knowledge of the daily tribulations of a woman's existence than of nuclear weapons or economics. But they resolved to try. With admirable persistence, they pursued this pastoral through multiple versions and a decade of protest. What they had not envisioned was a participation and revision process that would run amok and wrest control of the pastoral's contents. In previous pastorals they had assurance from the outset of the project that their position fulfilled Gospel mandates, and in spite of ideological debate with a small number of bishops and conservative pundits, they had not wavered from their original purpose in seeking to provide the basis for a new perspective on existing public policy. This time, however, no such clear-cut direction existed, and the opposing ideologies to which various bishops' and women's groups subscribed created a pastoral that swiveled from establishment of a new vision for women to one that merely reinforced the status quo.

This chapter examines the high hopes and dashed expectations that accompanied a document that began with supportive intentions and ended with rejection. To understand the fate of the pastoral on women, the pastoral process can be examined in its context as the apex of a trajectory of increasing rhetorical aspiration within the conference of bishops. The earlier pastorals had created an expectation of success, since the bishops' previous efforts at seeking an open dialogue had met with such praise. They felt confident that their strategy of listening and responding would meet with a similar positive outcome. During its long journey, the process used to gather input for the letter on women broadened into the widest and most democratic forum of any pastoral. So why did this pastoral become the only one to fail? While the trajectory leading *to* the women's pastoral had been a series of advancing public participation, press attention, and moral dialogue, this chapter will demonstrate that the trajectory *within* its process became a series of reversals and revisions.

THE BEST OF INTENTIONS

Although the proposal to draft a pastoral on the status of women was made in 1983, the issue had already been raised several years earlier. At the regular November meeting of the NCCB in 1975, Bishop Michael McAuliffe of Jefferson City, Missouri, proposed an office staffed full-time to research women's issues. As chair of the already standing Ad Hoc Committee on Women in Society and the Church, the bishop warned, "The seriousness of the issues demands urgent and extensive attention from the Church at these levels, and the failure to provide such attention, we believe, may prove costly."[1] The NCCB rejected funding the proposal on the ground that "it would isolate women's concerns from the rest of the conferences' activities . . . or it would establish little more than a visible but ineffective expression of the Church's willingness to deal with these issues."[2]

A task force consisting of secular and religious women issued a report to the bishops in June 1976 countering that view.

> If the U.S. Catholic Church is to be credible when it urges secular society toward justice, it will have to set the example. Today a genuine challenge forces us to exert responsible leadership in positively shaping public opinion on issues such as the condition of women on welfare, minority women . . . prostitution, rape, prison reform, abortion, just compensation for labor, and others.

The report went on to style the bishops as leaders whose obligation to shape attitudes toward justice called for the courage to take public stands on controversial issues.[3]

In 1977 the bishops decided to examine the conditions of women within their own institution. A bishops' subgroup within the NCCB, the Ad Hoc Committee on Women, conducted a survey of women's positions within Church administration.[4] They found that while women were represented in policymaking and executive-level jobs, these were in the areas of education and social services.[5] When the Equal Rights Amendment came up for adoption in 1978, the bishops opted to take no collective position in support or opposition.[6] Some individual bishops did take stands, such as Bishop McCauliffe, who spoke in support before his state legislature.[7]

A dozen individual pastorals on women were written by bishops, beginning with Bishop Leo T. Maher of San Diego in 1974 ("Women in the New World") to Archbishop Roger Mahony of Los Angeles in 1987 ("Just as the Women Said"). The bishops of Minnesota collaborated on "Woman: Pastoral Reflections" in 1979.[8] Archbishop Raymond A. Hunthausen of Seattle, Bishop Matthew Clark of Rochester, New York, and Archbishop Rembert Weakland of Milwaukee all created their pastorals in the early 1980s by conducting dialogues, interviews, surveys, and hearings. The interest stirred had prompted some dioceses to establish women's commissions and to implement objectives.[9]

However, American women sought to be heard on a national level. In 1981 *Origins,* the documentary organ of the NCCB, reported :

> Since the spring of 1976, women have been present at the National Conference of Catholic Bishops meetings to raise the issue of justice in the church. . . . The Women of the Church Coalition, a group of more that twenty national and local organizations attempted for the next two years to find an avenue for dialogue with and input into the NCCB.[10]

At the November 1978 annual meeting, Bishop Maurice Dingman of Des Moines asked for such dialogue, and then NCCB president Archbishop John Quinn directed the Committee on Women in Society and the Church to convene.[11] The committee responded by holding three sessions between December 1979 and July 1980. Bishop Michael McAuliffe of Jefferson City, Missouri, as chair, defined as their goal to "discover, understand, promote the full potential of women as persons in the life of the church."[12] By the spring of 1982, the Ad Hoc Committee on Women in Society and the Church had completed a thirteen-page report to the NCCB based on an additional series of dialogues, sessions with the Women's Ordination Conference (WOC), held in December 1980, March 1981, and August 1981, described by bishops as a "process marked by serious disagreements and moments of impasse" and a "painful, painful experience." The WOC challenged the members to recognize sexism as a sin and to acknowledge the need to update interpretation of Church teachings, even though the Vatican staunchly upheld the traditional understanding of those teachings.[13]

In the days just prior to the annual NCCB meeting, a conference on "Women in the Church" took place in Washington, and its timing allowed many bishops to attend. About one-third of the assembled hierarchy took advantage of the overlap to hear what women were saying. Workshops for the bishops were also scheduled by the NCCB committee on Women in Society. Concurrently, a meeting in Chicago, "Woman Church Speaks," was contending that it was "imperative . . . that women no longer remain voiceless." Their case was buttressed by the statement of Pope John Paul II to the U.S. bishops on September 5 that they should demonstrate support of the "dignity of women" and that exclusion from ordination was "extraneous to the issue of discrimination."[14] While the Washington conference heard a series of papers presented by female scholars, with male scholars responding, the Chicago group was denouncing sexism, along with militarism, classism, and racism in the report of the conference, titled "From Generation to Generation: Woman Church Speaks."[15]

Whether the presence of so much feminine input influenced the bishops or whether the publicity and presence of the issue highlighted a sense of urgency, the suggestion of a pastoral met with favor. Bishop McAuliffe as outgoing chair had proposed the pastoral at the November 1982 meeting, and the committee endorsed the proposal when they met in July 1983. It was the new chair of the Ad Hoc Committee on Women in Society and the Church, Bishop Joseph Imesch of Joliet, Illinois, who recommended proceeding with the project at the November 1983 meeting.[16] There was no dissent, and the projected time frame for completion was estimated to be four years. Cindy Wooden reported: "Despite the potential for controversy surrounding the pastoral letter, there was no discussion about the matter, and the proposal to produce a pastoral was passed unanimously."[17] It was the last time that the concepts of unanimity and the pastoral letter on women would ever be linked in the same sentence.

To Be or Not to Be

Although the passage of the proposed pastoral letter on women prompted no debate on the floor, contention about its legitimacy began immediately. As with previous pastorals, opposition to the idea of its existence began prior to the bishops' decision: "Even before the nation's bishops approved the project . . . the pastoral provoked controversy."[18] The bishops had heard the sentiments expressed at the Woman Church Speaks conference, acknowledging that "some women do not wish us to write" and that "women should be writing about women." Bishops were concerned about their lack of expertise on the topic, for which they had already been criticized with the peace and economic pastorals. Still others commented that there could not be a joint production with women, that any pastoral had to remain the responsibility of the NCCB. Other bishops recognized that the issue of women being ordained priests would inevitably overshadow all debate. Roman Catholic tradition restricts priestly ordination to men, but major denominations such as Lutherans and Episcopalians were joining other Churches in ordaining women. The intransigence of the Catholic Church on this issue infuriated radical feminists and bewildered middle-of-the-road Catholics who knew there was no scriptural prohibition to such ordination, but a strong heritage of tradition.

Despite these early warning signs of controversy, a drafting committee of four laywomen scholars and one religious sister joined the six bishops and other consulting specialists, and a target date for completion was set for 1988.[19] However, the drafting committee was not the only group that was forming. As with the economic pastoral, a conservative group was formed to preempt any report that might emerge from the bishops. Solely in response to the proposed pastoral, an organization founded in St. Louis, Women for Faith and Family, claimed its mission to be support for Church teaching and combating liberal feminism. Identified as a grassroots organization meant to give the ordinary woman a voice, its founder, Helen Hull, claimed to have obtained five hundred signatures of support in three days. Hull affirmed that a priesthood reserved for men was comparable to motherhood reserved for women.[20]

Mothers were not the only women ready to complain about the unwritten pastoral. When the bishops' committee held hearings on March 4–5, 1985, for representatives of national women's groups, the Leadership Conference of Women Religious (LCWR), which represented most U.S. nuns, called for an "indefinite postponement" because "a much more structured kind of dialogue" was needed.[21] The LCWR offered the sharpest critique of a pervasive and alienating patriarchal attitude that considered the male gender as "superior or normative" and expressed the irony of having a celibate patriarchy address the status of women, when some of their members participated in the devaluation of women. They pointed out that while men control war and the economy, "this pastoral is about our lives."[22] Instead, the bishops were asked to continue their listening session, which offered the respect "that comes from the telling of one's story and having it valued."[23]

Similar concerns about the need for a different kind of focus were expressed by representatives from other groups from around the country at the first hearing for the pastoral. Dolores Leckey of the U.S. Catholic Conference suggested that the bishops write a companion pastoral on men.[24] The Black Sisters Conference, arguing that "isms" were linked, asked for racism to be incorporated, and Las Hermanas claimed that Hispanic women also had double difficulties. An alternative hearing, denied permission to meet at a Catholic church, was offered quarters with the Lutherans and denounced Vatican intervention on sexual and reproductive morality as well as women's roles.[25] Such reactions prompted the bishops to admit to the Catholic Press Association that one document could not address the manifold concerns of American Catholic women and that the document was not meant to be a final word on the subject. They also revealed that despite vocal opposition, the mail they were receiving was "decidedly in favor of the status quo."[26]

Throughout the summer, regional hearings were held, and bishops were surprised and pained at the women's testimony. Bishop Francis R. Shea of Evansville, Indiana, was prompted to reveal: "The hurts are real, they are deep and much more widespread than I previously thought."[27] A thousand women at nine parishes in Orlando reiterated a constant theme: that women were not taken seriously in the Church, that they needed to be included in ministries and not merely serve quietly in the background.[28] Hearings in Chicago in August provided conflicting advice from national women's groups, which fell into two extreme camps. While one side agitated for support on the ordination of women and relief from alienation caused by a male-dominated Church, the other side asked the bishops to ignore what they considered a disaffected vocal minority. Sister Mariella Frye, lead committee advisor, conceded, "We won't ever come up with a document that will please everyone."[29] Fifteen hearings in Ohio allowed 450 women to claim "very different and sometimes conflicting views," among which were the desire to participate in liturgy and administration.[30] Women from seventy-eight parishes in the diocese of Joliet, Illinois, expressed their views, and nine hundred lined up to share their experiences in San Bernardino. Across the nation women were anxious to articulate their perceptions, which were divided between negative and positive positions on their perceived value in the Church.

In August, committee members, uneasy about the extreme reactions ranging from radical change to preservation of the status quo, began waffling on the pastoral's outcome. Sister Frye announced that instead of a pastoral, a document could be issued as a statement or an action plan: "Pastorals are too easily put on the shelf." Bishop Imesch, chair of the drafting committee, temporized, issuing comments that the final format had not been decided.[31]

By September, recognizing that the views expressed were "as diverse as the women expressing them," the drafting committee of bishops and their five female consultants felt that the pastoral letter should shift from centering on "women" to that of "women's concerns," and its scope restricted to matters that had already been raised during the hearings. This change reflected a response to the indignation of women who felt that they were being characterized as a "problem" to be solved.[32] In a move reminiscent of the preceding pastorals, Women for Faith and Family put together a statement entitled "Affirmation for Catholic Women," to which they appended seventeen thousand signatures, and sent it to the Pope, affirming their loyalty to the Church.[33] By the spring of 1986, the drafting committee reported that eighty-three dioceses, sixty-two colleges, and forty military bases had provided reports on the results of their local hearings on the letter.[34]

Nevertheless, rumors continued to circulate to the effect that the pastoral letter had been abandoned and the project was "off," and press reports that the bishops would be responding to specific concerns expressed by women at the hearings rather than providing a general pastoral led to the impression that the bishops had abandoned their effort.[35] To combat this, Bishop Imesch countered, "Every pastoral letter is a response to some concern." He provided a revised schedule in April 1986, promising a first draft in one year, May 1987, a second in the spring of 1988, and a final draft for the November 1988 general meeting.[36]

It was customary for staff to be assigned to assist the bishops, who still had to perform all the regular duties involved in running a diocese, in the preparation and writing of pastoral drafts. The drafting committee hired Susan Muto to write the draft pastoral. Ten other people were asked to comment privately on the draft, and in June 1987 Bishop Imesch reported that the rough draft had been well received by the initial reviewers.[37]

This good notice for the pastoral efforts was trumped, however, by Archbishop Roger Mahony of Los Angeles, who released his own sixteen-page pastoral, calling for an end to the prevalence of masculine references in the liturgy and asking for recognition of the "feminine side" of God, acknowledging the power of words: "While we human beings shape language, it is also true that language shapes us.[38] Archbishop Mahony's letter was also a collaborative effort, issued only ten months after 2,500 Catholic women in the Los Angeles area had spoken on the national pastoral. The speed of completion and the assertive tone of Archbishop Mahony's pastoral provided a marked contrast to the cumbersome process of committees, reviews, and approvals required by the national pastoral. His letter joined the earlier effort of Bishop Matthew Clark, one of the committee members, who had written an individual pastoral for his diocese, stating that women, in asking for what is "rightfully" theirs, were merely in a dialogue between believers and their culture.[39]

The First Draft

The first draft, entitled *Partners in the Mystery of Redemption: A Pastoral Response to Women's Concerns for Church and Society,* was released to the public on April 12, 1988.[40] The draft is divided into four chapters, each covering an aspect of partnership.[41] The introduction specifies that the document is not a final fiat, but a report on the consultations with Catholic American women, providing reflections on the Church's heritage regarding their comments, with the bishops' responses considered to be "contributions to the ongoing dialogue."[42] Each chapter is divided into four sections. Two of these sections are devoted to the views of women who felt affirmed and the ways they felt alienated or discriminated against. A third section presents Church teaching and tradition on the topic under discussion, and finally, the responses of the bishops to the views expressed on the topic by women are presented. Thus the pastoral itself constitutes a form of dialogue, in which the voices of both women and bishops can be heard.

Chapter One discusses personhood, the dignity and rights of women in business and public life to exercise their gifts and talents, and the protection of their prerogatives in their family roles. The draft contains an explicit admission from the bishops: "We therefore regret and confess our individual and collective failures to respond to women as they deserve."[43] Chapter Two looks at women in their personal relationships, espousing the ideal of family life, but including comments that reflect women's cynicism regarding men's sharing of responsibility and the alienation of the unmarried and divorced in parish life.[44] Chapter Three acknowledges the devaluation of women's work in the home and the marketplace, and their additional burdens of racism, poverty, and violence. It examines society's responsibility for legislation, affirmative action, and alleviation of poverty and raises the Church's tradition, which gives women the freedom to function in a public capacity or to work in the home.[45] Finally, the last chapter examines the role of the Church and its obligation to provide just wages and opportunities and to educate boys and men about the sins of violence and sexual exploitation.

Women acknowledged being affirmed by the Church's heritage of supporting education for both sexes and providing leadership opportunities for women religious to found and administer many of the Church's educational and social service institutions. Women also cited liturgical non-inclusive language, the attitudes of some clergy, and their exclusion from ordination as sources of alienation from the Church. Although they affirmed the Church's advocacy of a diversity of vocations, the bishops were also constrained to stipulate that, regarding the restriction of priestly ordination to males, "the church declares that its constant practice constitutes a tradition. . . . It is, therefore, normative, and the church is not free to depart from the tradition."[46] The draft recommends that consideration be given to allow women to be eligible for the diaconate (the rank preliminary to the priesthood, and with limited functions) and other ministries.[47]

In his presentation of the first draft to the summer session of the NCCB, Bishop Imesch explained the procedure that had been used. Because "we dared not presume what women thought or felt," a set of six open-ended questions allowed women to express the positive and negative aspects of their experience in the Church. Rather than define or proscribe women, Bishop Imesch continued, they were "the experts in their own lives." Women scholars in the areas of theology, sociology, anthropology, and psychology were consulted, but the chair stressed that the document was not to be an academic treatise nor a final coda, but initiation of an ongoing dialogue.[48] He emphasized that the letter sought to represent "ordinary" women, wives, mothers, singles, nuns, those involved in parishes.[49]

The reactions of the bishops were mixed. This first draft came to 164 pages, prompting some bishops to request a summary, as had been provided for the peace and economics letters. There were requests for more detailed analysis on sexism and longer expositions of Church teaching. Auxiliary Bishop P. Francis Murphy of Baltimore criticized the lack of vision in the document: "For the Church to look exclusively to its past teachings for its current policies on women is futile," like "planning a trip to the moon using pre-Copernican astronomy," referring to the Church's reliance on the teachings of St. Thomas Aquinas.[50] Others complained about the attention given to radical feminist views and objected to the attacks on clergy as "priest-bashing." Committee member Bishop Amedee Proulx of Maine encouraged his colleagues to participate personally in the hearings, telling them that while it was "one thing to read a report . . . [it was] quite another to hear women voice their concerns personally. It is important for us as bishops to listen to the voices."[51] Bishop Imesch called the letter "realistic" rather than radical, acknowledging that it would not be possible to please everyone.[52] Instead, the reaction to the draft seemed to indicate that the pastoral pleased no one.

Three organizations promoting religious tradition sent a statement asking the bishops to reject the draft: "The overall tone of the pastoral is excessively conciliatory" to those considering the Church sexist.[53] Phyllis Schlafly called sexism "a phony sin" and accused the bishops of adding a new element to the Ten Commandments. "I think these bishops are a bunch of wimps if they let these militant women pursue their agenda at the expense of tradition, propriety and even theology."[54] Other conservatives like Helen Hull accused the bishops of creating "further division and disunity within the church." On the other side, the National Assembly of Religious Women complained that the draft "fails to suggest substantive changes that would alleviate the sexism that women experience in their own church." They rejected the sense of compassion articulated by the bishops, demanding instead justice. Priests for Equality called the effort a "muddled statement which makes attempts to please everyone yet satisfies no one."[55] The Center of Concern in Washington cited a "lack of intellectual rigor."[56] Sister Maria Reilly, their spokesperson, discussed the difference between this pastoral and the previous two letters, calling the earlier essays "more systematic, informed and scholarly." The bishops were called upon to make a stand with women "regardless of what the Vatican says."[57]

Bishop Imesch had predicted that the press would focus on the most controversial item, women's ordination, to the detriment of attention to other issues. Admitting that "the number of women who do not receive any child support, that's astounding," the bishop lamented readers' neglect of other themes that the pastoral covered in depth, such as the feminization of poverty.[58] He also protested that the pastoral was not intended to promulgate foundational theological change, such as women's ordination.[59] The attachment of ideological partisanship to the neutral draft elicited concern among lay leaders: "The public strategic split between conservatives and liberals within the church's formal institutional structure scandalizes the society."[60]

Innovation in Style

While recent pastorals had established doctrinal, scriptural, and philosophical foundations for their recommendations, the women's letter used a different methodology, described by Bishop Imesch as listening to the actual experiences of women in the American Catholic Church and responding by relating the teachings of the Church to those experiences. While the peace and economic pastorals had held study sessions and collected comments, this pastoral was distinguished by the holding of hearings as the foundation for its text. The discourse of Catholic women had been elicited by open-ended questions addressing six areas about women's encounters within the Church and society. The lived actuality of 75,000 women in urban, suburban, and rural America was seen as the equivalent of the experts who had previously been consulted.[61] The bishops were not seeking the creation of an academic treatise. Their initial interest was in dialogue, in utilizing the pastoral as a document that shepherded, expressing care and direction. Such a format led to accusations of a lack of scholarship, but a number of bishops admitted that, with its simple, clear language, this was the first pastoral they actually enjoyed reading.[62] Some women, on the other hand, found it long and difficult.[63]

Another highly unusual aspect of this pastoral was its inclusion of women's voices. In keeping with their mission of contesting the Church's perceived silencing of women, the bishops' first draft included direct quotes taken from testimony given at the hearings held around the country. These vernacular sentences, italicized, anonymous, chosen as representing prevalent views, were liberally sprinkled throughout the first draft and provided a warmth and a human grounding that the previous intellectual pastoral letters had lacked. The brief statements performed the rhetorical task of enacting dialogue, of articulating the suppressed voices and views of women in the Church. They also provided the document with an apt personalization in ways that the economic pastoral had not. Women remarked that they were glad to see the incorporation of sections entitled "Voices of Affirmation" and "Voices of Alienation."[64] A few commentators had pointed out that the voices of the poor appeared nowhere in *Economic Justice for All*, and the bishops endeavored in this next project to remedy that lack. In defending this process as "relevant and representative," Bishop Imesch noted, "Feelings are real, and perceptions are powerful indicators of experience."[65]

The importance the bishops attached to listening indicated their response to the praise they had received for democratizing their pastoral process and their desire to proceed along this rhetorical course. Unfortunately, multiple strident voices sought to co-opt the document for opposing reasons. The bishops sought to respond to conservative, liberal, religious, and lay interests, division within their own ranks, and the need to conform to Vatican strictures, tensions that distorted the shape of the document.

Papal Preemption

The attention of the public on the pastoral was diverted in the summer of 1988 when Pope John Paul II announced that he would issue his own pronouncement. During an *ad limina* meeting (required visit every five years) with twenty-two American bishops from the western states, the Pope referred to the Americans' first draft as demonstrating "sensitivity," but his comments focused on the importance of marriage and family stability.[66] While avoiding any reference to the pastoral's specific recommendations, his repeated use of the term "complementarity" foretold the Vatican's direction. Although the papal document was framed in the context of an upcoming Marian year (devoted to Mary), the Pope's statement on the "dignity and vocation of women" came out only a few months after the Americans' first draft. The papal letter on women, *Mulieris Dignitatem*, a 119-page "meditation about the bases of equal dignity between humans," was released on September 30, 1988. The Pope affirmed that in the words and actions of Christ "one can find nothing which reflects the discrimination against women prevalent in his day."[67] Its issuance immediately gained more attention than the American pastoral and caused more restriction for it.

THE CONTROVERSY CONTINUES

As early as January, Bishop Imesch acknowledged that there was "no way in the world" that the second draft would be completed in 1989.[68] It had originally been assumed that the second draft would be the final version, incorporating the requested revisions. However, plans for a revised format included eliminating the actual quotes representing the voices of women and adding an explanation of Christian anthropology similar to the Pope's. Fearful that the Pope's views would outweigh the tenor of the women's comments, women asked for another round of discussion.[69]

Instead, bishops convened a gathering of women from thirty-three dioceses along the East Coast in January 1989, during which women were asked to share their own stories and to suggest ways in which dioceses could contribute to meeting women's needs.[70] Women responded by asking for a national women's conference in 1990. They also wanted the bishops to integrate ideas from the peace and economic pastorals into the letter on women's letter. They requested establishment of permanent diocesan women's commissions. Finally, they wanted the drafting committee to publish the reports received from professional women's groups regarding the pastoral.[71]

The first draft was criticized for failing to acknowledge the double burden of sexism and racism to which American women of African, Hispanic, Asian, and Indian descent were subject. The lack of sufficient minority input led it to be characterized as a "white, middle-class, women's pastoral,"[72] although this tended more to describe the women on both ends of the ideological spectrum who responded to and critiqued the pastoral. At the end of the conference, Sister Mariella Frye, staff to the drafting committee, reported to the press that the new draft would be "radically" changed and that it would present a theme of friendship as a model for women's relationships, aimed toward seeking "solidarity" among men and women. Women had objected to the first draft's title "Partners in Redemption" as a "misnomer." She also revealed that the voices of women would be removed, to be merged with Church teaching and the Pope's recent explanation of Christian anthropology, in which the "equivalence" of women and men was affirmed by their differences.[73]

The following month, women representing thirty-eight Midwestern and Western dioceses met in California. They requested a more scholarly foundation for the pastoral and more specificity in the recommendations. Bishop Thomas Grady of Orlando, a member of the drafting committee, reflected on the committee's dilemma: "It seems almost impossible to produce one document which would seem satisfactory to very conservative women and to the more radical feminists." He also stated that the fragmentation of ideas in the first draft did not allow for elaboration of the concept of personhood and acknowledged the importance of the Pope's document in establishing the theological foundation for human dignity.[74]

During that same week, twenty cities were the scene of Lenten vigils, as women and priests protested sexism and patriarchy in the Church outside diocesan cathedrals on Ash Wednesday to remind the bishops of these issues as they continued revising the second draft.[75]

The most outstanding example of gender restriction within the Church was the ordination of women. The bishops had hoped to skirt this issue and limit discussion to other, socially pervasive forms of sexism. They were foiled, because ordination became the main issue of the debate. The laity—women in particular—who had never been asked for their views, took the bishops by surprise in the depth of feeling expressed.[76] The intended audience for the pastoral had been centrists, particularly men, to underscore the debilitating effects of daily sexism, but as ordination of women became associated in the public's mind as the keystone of the pastoral, the bishops were forced to change their previous strategy of sidestepping the ordination issue. Even Catholic Americans had a difficult time understanding the Church's practice of ordaining only men. Bishop Imesch remarked, "Bishops told me: I'm out in the middle of a farm community and the concerns I'm hearing are the same as if I were in the middle of New York." Among the issues raised at every hearing were birth control and ordination.[77] Still less, then, did the general American public, with a national emphasis on equality, comprehend why the door to the priesthood needed to be so firmly closed to women. Trying to ignore what seemed so alien to American secular culture, the bishops, because

of the public clamor, were forced, in the second draft, to come into the open
and explicitly state their support of Church teaching on ordination.[78]

The Second Draft

The second draft, newly entitled *One in Christ Jesus: A Pastoral Response
to the Concerns of Women for Church and Society,* was released on April 3,
1990, for consideration at the November general meeting.[79] Although still
containing four chapters, the parallel subdivisions of the first draft have
disappeared, and the second version is sixty-five pages less than the first.[80]
Quotes from women are now scattered in italics throughout the text, minus
the geographic identification in the first draft. The sense of synthesizing
what women had said is lessened, while the pronouncements of Church
teaching are heightened, interwoven with scriptural and biblical citations.

The chapters continue to be oriented as before, beginning with "Equal
as Persons," in which Christian anthropology is explained: "There are two
realities that must be held in tension: 1) men and women have the same nature, a common humanity, fundamental equality; 2) nevertheless, women
and men are different because their identical natures are embodied in different ways."[81] The characterization of discrimination as evil is retained in
this draft: "The corrosive power of the sin of sexism has seeped into the
fabric of our civilization, invading economic and governmental systems as
social and ecclesiastical structures. Historically, women have borne the
brunt of this prejudice."[82]

In Chapter Two, "Equal as Persons in Relationships," the draft addresses
the variety of vocations in family life, marriage, parenting, family planning,
and single life. The letter acknowledges the double burden of working
women, of the need for intimacy rather than apathy, the need for both parents to prioritize the parenting role, the need for sensitivity toward those
who are single, divorced, or homosexual, and the importance of friendship.

Chapter Three, "Equal as Persons in the Church," addresses the strain
engendered by the call to use one's talents under a system that imposes limitations on who can minister. Tracing the participation of women in the
Church through the New Testament and beyond, the bishops focus specifically on American women who have achieved sainthood and the pioneering
work performed by religious and laywomen: "American Catholic women are
characteristically independent and imaginative."[83] Acknowledging the limitation of access to Church ministries, the question of priesthood naturally
follows: "Many ask what prevents them from being ordained as priests."[84]
The paragraph that follows disclaims responsibility for the issue: "It is not
the purpose of this letter to address in detail the ordination of women . . . .

The teaching is clear and consistent." However, another three columns are devoted to justifying the Church's tradition but admitting a need for continued reflection and dialogue. The clergy are enjoined to examine their communication with women: "An incapacity to deal with women as equals should be considered a negative indication for fitness for ordination."[85] As in the first draft, this version encourages inclusive language in liturgical texts but adds a section on "Christian" feminism, supporting efforts to liberate women to use their talents.

In the final chapter, dealing with society, the letter raises the specter of poverty, old age, racism, violence, double workload, and other inequities to which women are subject. The Church's role as a social institution is acknowledged: "Women's plea for justice is not a passing complaint, but a clear mandate for the church. We must undertake an examination of practices, possessions, power structures and lifestyles found within our own house that prevent the proper advancement of women."[86]

In style and tone, the second draft created a greater sense of distance; women were no longer "partners" with the sense of active participation that word connotes. Now they were "equals" inhabiting separate spheres of existence. The second draft contained more pastoral text and fewer quotes, which gave a sense of greater editorializing. Six columns of this draft were devoted to the image of God, the initial rupture of Edenic human relationships, and consequent restoration through redemption.[87] Yet, while asserting everyone's equality in dignity before God, the letter circumscribed that assertion in distinguishing their "distinctive embodiments."[88]

The range of the draft's reception is exemplified in the diverse comments issued from the National Council of Catholic Women: "Marvelous, marvelous first step,"[89] to the Women's Ordination Conference, which judged it to be inferior to the first draft and hoped it would "mold on the shelf."[90] For Susan Muto, its principal author, the pastoral represented a starting point, not a conclusion, and the "truckload" of feedback constituted evidence of its responsiveness to women's voices.[91]

The Center for Concern, a Catholic action lobby, recommended calling a halt to the process. Their 10,000-word report, issued in June 1990, rejected even the attempt to amend the draft. Their fundamental objection focused on the way the pastoral affirmed equality, yet at the same time used gender to justify differences in Church policies.[92] By August the Leadership Conference of Women Religious had joined the chorus, claiming that the bishops were not ready to do the kind of critical analysis needed to examine Church policies. To the sisters who headed their religious congregations, the fact that Church patriarchs seemed to be exempt from its critique of sexist practitioners constituted an intrinsic contradiction. They also pointed out that the bishops' assumptions that "women's issues" were a monolithic entity were condescending. The group averred that family and reproduction were everyone's concerns and not confined to women.[93]

Even their fellow bishops were not altogether complimentary of the drafting committee's efforts. In his diocesan column, Archbishop Rembert Weakland, who had headed the drafting committee for the economic pastoral, called this pastoral draft "preachy" and "not inspired," having a "strident, negative, judgmental tone." He added that its stress on "equality" made the internal contradiction of the section on ordination even more chilling.[94] Archbishop Weakland likened the authors' position to being in the ring with Mike Tyson with their hands tied, because the bishops did not have jurisdiction or power to change or affect the ordination question, but were receiving the blame for not fixing the problem. He complained that the issue of leadership was absent from the document, and would continue to be if it remained linked to ordination. He recommended scrapping the pastoral.[95]

Certainly the unanimity that had characterized previous pastorals was lacking for this one, and a number of bishops had already announced that they would vote against the document should it reach the floor. After Archbishop Weakland, seven other bishops added their voices to the call to drop the pastoral effort.[96] Without the majority support that the other pastorals had enjoyed, Bishop Imesch recognized that this pastoral might make history by being the first not to win approval. He continued his defense in press interviews, insisting that something was wrong if, after seven years, the bishops had nothing to say and could speak to women only through their silence.[97] Yet to conservative bishops, calls for abandoning the pastoral were tantamount to professing that the bishops could not support the Church's ban on the ordination of women, which the second draft clearly stipulated.[98]

The open divisiveness and inability to present a coherent vision in this pastoral caused concern about perceptions of the bishops' role in public affairs. Not only was the mangled pastoral problematic in itself, it also had the potential to diminish their effectiveness in implementing other public policy objectives. Priests for Equality collected 241 signatures asking the bishops to drop the effort "before your role of effective leadership is destroyed."[99] Auxiliary Bishop P. Francis Murphy of Baltimore expressed a similar concern that the "loss of credibility in any sphere negatively affects the full range of bishops' public policy efforts, including our pro-life agenda, our peace and economic agenda, parochial school issues and global matters."[100] Thus the stakes of the outcome of this pastoral were not limited to the moment but had repercussions for the future.

The Voice of the Vatican

In mid-September the decision was made to defer any vote on the women's letter. Archbishop Daniel E. Pilarczyk of Cincinnati and NCCB president, denied direct Vatican intervention but conceded that Rome had suggested the benefits of an additional consultation with the bishops of other nations. Although not an order, the idea certainly did reveal the Vatican's concern about the international attention given to the documents issued by the American bishops. Deflecting the idea of interference by the Holy See, Archbishop Pilarczyk defended the postponement on the grounds both of the precedent set by the peace pastoral and the greater opportunity provided to collect the additional responses that were still being received.[101] However, committee chair Bishop Imesch revealed a glimpse behind the scenes of hierarchical power. When asked if Vatican Secretary of State Agostino Casaroli had made a "strong" suggestion for consultation in his letter commenting on the second draft, he replied, "I don't think it has to be strong. I think a suggestion is sufficient."[102]

In November 1990 some American women had initially planned a demonstration called a "block party," because their purpose had been to block the pastoral from being approved; instead, they met to praise the bishops for their delay in voting, attributing the action to the bishops' listening to their concerns.[103] They seemed to be unaware that the decision owed less to the threat of demonstration and more to a Vatican mandate.

The Vatican Secretariat of State scheduled a two-day conference on May 28–29, 1991. Over a dozen nations were represented. Although the Vatican's attention may have been an unwelcome interference in the independence of the American hierarchy, it also validated the growth in the public influence of the American pastoral process. This was only the second time such a conference had been called on the pastoral letter of a single nation; the first had been for the peace pastoral. The Catholic News Service reported that since it was unusual for the Church to listen to the teaching voice of a single national hierarchy, which would represent a change from the traditional "top-down" model, the issue had been pushed into the arena of the universal Church.[104] The Vatican itself acknowledged that the meeting indicated the increasing influence of the U.S. culture and the importance of pronouncements by American bishops. One Vatican official conceded Rome's awareness of the U.S. hierarchy's influence beyond its borders, and another explained that the special attention given by the Vatican to the U.S. conference was because "everything it does gets publicized and filtered around."[105]

Thus the consultation provided international "balance" but also gave the Vatican an opportunity for direct input into the pastoral: "Rome is uncomfortable sitting on the sidelines while a national conference breaks new ground."[106] Moreover, because of the dominance of women's issues on the American cultural scene, the United States was dealing with this issue far in advance of other nations.[107] However, while in Rome, the Americans pointed out that while their pastoral was reflective of American women, who were accustomed to "participation and partnership," in time other nations would be confronted with similar issues.[108]

While the other thirteen countries represented at the conference praised the American bishops for their pastoral "solicitude" and their listening process, they also noted three areas of concern: the methodology by which the letter had been developed and the level of authority the document would carry; the need for a "more profound anthropology" on the roles of women and men; and the development of Mary as the feminine model for the Church.[109] Bishop Imesch interpreted that as "I think that what they were trying to say was let's not stress the authoritative leadership role" but Mary as servant.[110] Archbishop Pilarczyk stated that these observations were identical to the reservations about the pastoral that had been expressed earlier by Cardinal Joseph Ratzinger, prefect of the Congregation for the Doctrine of the Faith.[111]

By the end of the meeting, the American bishops had been advised to exercise caution by diluting the pastoral letter to a statement or other documentary form "with a lesser value of authority," Archbishop Pilarczyk reported.[112] To the Vatican, the form of the pastoral letter was meant to contain authoritative, magisterial Church teaching. Cardinal Ratzinger's concerns about the letter's methodology of holding hearings with women and reflecting their responses in the pastoral reflected unease about the potential influence of radical feminism and use of the letter as a forum for women's voices rather than those of the bishops.[113]

The *Boston Globe* reported consternation on the part of the Americans attending the conference; they would need agreement within their national conference to change the status of the pastoral as suggested by Rome.[114] Archbishop Pilarczyk noted that the final decision was left to the Americans and conceded that downgrading the status of the letter could create the impression that women's issues were not as important as peace or the economy. On the other hand, the archbishop admitted, "If we have our heads screwed on tight, we're going to listen to the input," because of the lack of theological clarity on issues such as women in the diaconate.[115]

Intercultural differences highlighted the unique perspective of the American context in creating pastoral discourse. While the American bishops had been subjected to criticism from their brethren of other nationalities, Bishop Imesch noted that the bishops of other nations simply had not been forced to confront the issues facing the American Church, and that aside from Canadian and English bishops, other nations were two decades behind the U.S. Moreover, he bluntly said of the Roman officials and their emphasis on Mary as servant: "It's always easy for people who hold positions of power to talk about how wonderful humility and service are for the people who don't have any power, encouraging them to be patient. That's what we did to the blacks." Regarding the requirement that the letter be authoritative teaching, Bishop Imesch retorted in a press interview, "Cannot bishops be learners as well as teachers in a document? . . . Might not some legitimate concerns be expressed without giving an authoritative response?"[116]

The Third Draft

The new schedule pushed the release of the third draft to November 1991, with a vote at the general meeting in November 1992. Thus work on the third draft was already underway during the meeting in Rome. However, by the time the next version was released, it was overtly crafted to respond to Vatican comments.[117] A press release issued on April 9, 1992, announced the publication of *Called to Be One in Christ Jesus: A Pastoral Response to the Concerns of Women for Church and Society.*[118] The publication of drafts had faithfully followed a biannual pattern, appearing in April 1988, April 1990, and now April 1992.

At the outset, the long summary that discussed the precedents for, and the process of, the pastoral was dropped. There were now only three chapters, because those discussing personal and social relationships are combined. This version deleted the sections on Christian feminism, the quoted testimony of women, encouragement of women in non-ordained ministries, and the rationale for not ordaining women but expands the comparisons to Mary as exemplar of womanhood.[119] These deletions reflected a continual reduction in the pastoral's content. As the bishops found themselves unable to please Americans, women, other bishops, or the Vatican, their response was to offer a smaller target for attack.[120] While the first draft, issued in April 1988, had undergone five sets of revision and consisted of 164 pages, two years later, after four more revisions, the second draft had been reduced to ninety-nine pages. Continuing the trend toward slimness, this draft had shrunk to eighty-one pages, eighteen pages less than its predecessor and half the size of the first try.

Chapter One, "Called to Equality in Dignity," provides the scriptural basis for the Church's teaching and repeats the Pope's view of Christian anthropology of humans as "different yet equal." It also discusses the virtues of Mary—fidelity, creativity, genuineness. Chapter Two, regarding relationships, discusses social inequities in the third person of the bishops' voice. They acknowledge the injustice inflicted on society's caretakers by poverty and sexual, physical, and visual assault. While the second draft had prioritized family and married life, this draft moves singles to the forefront and truncates the other sections. Language is softened, as when presenting the grievances of married women. The second draft had used the phrase "inexcusable insensitivity," which is replaced in the third draft by "Some husbands seem unaware of the complex activities involved in homeworking." While references to family planning, divorce, and homosexuality are carried over from the second draft, abortion is added in the third draft. The final chapter, "Called to Be Church in a Unity of Service," asks for a "collaborative ministry," particularly for young single women whose gifts are unused. The same text is retained regarding the issue of ordination, but expressions of dissatisfaction with the attitudes of some clergy are dropped. This draft also ends differently from its predecessors. A list of twenty-five objectives is added to the conclusion, beginning with education regarding respect in relationships, promoting marriage and parenthood, and implementation of respectful practices within the Church.

The draft was greeted temperately ("not as strong as we would have liked," but "as good a job as they possibly could") by the National Council of Catholic Women, representing eight thousand women's groups, despite the elimination of a recommendation for a study of the diaconate for women.[121] The Center of Concern pointed out that the restriction of power made male clergy the only source for changing the system. They listed several areas of deficiency, two of which focused on the disconnection between American equality and Vatican hierarchy, and between Roman expectations of a passive laity versus a progressive understanding of Church. Moreover, the Center considered that the bishops' failure to criticize the Church's patriarchal structures and their critique of society for the very offenses perpetrated by the Church created a gap in their credibility.[122] In addition, women from twenty-four Catholic feminine and reform groups asked for new hearings, claiming the present draft was a "major embarrassment for the U.S. Church."[123] The reactions caused Bishop Imesch to lament that the committee's desire to create a workable, "middle-of-the-road" document created disappointment in those expecting resolution of key issues, saying that the public "expected a Lexus, and got a Taurus."[124] The third attempt was discussed at the NCCB's summer session on June 18–20, 1992, at Notre Dame University. Ordination (which Cardinal Bernardin called the pastoral's "neuralgic issue") and the need to explain the reasons for its restriction remained a chief stumbling block. Yet not all the bishops were entirely comfortable about that and held reservations about the Church's position. Even the venue for discussion became a point of contention. The bishops argued over whether executive session, which shielded them from public scrutiny and might allow franker dialogue, was to be weighed against exacerbating already sensitive controversy about Church power and exclusion. The voice vote on the motion was too close to count, and only a standing count kept meetings open to the press. Even the status of the pastoral—whether it should be a letter, a general statement, or a committee report—after two hours of debate remained unresolved. Yet the majority were opposed to simply dropping the effort. Bishop Imesch, the committee's chair who had staunchly supported the continuance of the pastoral in its present form, made an uncharacteristic remark, comparing his experience to a twenty-inning baseball game: "After 10 years, you don't care who wins anymore, you just want to get the game over."[125]

The one area none of the bishops complained about was the process. It was repeatedly called "constructive and beneficial."[126] The bishops' widespread praise for increasing openness of the pastoral process confirmed the positive benefits of their becoming more oriented toward lay participation. At least in public, none of the bishops blamed the process of open dialogue and willingness to listen for the onslaught of criticism aimed at the pastoral.

THE FINAL OUTCOME

The fourth draft of the pastoral on women began to receive press coverage when it was mailed to a number of bishops in August 1992, although it had not yet been made available to the public.[127] The revised version appeared to be conciliatory to conservative bishops, reducing discussion of sexism and magnifying the issue of ordination.[128] Sexism was declared "evil," but all reference to "sin" was dropped.[129]

The third draft had taken the position that the pastoral letter was not the appropriate vehicle for discussion about women's ordination, devoting only four out of 132 paragraphs to the subject. The fourth draft, by contrast, firmly avows the traditional Church rule about a male-only priesthood. Bishops' requests for a fuller defense of the position are amply provided in fifteen paragraphs.[130] While the third draft had briefly synthesized the Vatican's statement on ordination, the fourth draft details and defends that document, arguing that the Church itself does not have the authority to amend the sacrament of holy orders.[131] The draft discards the concept of sexism embedded in social institutions and merely lists it as an "error" among other evils like individualism and radical feminism. The critique of the third draft as "priest bashing" caused deletion of statements promoting positive clerical attitudes toward women.

The reaction to the drastically orthodox pastoral was swift and passionate. The fourth draft seemed to transfer the contamination of ideological polarization from the public to the bishops. Conservative bishops claimed it exalted the traits and gifts of women while belittling men, and Bishop John Sheets of Fort Wayne announced he would vote against it unless there was more on combating "radical feminism." Auxiliary Bishop Austin Vaughn of New York saw "a lot of improvements" but announced he still had objections that would preclude his vote to approve.

On the other side, Auxiliary Bishop P. Francis Murphy of Baltimore said the draft eroded the bishops' credibility as moral teachers and would further alienate women, while Bishop Raymond Lucker of New Ulm, Minnesota, said that the pastoral itself was an example of sexism in the Church. He commented on the fact that several pages of the pastoral addressed sexual morality, a matter that involved men as much as women.[132] Bishop Lucker would go on to demand reinstatement of sections that had been dropped in later versions, regarding the importance of listening and consulting, blunt criticisms of sexist attitudes, and recognition of Catholic failings on both individual and institutional levels.[133] Bishop Walter Sullivan of Richmond concurred, saying the first draft had "listened to the voices of women . . . and attempted to respond to them respectfully and pastorally," but that subsequently it "shifted from a 'listening' mode to a 'telling' mode." He also complained about the intrusion of sexual morality as a woman's issue, calling it "preachy and patronizing."[134]

A few American bishops were blunt about Vatican interference on the issue. Bishop Murphy urged that the ordination of women issue not be restricted to the U.S. but be subject to an international review by the universal Church. He also wanted a release of the Vatican critiques of the second and third drafts, to which even the body of American bishops had not been privy, so that the conference could see "the harmful pressure being exerted by Rome."[135] In the Catholic journal *Commonweal,* he wrote that it had become "a pastoral letter on the concerns of the bishops over what the Vatican would tolerate them saying on the question of women."[136] Archbishop Weakland's *Catholic Herald* column of October 22 predicted that documents such as the peace and economic pastorals had become a thing of the past: "At present the Roman congregations critique the drafts during the process and do not wait until the bishops have finished their work. A new dynamic thus ensues. . . . [T]he results, if dictated from the top, cannot be called a document of the American bishops."[137]

The press chimed in the chorus. Reflecting a division of opinion similar to the nation's bishops, Catholic publications printed editorials that in turn supported adoption, tabling, rejection of the pastoral, creating a straightforward brief alternative statement, or continued revision. Many agreed that the process itself had been valuable in initiating dialogue and creating a learning forum for bishops.[138] One publication, acknowledging that the pastoral had "focused the issues even as it polarized the camps," suggested retaining only the twenty-five action points at the end of the pastoral, which had remained intact since draft two.[139] On the public front, five pages of signatures appeared in the *National Catholic Reporter* calling the draft a "scandal" and urging rejection. It was signed by over one hundred groups and three thousand individuals. Four hundred priests and two bishops signed a letter that went to each bishop asking for its rejection. Demonstrations were held at the chancery offices in Denver and other cites around the nation.[140] In interviews bishops predicted different outcomes for its ratification or rejection.[141]

The November 16, 1992, general meeting of the NCCB began ominously. Archbishop Daniel E. Pilarczyk of Cincinnati, president of the conference, opened by announcing the conference rules for postponing an agenda item or sending it back to committee. Cardinal Bernardin of Chicago had indicated his intention of forestalling both action and discussion on the pastoral by making such a motion. However, when the members of the drafting committee and those wanting approval prevailed on him to allow debate and a vote on the item, he withdrew it.[142]

Bishop Imesch presented the pastoral, saying that whatever the outcome, women needed to be taken seriously. The ensuing discussion raised the question of why, since no bishop had requested a section on sexual morality after the third draft, it unexpectedly appeared in the fourth. Bishop Thomas Grady of Orlando mourned the missing sense of listening to women's voices that had distinguished the earlier drafts, and Bishop Anthony Bosco of Pennsylvania asked for an assessment of "the Roman impact" on the letter, since the Vatican's comments had not been released.[143] Auxiliary Bishop Alfred Hughes of Boston noted, "The public discussion to this moment seems to have become political and ideological rather than focusing on the content of the document."[144]

On November 17, Cardinal Bernardin again attempted to preempt discussion on the pastoral by making a motion to forward the pastoral to the Executive Committee. The cardinal offered as his motive a desire to bypass approval or rejection of the pastoral: "My concern, as expressed yesterday, is that the present draft has become so controversial and politicized by persons on both sides of the ideological spectrum that its passage or non-passage will have certain implications, not all of which are to our liking."[145] His idea of replacing contention with a solution that would salvage the text and unify the divided bishops was not immediately accepted.[146]

Instead, Cardinal Bernardin's statement itself elicited debate. The bishops fretted about the message the public would receive, not from the pastoral text, but from their treatment of the document. Bishops expressed a concern that a return to committee would signal rejection of the pastoral's strong support for traditional priesthood. Copious comments were made about the need to pass or reject the pastoral based on either the need to support women or male ordination. Bishop Imesch (who had suffered a heart attack during the pastoral effort) thanked key staff for ten years of effort. Urging its adoption, he reminded the bishops of the pastoral's initial purpose: "The reality of women's concerns does not depend on a vote of the bishops."[147]

Finally, on November 18, after two days of debate, the vote on the pastoral was taken. The count came to 137 in favor of the pastoral and 110 against. Although the pastoral had received more than half the vote, it failed to attain the two-thirds majority needed for adoption. For the first time in its history, the body of American bishops had rejected a pastoral letter.[148]

Cardinal Bernardin's motion to send the document to the bishops' Executive Committee was then taken up. By a vote of 185 to 51, it was agreed to publish the letter as a report of the Ad Hoc Committee for a Pastoral Response to Women's Concerns and to forward the text for study and action on various sections to the Executive Committee for assignment to appropriate groups.[149] The post-meeting press conference stressed that the pastoral's lack of majority did not indicate disagreement with Rome's stance on the ordination issue.[150] Women's advocacy groups who had lobbied for its defeat were "popping champagne corks," while "the Vatican declined to comment on the vote, calling it a decision of the American bishops."[151]

Immediately the press headlines highlighted the "failure." As Bishop Imesch, at the end of his ten year tenure as chair, wryly observed, "We have managed to alienate at one time or another every identifiable male or female group along the way."[152] Almost every change designed to appease one group had alienated another. Even the fact that its passage had differing implications regarding Church policy indicated that the pastoral had ceased to be a teaching document and had become almost a referendum on women's ordination. The pastoral on women was the longest effort undertaken by the NCCB, and the only one to that failed to be adopted. Certainly no lack of persistence by the committee could account for the outcome. nor could the initial willingness of the bishops' committee to maximize opportunities for lay input.

The path of the previous pastorals had established a trajectory toward such increasing responsiveness to lay voices. The acclaim that greeted the bishops' efforts arose not only from appreciation for the courage of their convictions but also from the Church's apparent acculturation to American democracy. John Deedy, referring to the bishops' reception outside the Palmer House in Chicago when finalizing the peace pastoral asked, "How long had it been—indeed, had American bishops ever heard themselves applauded, literally applauded, as a hierarchical group for a particular action?"[153] Thus both the bishops and the public had come to expect a similar outcome for their latest effort.

The difference with this project was that expectations were raised that had no chance of being fulfilled. First of all, the bishops in other efforts had listened to voices without making a commitment to heed any particular side. Regarding women's concerns, however, there was an implicit understanding that women would express their views to a receptive audience who would be able to act on them. Secondly, the presumption that the bishops could respond to women's concerns created a sense of public anticipation for change that could not be met. Ironically, the bishops were powerful advocates for change in national government, an institution over which they had no control, but they were powerless to make changes within the Church, the institution in which they were leaders. Thirdly, assumptions about the bishops' autonomy and willingness to revolt against Vatican injunctions were based on the bishops' previously liberal stances. Again, liberality in proposing abstract social changes was not synonymous with relinquishing traditional power in one's own house.

The past trajectory of success experienced by the bishops had created a process of commenting on current issues. In tune with the times, the idea of addressing women's concerns did not raise alarms, and few bishops posed objections. Yet the Church's anomalous position with regard to its own gender restrictions created a precarious slope that was not foreseen. As a practitioner of an exclusive hierarchical governance, the Church, even in its American mode, could not meet the national standards for independence, initiative, and individuality that are so prized. The bishops were all too vulnerable to the finger-pointing that would come with calls to examine their own institution.

During its composition, the women's pastoral became transformed from its intended purpose as a teaching tool and social exhortation to a structural symbol. It became associated in the eyes of the public as a litmus test for the American Church's liberality, its independence from Rome, and its worldwide leadership in establishing new norms. But the American values of equality and independence belied the Church's competing values of tradition and orthodoxy. The Vatican prohibition of any official discussion of women's ordination was the antithesis of the American premium on free speech and exacerbated the discomfort liberal bishops felt about the Church's intransigence, while it hardened the convictions of conservative bishops. Eventually, even the act of voting for or failing to adopt the pastoral developed political ramifications. Conservatives were afraid that rejecting the pastoral would seem to be rejecting the Church's position on ordination, while liberals were concerned about seeming to have nothing to say to women. The effort to be representative of women's views led the various drafts to reel from liberal to conservative, from being progressive to guarding tradition.

The laudable aims of the bishops to respond to women's concerns were sabotaged by their own desire to listen to all voices, including the Vatican. In trying to be participatory, the bishops forfeited a sense of harmony that had previously united them, and in seeking too many voices, they arrived at dissonance. In the end, the bishops were left only with silence.

Chapter Six

Contributions to
Public Discourse ════════════

THIS STUDY HAS EXAMINED THE RHETORICAL TRAJECTORY of a series of institutional texts issued by the bishops of the American Catholic Church and the ways in which the authors extended their range. This expansion encompassed shifts in form, subject, audience, argument, and process. As discussed in the first chapter, the transformation in the aim of the pastorals was in response to the expanding opportunities provided by changes in Church policy and the changing American scene. The growth of influence they exerted over a wider public evolved as an adaptation to the Church's acculturation to American norms and its acceptance as a part of American society.

The bishops' first joint pastoral letters were pragmatic, conveying appreciation for the constitutional separation of Church and State as a means of avoiding official persecution. The letters also defended the faith against acts of unofficial intoleration. The primary interest of these letters was to exhort, admonish, and solicit resources, all in an effort to ensure survival of the faith in hostile surroundings. Throughout the nineteenth century, as immigrants flocked to this nation in search of economic opportunity, the tenor of the bishops' statements offered a tentative admonishment of the "public" in the sense of social inequities as it affected their own flock, while stoutly affirming American governance. Their critique of the mores of American society focused on cultural trends, pointing out areas of conflict with Christian teaching: education, child-raising, divorce, and materialism.

The twentieth century brought a significant shift in the bishops' advocacy; their focus shifted from rhetorical reproaches for the persecution of Catholics to proposals designed to contribute to an improved quality of life. The time lapse between the last letter of the nineteenth century to the post–World War I pastoral is notable for the nation's emergence as a primary power and the gradual legitimation of Catholicism in the public eye. The bishops' influence as a commenting force paralleled the escalation of the importance of the United States as a global force. They managed to project a unified patriotic image in spite of a polyglot constituency, and they framed their proposals for moral national policy as benefiting all the nation's citizenry. The establishment of a permanent national organization allowed for more frequent production of pastoral discourse. The types of statements also proliferated, distinguished by a variety of lengths and forms, and broadened the scope of issues to include matters of universal concern. However, Church policy limited the autonomy of the bishops' conference to participate in secular matters.

Finally, in the later decades of the twentieth century, the universal Church's new openness, under the leadership of Pope John XXIII, coupled with the social activism then prevalent, freed the bishops to speak in support of the American ideals of justice for the disenfranchised and equality in the fulfillment of economic and social goals. Their statements, no longer encyclopedic commentaries, became focused and topical explorations of a particular issue. This discourse aimed at teaching Catholic social thought in a reasoned manner that could resonate with other Americans. The letters on peace and economics were notable for their global perspective of interdependency and garnered international attention. The participatory process of consulting with experts and laypersons was lauded as a model for the creation of future Church statements.

However, that model, so successful previously in addressing public policy, could not secure consensus on the subject of women, either from the laity or from the bishops. The many accolades the bishops had received for making the Church more democratic and participatory led them to maximize the inclusion of women's voices, but the ideological debates that had greeted earlier pastorals became, in the case of the letter on women, acrimonious among women themselves, leaving the bishops unable to satisfy multiple constituencies. The uneasy position of women within the Church put American bishops who asked for greater equality in a rhetorical bind that could not be resolved.

This chapter reviews the joint pastoral discourse that has occurred since 1985. It then offers some thoughts on the contributions made by the joint pastoral letters to three elements of civic discourse: their enhancement of public dialogue, their moral interjections, and the uniquely American nature of their argumentation.

THE WORK CONTINUES

In 1998 a sixth volume was added to the compendium of pastoral statements, covering documents issued between 1989 and 1997. In contrast to previous volumes, each of which covers decades, this single volume, comprising only eight years of pastoral output, features sixty-four statements, representing a mere third of the 185 documents produced by the bishops during that period.[1] The proliferation of pastoral publications—fifteen for the year 2000 alone—is accompanied by an increase in the types of labels under which they are issued.[2] Documents called "Responses" address ongoing social exploitation, such as domestic violence (*When I Call for Help,* September 1992) and child sexual abuse (*Walk in the Light,* September 1995). The use of "Statements" relates to issues calling for public intervention (*On Kosovo,* March 1999; *Kosovo Refugee Crisis,* April 1999; *East Timor,* June 1999; *Cologne Initiative from the G-8 Summit, On the Congo, Debt Relief,* all in October, 1999). This variety gives the bishops additional flexibility to respond to current conditions in a timely manner.

The pastoral discourse of the late 1980s and early 1990s reflected a focus on deepening the commitment of the diverse membership within American Catholicism. In 1985 and 1987, respectively, publication of *Empowered by the Spirit,* on campus ministry, and *National Plan on Hispanic Ministry* flanked 1986's *Economic Justice for All.* Plans for evangelization expanded to African Americans in 1989 with *Here I Am, Send Me* and to Native Americans with *1992: A Time for Remembering, Reconciling and Recommitting Ourselves as a People* in 1992. The bishops wanted to reach out to seventeen million inactive Catholics and curb the high rate of Hispanic attrition.

Although the bishops reached outside national borders by visiting global concerns in statements addressing food, Third World debt, normalization of relations with Vietnam, and the Middle East, all in 1989, the following decade concentrated on domestic unity. New initiatives were established in *Heritage and Hope: Evangelization in the United States* (1990) and *Go and Make Disciples* (1992). The Hispanic experience of integrating faith and culture was held up as a model in 1995's *Hispanic Presence in the New Evangelism in the United States.* Thus the bishops' rhetorical route of examining public and global issues appears to have turned back to the welfare of groups within their own membership in a manner reminiscent of the first pastorals.

As their body of discourse has grown, the bishops more frequently invoke previous statements as precedents and create anniversary statements that update former publications. NCCB president Bishop Anthony Pilla of Cleveland also noted that enough history had accumulated for assessments to be conducted on past pastorals.[3] The bishops revisited their pastoral on nuclear arms in 1989's statement *Toward Peace in the Middle East,* and 1993's *Harvest of Justice* reflected on the tenth anniversary of the *Challenge of Peace* pastoral. The economic pastoral received an assessment on its tenth anniversary in 1995, and a brief articulation of economic principles appeared a year later.

The work on women's issues was acknowledged in a general pastoral statement, *Strengthening the Bonds of Peace,* in 1994, which, despite its title, comments on the participation of women in the mission of the Church in terms of leadership, equality, and diversity of talents. Increased roles for women in Church governance and the use of inclusive language are recommended, while extreme views on either side of the ideological spectrum are called alienating. The pastoral is called an appreciative "reflection" rather than a theological pastoral letter.[4] The contributions of the laity in general are acknowledged in *Called and Gifted for the Third Millennium,* in 1995, which updated 1980's *Called and Gifted.* The earlier statement had invited the laity to respond to its message in "structured dialogue," and the latter sought to continue it. Thus the practice of continuously producing pastorals occasionally breaks forward momentum to allow for review and assessment.

The nation's preoccupations with physical well-being and various forms of peril are reflected in statements that parallel secular headlines: AIDS (1987, 1989); substance abuse, "the new slavery" (1990); dying (1992); health care reform and human sexuality (both 1993); violence (1994); the American "culture of death" regarding abortion and euthanasia; and condemnations of land mines and arms trading (both 1995). The bishops called for compassion and acceptance by Catholic parents and pastors toward homosexual children in a brief statement in 1997, which garnered public attention when the press misrepresented it as a potential reversal in Church policy. *The Blessings of Age: A Message for Parishes and Caregivers* sought to avoid marginalizing the elderly within their communities (November 1999). These messages are aimed at raising consciousness about issues specific to vulnerable groups.

The focus for 1998 was on actuating Christianity and reminding the laity of their social mission through two statements issued that year. *Sharing Catholic Social Teaching* (June 1998) addresses the need to educate Catholics about the social demands of the Gospel and Catholic teaching. It is in *Living the Gospel of Life: A Challenge to American Catholics* (November 1998) that the bishops make their strongest assessment of the American century. They castigate the dominant marketplace characteristics of "utility, productivity and cost-effectiveness" in all spheres of American culture, which shunt into silence the elderly, poor, disabled, infirm, unborn, and dying. The bishops liken nations to an ecosystem, in which "habits, beliefs, values and institutions intertwine like a root system" and reiterate their consistent pastoral message: "'Citizenship' in the work of the Gospel is also a sure guarantee of responsible citizenship in American civic affairs."[5] The theme was continued the following year in *Faithful Citizenship: Civic Responsibility for a New Millennium* (September 1999), in which the bishops include a section titled "Catholic Assets in the Public Square," which stresses the belief that "major public issues have clear moral dimensions and that religious values have significant public consequences."[6]

Everyday Christianity: To Hunger and Thirst for Justice (November 1998), reminds Catholics that their faith calls them not to abandon the world, but to transform it by living out their values in the public square, whatever their roles as workers, consumers, investors, and citizens. During that annual meeting the bishops also adopted *In All Things Charity: A Pastoral Challenge for the New Millennium* (November 1999), in which the bishops, recognizing that the assimilation of Catholics into society had created a fissure between the tenets of their faith and the appeal of materialism, remind their readers that while the nation's gross national product grew by 25 percent, the number of those living in poverty soared by seven million between 1980 and 1995. These statements tended to be more abstract and global but retained their activist thrust in advocating social justice.

In *Responsibility, Rehabilitation, and Restoration: A Catholic Perspective on Crime and Criminal Justice* (November 2000) the bishops again aim to educate their readers on the principles of Catholic social teaching, human life and responsibility, social community, the common good, and consideration for the neediest. The bishops reject simplistic "three strikes" solutions and call for "a new national dialogue on crime and corrections, justice and mercy, responsibility and treatment." They call for a cultural shift from violence, a role for victims, for restitution, and for constructive punishment. Their emphasis on restoring unity for the community counters the current trend toward increased incarceration.

In another loop of the trajectory, the bishops of the twenty-first century find themselves reiterating protests against nativism, this time emanating from their own membership. *Welcoming the Stranger Among Us: Unity in Diversity* (November 2000) revisits their twenty-year-old statement *Beyond the Melting Pot: Cultural Pluralism in the United States* and rejects the anti-immigrant bias that has reemerged in the nation. While the earlier statement celebrated diversity of heritage, the current statement focuses on global changes that have altered the profile of contemporary migration.

The bishops address the cultural disdain directed toward newcomers who are "different" (now expressed by the descendants of the same immigrants who had been plagued by such nativism) and stress the importance of communication to unite people of different cultures. Continuing the tradition begun with the peace pastoral of fostering discussion groups facilitated by ancillary pastoral materials, the bishops again produced a program of lay dialogue. Titled *Encuentro 2000: Many Faces in God's House,* it created multicultural discussion groups throughout the country, using a special text and a "mutual invitation process" to maximize communication.

These recent pastoral statements also reflect expansion not only of topical issues but adaptation in rhetorical style, suitable for a democratic audience. Cardinal Avery Dulles has written:

> The question of style is an important feature of the teaching of the U.S. bishops' conference. . . . Episcopal conferences, having only an essentially pastoral magisterium, can rarely impose assent by the juridical force of their documents. In an society such as our own, authority is best accepted when it commends itself by reason. Most Americans expect to be informed about the process and the rationale behind the teachings of their bishops.[7]

Archbishop Weakland amplified, "Our people are well-educated and used to forming their own opinions with the evidence at hand. They are less impressed by who says something than by how they understand the inner arguments for it."[8] Acculturation of the national traits of freedom and independence, frank and open communication, and accountability by public leaders, according to Cardinal Dulles, explains why "Catholics are inevitably, and perhaps rightly, affected by these national traits. American church authorities . . . have to speak and act in a style that takes cognizance of such expectations. Roman documents often show signs of emanating from a more authoritarian and hierarchical culture, and must be adapted to the American situation in order to be well-received."[9]

The bishops have appeared to heed the lessons learned from the volumes of commentary they solicited on former pastorals about readability in terms of vocabulary and length. Their commitment to reaching lay audiences is evidenced by recent trends in brevity and simplicity. *Because God Loves You, A Message for the Year 2000* (November 1999) was issued in two versions. A page of brief paragraphs reminding readers of the presence of God at work in daily life omits the quotations from Scripture and papal encyclicals that added eleven pages to the more formal version. Various other contemporary issues have received brief commentary of three to five pages, such as genetic testing (*Critical Decisions,* March 1996), *Civility in Media* and *Your Family and Cyberspace* (both June 2000).

One contribution made by the pastoral on women was the evocation of individual voices, brief excerpts of first-person narratives. In spite of the outcome of that document, the practice of using sidebars to provide individual stories and experiences has continued to liven recent reports. This practice has the advantage of breaking up the text, providing variations in tone, font, size, and color, and illustrates the concepts under discussion. A number of newer documents addressing social justice issues used this approach, including *Welcoming the Stranger* and the statement on prison reform, *Responsibility, Rehabilitation, and Restoration: A Catholic Perspective on Crime and Criminal Justice.*

Thus the lessons of the past in shaping pastoral discourse have been heeded in terms of focused topic, stylistic format, readability, argument, and narrative. However, the desire to exercise a direct influence on public policy appears to have been curtailed. The consequences of the pastoral on women appears to have had deleterious effects on the efforts to foster lay participation and gain public attention. The Roman alarm over such activities has been raised by their fear of diluting hierarchical control over doctrinal interpretation and seems to indicate that pastoral ambitions, as at the end of the nineteenth century, must again become quiescent.

On the other hand, the advent of the Internet age means that recent pastoral statements are more accessible than ever as they become available online. While only one statement is listed from 1992, twenty-two statements on assorted topics can be retrieved for the year 2000 on the bishops' website.

On July 1, 2001, the National Conference of Catholic Bishops (NCCB) and its lobbying arm, the United States Catholic Conference (USCC), merged to become the United States Conference of Catholic Bishops (USCCB).

CONTRIBUTIONS TO CIVIC DISCOURSE

The bishops' stated aim in the introductions to the peace and economic pastorals was to set a new standard for civic dialogue. Through time they had arrived at this objective by expanding previous rhetorical boundaries regarding topics, audience, and scholarship in pastoral statements. As a major institution other than a political party, the bishops' conference was in a unique position to raise matters of crucial importance to the well-being of the average citizen. The astuteness of their critique and the publicity given to their comments forced those in power to provide a spirited defense of the status quo. In raising the moral foundations of public policy, the bishops provided an alternative grounding for debate and evoked an ecumenical response from leaders of other faiths. Finally, the bishops sought to surmount the divisiveness of diversity by returning to the nation's founding principles as a basis for consensus.

Public Discourse

One of the themes reiterated in public commentary about the pastoral letters was recognition of their importance in raising questions. The previous chapters cited acknowledgments of the contributions made by the bishops in providing a public square for discussion of national policy issues. By questioning fundamental assumptions about issues such as weapons and work, the bishops were willing to probe into the unquestioned bases upon which rested numerous policies. Seeking to educate the Catholic conscience and raise public consciousness, the bishops created a space for the citizenry to ponder the values that constituted the nation's collective wisdom. Even if there was disagreement on solutions, mutual consent that a problem even existed was a valuable contribution. In 1984, NCCB president Bishop Malone depicted his organization as the vehicle by which the Church could speak to the nation, filling in the gap between the citizenry and the government.[10] By probing into the basic foundations supporting governmental policy, the bishops opened the arena of public discussion on a more profound level than usually heard in presidential debates or on television talk shows.

Moreover, two elements contributed to the participatory nature of later pastorals. First was the solicitation of lay contributions to the debate; input was received from experts in the research phase and from parishioners in the review stages. These occasions represented opportunities for comment akin to that of town hall meetings. By creating a forum that encouraged ordinary citizens to ponder choices, the bishops satisfied a need neglected by formal levels of governance. Second, the controversy attached to selected pastorals attracted press attention, which in turn brought the statements to the public eye. The vocal and often vitriolic comment directed toward the bishops served to publicize their work as effectively as any public relations effort.

In the final analysis, the stance of invitational public dialogue can be considered an important contribution by American pastoral discourse. The corporate voice of the bishops sought to augment the technical authority of public policymakers with the authority of their own moral voice. The predictable howls of outrage regarding trespass of authority when the bishops dared to comment on Washington's willingness to bomb the planet or on industry's pursuit of profit acknowledged the force of their potential power in the public eye. The movers and shakers understood that if the liberal/conservative fissure had been spanned, the bishops would have been able to harness the support of a significant portion of the populace. As it was, the bishops did not achieve their influence through the mere presence of their authority, but through their desire to create a rhetorical intervention in the rift between public and private spheres. Many acknowledged the power inherent in their collegial voice; the bishops wanted not only to promulgate their views but to establish an effective communicative forum for general public debate.

The proliferation of scholarly essays that ensued attested to the interest raised among the intellectual elite. Yet, although the bishops were lauded for raising the principles underlying contemporary issues, the abstract and philosophical nature of such discussion was alien to many Americans. Previous chapters pointed out the limitations inherent in long and scholarly documents for a general audience. Recognizing this, the bishops extended their effort beyond issuance of their pastorals. Their educational outreach included summaries, supplemental educational materials, and symposia. Nevertheless, they found it difficult to escape the rhetorical double bind with which critics confronted them: their pastorals were criticized for lacking the requisite technical expertise pertaining to their subject matter, yet were considered too long and too learned to be accessible.

While the bishops' primary purpose in writing the pastoral letters was the exercise of their collective magisterium, they also succeeded in challenging limitations of contemporary rhetorical argument. Their willingness to tackle topics formerly reserved to technical experts indicated their confidence in the abilities of an educated public to cope with the intricacies of current issues. They also contributed a deeper dimension to rhetorical argumentation in the public square by raising a neglected aspect—the moral dimension.

Moral Discourse

Beyond the provision of a non-governmental forum for discussion of national policy, the bishops introduced an ethical perspective to the debate that transcended typical ideological disagreements. By elevating the gravity of secular issues to the standing of a moral imperative, they blurred the distinction between institutional values.

The criticism most readily launched against the bishops was by those who decried the violation of separation of Church and State. Such censure served to exacerbate the divide between institutions which, in previous eras, had exhibited mutual support. Those whose rebuttal to the bishops consisted only of invoking the First Amendment attempted to further polarize public dissension. The views expressed in the press forced Church and State into opposing corners, depicting contested issues as a bout between God and Mammon. Yet the rhetorical trajectory clearly shows that the bishops had no history of opposition to government, but only a stance of encouraging participation in enhancing public life. Throughout the history shown in this study, the bishops regarded their pastoral statements as contributing toward negotiating Catholic life in the United States. The corporate action authorized by their national organization allowed them to address their "multi-issue moral vision" to matters of national significance.[11]

The range of topics covered by pastoral statements since then attests to the profusion of issues the bishops have selected to comment on. The pastorals have become topical essays, presenting theological tradition as applied to contemporary issues. Thus the bishops seek to educate the consciences of American Catholics in regard to their beliefs and positions about public policy, raising the awareness of the moral consequences of public action. Archbishop Weakland concurred, "We have to learn to critique our culture as we interact with it."[12] In this the bishops succeeded in securing ecumenical support and affirmation from other religious leaders. The voice of the bishops sought to counter the extreme individualism of modern culture and the subsequent erosion of public life by returning attention to the principles on which this nation was founded.

American Discourse

The early theme of praising the American ideal instantiated in the first pastoral evolved to the bishops' present desire to enact good citizenship through their magisterium. The application of their teaching mission has meant calling the Catholic citizens of their homeland to a higher standard of civic duty. They accomplish this not only by invoking religious concepts but by recalling the principles upon which the American proposition rests, such as natural law and the common good. Their references to the work of theologian John Courtney Murray underlie the promulgation of his idea that the phrase "We hold these truths . . ." establishes the concept of a consensual public life.[13]

The bishops have made it their pastoral mission to demonstrate that Christian precepts and the nation's founding principles express mutual goals: the maximization of human potential through a common regard for individual rights. Such mutual understanding could help span the fissures that are the corollaries of diversity and ideological debate. Moreover, Murray argued, such consensus derives not only from majority opinion, because it is not the mere preponderance of belief that warrants the truth of the propositions that follow; instead, Murray claims, their acceptance is based on "the moral experience made public."[14]

In an address commemorating Murray at Georgetown University, Cardinal Joseph Bernardin commented on the writer's contributions in articulating the need for a civic consensus as a foundation for democratic life, pointing out that Murray's position took issue not with whether moral leaders should enter the debate but how best to advocate a public case.[15] Murray understood the role of reason and rhetoric, the need both to articulate an accounting for reaching one's moral conclusions and the need to translate religious vernacular into the vocabulary and arguments accessible to a pluralistic society. The achievement of consensus regarding both mutual acceptance of moral principles and acknowledgment of the significance of a public problem are necessary corollaries to democracy. Reminiscent of the bishops who espoused Americanism at the end of the nineteenth century, the late twentieth-century body of bishops has utilized the pastorals as its means of participating in the democratic concept as a work in progress, of perfecting the Puritan ideal of America as the city on the hill.

Thus, despite the constant reminders of the separation of Church and State, the Catholic experience in the United States has experienced an increasing penetration into the public sphere. As American culture has shaped the Church, the Church in turn seeks to contribute its vision toward the fulfillment of Christian and founding ideals.

In a strong echo of early pastorals, the bishops remind readers of the constant tension confronting their membership: "American Catholics have long sought to assimilate into U.S. cultural life. But in assimilating, we have too often been digested. We have been changed by our culture too much, and we have changed it not enough."[16] Citing Pope John Paul II's statement that "democracy is . . . a moral adventure, a continuing test of a people's capacity to govern themselves in ways that serve the common good and the good of individual citizens,"[17] the statement continues, "We encourage *all citizens,* particularly Catholics, to embrace their citizenship . . . as an opportunity meaningfully to participate *in building the culture of life*" (original emphasis).[18]

The pastoral trajectory launched by John Carroll two hundred years ago has penetrated the strata separating the Church and the world in two directions—first, from the outside in, as the pastoral process became invitatory and responsive; second, from the inside out, in attempting to conciliate religious and public interests. The United States and Catholicism have exercised mutual influences; American Catholicism has been shaped by democratic principles of participation and progress, and the faithful are being called upon to shape national values by collaborating in the mission of the Church.

Notes ==

NOTES TO THE INTRODUCTION, PAGES XI–XXII

1. *Harper Collins Encyclopedia of Catholicism,* ed. R. P. McBrien (San Francisco: Harper, 1995) 964.

2. Thomas T. McAvoy, C.S.C. *A History of the Catholic Church in the United States* (Notre Dame: University Press, 1969); Robert Leckie, *American and Catholic* (Garden City, N.Y.: Doubleday, 1970); Jay Dolan, *The American Catholic Experience: A History from Colonial Times to the Present* (Garden City, N.Y.: Doubleday, 1985).

3. Theodore Maynard, *The Story of American Catholicism,* 2 vols. (Garden City, N.Y.: Image Books, 1941, 1960); Stephen J. Vicchio,"The Origins and Development of Anti-Catholicism in America," in *Perspectives on the American Catholic Church, 1789–1989* (Westminster, Md.: Christian Classics, 1989) 85–103.

4. All cited above in footnotes 1–3 except John Tracy Ellis, *American Catholicism* (Chicago: University of Chicago Press, 1969).

5. Peter Guilday, *A History of the Councils of Baltimore, 1791–1884* (New York: Arno Press, 1969).

6. Hugh Nolan, *Pastoral Letters of the American Hierarchy, 1792–1970* (Huntington, Ind.: Our Sunday Visitor, 1971); *Pastoral Letters of the United States Catholic Bishops,* 5 vols. (Washington: United States Catholic Conference, 1984).

7. Walter J. Woods, "Pastoral Care, Moral Issues, Basic Approaches: The National Pastoral Texts of the American Bishops from the Perspective of Moral Theology" (Ph.D. diss., Pontificia Universita Gregoriana, 1979).

8. John E. MacInnis,"Catechesis in the United States: Church Texts in the Catholic Context, The National Documents of the U.S. Bishops in Light of Catechetical Developments in the U.S.A. and Official Texts of the Holy See, 1792–1979" (Ph.D. diss., Pontificia Universita Gregoriana, 1984).

9. Gene Burns, *The Frontiers of Catholicism: The Politics of Ideology in a Liberal World* (Berkeley: University of California, 1992) 114.

10. Joseph McShane, S.J. *Sufficiently Radical: Catholicism, Progressivism, and the Bishops' Program of 1919* (Washington: Catholic University of America, 1986).

11. Elizabeth McKeown, "The Seamless Garment: The Bishops' Letter in the Light of the American Catholic Pastoral Tradition," in *The Deeper Meaning of Economic Life: Critical Essays on the U.S. Catholic Bishops' Pastoral Letter on the Economy* (Washington: Georgetown University, 1986) 117–138.

12. Brian Benestad, *The Pursuit of a Just Social Order: Policy Statements of the U.S. Catholic Bishops, 1966–1980* (Washington: Ethics and Public Policy Center, 1982).

13. Phillip Berryman, *Our Unfinished Business: The U.S. Catholic Bishops' Letters on Peace and the Economy* (New York: Pantheon, 1989).

14. Michael Warner, "A New Ethic: The Social Teaching of the American Catholic Bishops, 1960–1986" (Ph.D. diss., University of Chicago, 1990).

15. *Changing Witness: Catholic Bishops and Public Policy, 1917–1994* (Washington: Ethics and Public Policy Center, 1995).

16. Timothy A. Byrnes, *Catholic Bishops in American Politics* (Princeton: Princeton University Press, 1991).

17. David P. Schultz, "Retrieving the Importance of Social Justice Themes in the Pastoral Letters of the United States Catholic Bishops" (Ph.D. diss., Marquette University, 1998).

18. Jim Castelli, *The Bishops and the Bomb* (Garden City, N.Y.: Image Books, 1983).

19. Philip Lawler, *Re-Imagining American Catholicism: The American Bishops and Their Pastoral Letters* (New York: Random House, 1985).

20. *How Bishops Decide: An American Catholic Case Study* (Washington: Ethics and Public Policy Center, 1986).

21. Anne K. Shepard, "An Adventure in Process: An Inquiry into the Process of Drafting 'The Challenge of Peace' and How the Bishops Were Educated in That Process" (Ph.D. diss., Columbia University, 1991).

22. George Cheney, "Speaking of Who 'We' Are: The Development of the U.S. Catholic Bishops' Pastoral Letter 'The Challenge of Peace' as a Case Study in Identity, Organization, and Rhetoric" (Ph.D. diss., Purdue University, 1985).

23. James E. Dougherty, *The Bishops and Nuclear Weapons: The Catholic Pastoral Letter on War and Peace* (Hamden, Conn.: Archon Books, 1984).

24. Charles J. Reid, Jr. ed., *Peace in a Nuclear Age: The Bishops' Pastoral Letter in Perspective* (Washington: Catholic University of America, 1986) ix.

25. R. Bruce Douglass, ed., *The Deeper Meaning of Economic Life: Critical Essays on the U.S. Catholic Bishops' Pastoral Letter on the Economy* (Washington: Georgetown University, 1986) xiv.

26. Charles R. Strain, ed., *Prophetic Visions and Economic Realities: Protestants, Jews and Catholics Confront the Bishops' Letter on the Economy* (Grand Rapids, Mich.: Wm. B. Eerdmans, 1989).

27. Dean C. Curry, ed., *Evangelicals and the Bishops' Pastoral Letter* (Grand Rapids, Mich.: Wm. B. Eerdmans, 1984).

28. Charles P. Lutz, ed., *God, Goods and the Common Good: Eleven Perspectives on Economic Justice in Dialog with the Roman Catholic Bishops' Pastoral Letter* (Minneapolis: Augsburg, 1987).

29. Georgia Masters Keightley, "Women's Issues are Laity Issues," *America* (August 6–13, 1988) 77–83.

30. Maria Riley, "One in Christ Jesus?: Women Critique the Pastoral," *The Catholic World* (November/December 1991) 282–286 ; "Women, Church and Patriarchy," *America* (May 5, 1984) 333–338.

31. Julie Fontenot, "A Content Analysis on NCCB's *One in Christ*: A Communication Perspective" (Thesis, Texas at El Paso, 1994).

32. Carol J. Jablonski, "Promoting Radical Change in the Roman Catholic Church: Rhetorical Requirements, Problems and Strategies of the American Bishops," *Central States Speech Journal* 31 (1980) 282–289.

33. "*Aggiornamento* and the American Catholic Bishops: A Rhetoric of Institutional Continuity and Change," *Quarterly Journal of Speech* 75 (1989) 416–432.

34. George Cheney, "The U.S. Catholic Bishops on Nuclear Arms: Corporate Advocacy, Role Redefinition, and Rhetorical Adaptation," *Central States Speech Journal* 35 (Spring 1984) 8–23.

35. *Rhetoric in an Organizational Society: Managing Multiple Identities* (Columbia: University of South Carolina, 1991).

36. Edward R. Sunshine, "Moral Argument and American Consensus: An Examination of Statements by U.S. Catholic Bishops on Three Public Policy Issues, 1973–1986" (Ph.D. diss., Graduate Theological Union, 1988).

37. J. Michael Hogan, "The Bishops as 'Revolutionaries': An Ideological Debate?" *Quarterly Journal of Speech* 76 (1990) 312–314; "Managing Dissent in the Catholic Church: A Reinterpretation of the Pastoral Letter on War and Peace," *Quarterly Journal of Speech* 75 (1989) 400–415.

38. Nolan, *Pastoral Letters of the American Hierarchy,* 1:9.

39. Ibid., 1:8.

40. "Holy See": " . . . the term usually refers to the authority, jurisdiction, and functions of government exercised by the pope, with the assistance of the Roman Curia, in administering the affairs of the Church around the world" (Michael Glazier and Monika K. Hellwig, *Modern Catholic Encyclopedia* [Collegeville, Minn.: Liturgical Press, 1994] 391).

NOTES TO CHAPTER 1, PAGES 1–33

1. James Hennesey, S.J. "The Baltimore Council of 1866: An American Syllabus," *Records of the American Catholic Historical Society* 76 (1965) 165.

2. Thomas Bokenkotter, *A Concise History of the Catholic Church* (Garden City, N.Y.: Image Books, 1979) 244–245.

3. Ibid., 246–247.

4. John Tracy Ellis, *American Catholicism* (Chicago: University of Chicago Press, 1969) 19–20.

5. Ibid.

6. John Cogley, *Catholic America* (Garden City, N.Y.: Doubleday, 1973) 9.

7. Catholics were prohibited by English penal laws from "the right to bear arms, to vote, to argue law, to inherit or own land . . . and made all priests liable to life imprisonment " (Robert Leckie, *American and Catholic* [Garden City, N.Y.: Doubleday, 1970] 32).

8. Ellis, *American Catholicism,* 22–24; Stephen J. Vicchio, "The Origins and Development of Anti-Catholicism in America," in *Perspectives on the American Catholic Church, 1789–1989* (Westminster, Md.: Christian Classics, 1989) 86.

9. Ellis, *American Catholicism,* 22–24; Thomas T. McAvoy, *A History of the Catholic Church in the United States* (Notre Dame: Notre Dame University Press, 1969) 6–10.

10. Leckie, *American and Catholic,* 27–32; Theodore Maynard, *The Story of American Catholicism,* 2 vols. (Garden City, N.Y.: Image Books, 1960) 1:71–77. Maryland created bans on conducting public services, the Catholic education of children, holding public office, the right to vote; it also imposed double taxation and called for destruction of the original church building (Leckie, *American and Catholic,* 32; Cogley, *Catholic America,* 12). Sheriffs of the counties reported on the locations of lay Catholics, of those in religious life, and of private chapels (McAvoy, *A History of the Catholic Church,* 15).

11. Maynard, *Story of American Catholicism,* 1:102.

12. McAvoy, *A History of the Catholic Church,* 16. Don Brophy and Edythe Westenhaver note that St. Joseph's, the first Catholic chapel in Philadelphia, a room tucked away from the main street, was, in 1734, the only Catholic church legally open for public worship in the entire British Empire (*The Story of Catholics in America* [New York: Paulist Press, 1978] 9).

13. Cogley, *Catholic America,* 2–5.

14. Ellis, *American Catholicism,* 340.

15. Leckie, *American and Catholic,* 36.

16. Ellis, *American Catholicism,* 32.

17. Also, only a bishop could administer the sacraments of confirmation (a rite received by all Catholics) without special dispensation and holy orders (the ordination of priests).

18. Cogley, *Catholic America,* 20.

19. Ellis, *American Catholicism,* 32; Leckie, *American and Catholic,* 57; Maynard, *Story of American Catholicism,* 1:163; Joseph Agonito, *The Building of an American Catholic Church: The Episcopacy of John Carroll* (New York: Garland, 1988) 30.

20. Maynard, *Story of American Catholicism,* 1:162–163.

21. Jay Dolan, *The American Catholic Experience: A History from Colonial Times to the Present* (Garden City, N.Y.: Doubleday, 1985) 103.

22. Ellis, *American Catholicism,* 38.

23. The Vatican was understanding of the position of American Catholics. Carroll had fretted to Rome that "Protestants would be confirmed in their prejudices" if a superior was appointed by a foreign power and that new clergy might impose measures contrary to American mores. Cardinal Antonelli, in a letter to Carroll dated July 23, 1785, concurred: "If, however, you judge it more expedient and more consistent with the constitution of the Republic that the missionaries themselves, at least for the first time, recommend some individual . . . the Sacred Congregation will not hesitate to perform whatever you consider to be most expedient" (Vol. 246, fol. 437, Guilday transcripts, Catholic University Archives, in Agonito, *The Building of an American Catholic Church,* 31).

24. Leckie, *American and Catholic,* 71.

25. McAvoy, *A History of the Catholic Church,* 69.

26. Peter Guilday, *A History of the Councils of Baltimore, 1791–1884* (New York: Arno Press, 1969) 58.

27. Leckie, *American and Catholic,* 80.

28. Carroll considered the use of Latin a hindrance in efforts to disseminate the faith throughout America. Rome had granted use of the vernacular to other, smaller national churches. For Carroll, Latin created prejudice among the general public, because prayers were not understandable to the hearers and because "many poor people, and Negroes generally, are not able to read, therefore have no help to confine their attention." However, his view did not prevail. He was outvoted by his clergy, a majority of whom preferred Latin as universal and fittingly mysterious (Agonito, *The Building of an American Catholic Church,* 125).

29. All citations of pastoral texts are from the series published by the United States Catholic Conference (USCC); therefore only the volume and page numbers will be referenced hereafter. Citations naming Nolan, who edited most of the volumes, refer to his commentary material.

30. Michael Glazier and Monika K. Hellwig, *Modern Catholic Encyclopedia* (Collegeville, Minn: Liturgical Press, 1994) 536–537.

31. In his entire jurisdiction, Carroll had ninety-two priests: Maine, Virginia, South Carolina had one each, Massachusetts had three. No other New England state had any, nor did

New Jersey, Delaware, North Carolina, or Tennessee. Half the country's clergy were posted in Maryland. Carroll's response was to establish St. Mary's Seminary in Baltimore and Georgetown College near Washington (Maynard, *Story of American Catholicism,* 1:203).

32. Letter to a Vatican official, in Dolan, *The American Catholic Experience,* 121.

33. Dolan, *The American Catholic Experience,* 105–109.

34. In Agonito, *The Building of an American Catholic Church,* 207.

35. Ibid., 55.

36. Ibid., 52. Letter of June 25, 1815, from Carroll to long-time English friend Father Charles Plowden on European attempts to influence the appointment of Philadelphia's bishop (Guilday Collection, Catholic University Archives).

37. Hugh J. Nolan, ed., *Pastoral Letters of the United States Catholic Bishops* (Washington: United States Catholic Conference, 1984) 1:14.

38. McAvoy, *A History of the Catholic Church,* 121–125.

39. In Guilday, *A History of the Councils of Baltimore, 1791–1884,* 84.

40. Maynard, *Story of American Catholicism,* 1:223–228.

41. Ibid., 1:177.

42. Ibid., 1:217–218.

43. Leckie, *American and Catholic,* 90–92; Maynard, *Story of American Catholicism,* 1:175–177; Ellis, *American Catholicism,* 50.

44. Cogley, *Catholic America,* 29–32. In 1826, four of the five Catholic bishops in this country had been born in France. Moreover, the seminary was staffed by a French order, the Sulpicians. However, by 1830, four of ten bishops were Irish (Leckie, *American and Catholic,* 90–96).

45. Cogley, *Catholic America,* 29–32.

46. In Maynard, *Story of American Catholicism,* 1:217.

47. Agonito, *The Building of an American Catholic Church,* 82–89; Maynard, *Story of American Catholicism,* 1:66–67.

48. Dolan, *The American Catholic Experience,* 168–173; Cogley, *Catholic America,* 50–51.

49. Leckie, *American and Catholic,* 96–98; Maynard, *Story of American Catholicism,* 1:174–176.

50. This contrasts with John Carroll's "Report for the Eminent Cardinal Antonelli Concerning the State of Religion in the United States of America" (March 1, 1785), where he wrote: "In Maryland, a few of the leading more wealthy families still profess the Catholic faith. . . . The greater part of them are planters and in Pennsylvania almost all are farmers except the merchants and mechanics living in Philadelphia" (Philip Gleason, ed., *Documentary Reports on Early American Catholicism* [New York: Arno Press, 1978] 153).

51. Maynard, *Story of American Catholicism,* 1:242, 256; Leckie, *American and Catholic,* 100–102; David J. O'Brien, *Public Catholicism* (New York: Macmillan, 1989) 42.

52. Maynard, *Story of American Catholicism,* 1:260.

53. Agonito, *The Building of an American Catholic Church,* 75.

54. Guilday, *A History of the Councils of Baltimore, 1791–1884,* 87–88.

55. McAvoy, *A History of the Catholic Church,* 93; Dolan, *The American Catholic Experience,* 171–172.

56. Leckie, *American and Catholic,* 89.

57. Agonito, *The Building of an American Catholic Church,* 82–89. Agonito, *The Building of an American Catholic Church,* 75–123, and Maynard, *Story of American Catholicism,* 1:174–185; 207–223, contain extended discussions about the complex and intertwined relationships between clerical intransigence, ethnic rivalry, and lay power.

58. Dolan, *The American Catholic Experience,* 172. It should be noted as a matter of process that the meetings of the bishops were divided equally between private and public sessions. During this council three prominent attorneys, including then U.S. Attorney General Roger Taney, were invited to consult with the bishops on legal questions of property incorporation (McAvoy, *A History of the Catholic Church,* 127–129).

59. Cogley points out that ownership of church property and meting out the pastor's salary gave trustees the ability to starve a priest out if he failed to please the congregation (*Catholic America,* 30). It should be noted that some churches were physically stormed with muskets or barricaded against competing factions, and at times disputes had to be adjudicated in civil court (Maynard, *Story of American Catholicism,* 1:168; 180).

60. The legislative decrees passed by councils were laws and rules for the diocese. They involved matters such as prohibiting priests from migrating at will, the use of the vernacular for baptism and burial, the keeping of parish registers, the cleanliness of altar linens, and the clothing and conduct of priests. These rules, which were the basic work of a council, unified Church practices throughout the nation (McAvoy, *A History of the Catholic Church,* 128–129). Such legalities however, were usually not mentioned in pastoral letters to the populace.

61. Harold A. Buetow, "The United States Catholic School Phenomenon," in *Perspectives on the American Catholic Church, 1789–1989* (Westminster, Md.: Christian Classics, 1989) 204.

62. Ray Allen Billington, *The Protestant Crusade, 1800–1860: A Study in the Origins of American Nativism* (Chicago: Quadrangle Books, 1964) 37.

63. Ibid., 39.

64. Ibid., 42.

65. Ibid., 92–93.

66. Leckie, *American and Catholic,* 105–107; Vicchio, "The Origins and Development of Anti-Catholicism in America," 91.

67. Leckie, *American and Catholic,* 108–109; McAvoy, *A History of the Catholic Church,* 134.

68. Vicchio, "The Origins and Development of Anti-Catholicism in America," 92–93.

69. Billington, *The Protestant Crusade,* 101; Leckie, *American and Catholic,* 111–113.

70. Billington, *The Protestant Crusade,* 107–110.

71. McAvoy reports that as of 1830, there were 600,000 Catholics served by 300 priests (*A History of the Catholic Church,* 133).

72. Dubuque and Nashville, for a total of twelve sees.

73. O'Brien, *Public Catholicism,* 44.

74. Ibid., 44–49.

75. Spiritual and financial support from Catholics of the Austro-Hungarian Empire was initially requested by Bishop Edward Fenwick of Cincinnati. The Leopold Association eventually sent monies to all American bishops. The Association for the Propagation of the Faith arose in France in 1832 especially to aid American missions (Billington, *The Protestant Crusade,* 121).

76. Edward Duff, S.J., "The Church and American Public Life," in *Contemporary Catholicism in the United States* (Notre Dame: Notre Dame University Press, 1969) 104.

77. Billington, *The Protestant Crusade,* 45.

78. The refusal of Pope Pius IX to join the cause of Italian unification created riots, necessitating the Pope's escape prior to Garibaldi's entry into Rome. The Pope was reinstated by the French in 1850 (Thomas Bokenkotter, *A Concise History of the Catholic Church* [Garden City, N.Y.: Image Books, 1979] 314–315).

79. Mel Piehl, "American Catholics and Social Reform,"in *Perspectives on the American Catholic Church, 1789–1989* (Westminster, Md.: Christian Classics, 1989) 204; Timothy A. Byrnes, *Catholic Bishops in American Politics* (Princeton: Princeton University Press, 1991) 16.

80. Billington, *The Protestant Crusade,* 221.

81. Notable expansions could be attributed to the immigration caused by the Irish potato famine (1846–1850) and the land acquired in the Mexican War (1848). From a base population of 35,000 Catholics in 1790 (Maynard, *Story of American Catholicism,* 1:277; Ellis, *American Catholicism,* 43), Catholic immigrants increased from 250,000 by 1820 to 650,000 by 1840 and 1.75 million in 1850, which figure had doubled again by 1860 (Maynard, ibid.). Chester Gillis states they were the largest Christian group in the nation by 1850 (*Roman Catholicism in America* [New York: Columbia University Press, 1999] 60). Dolores Liptak calculates that by 1866, Catholics constituted 4 million of the 30 million American population (*Immigrants and Their Church* [New York: Macmillan, 1989] 60). The number of dioceses had grown from one to seventeen within fifty years, numbered 21 dioceses in 1844, and 41 ten years later, served by 1,500 priests (Maynard, ibid.) Cogley cites 43 dioceses with 2,000 clergy by 1860 (*Catholic America,* 49).

82. Thomas McAvoy, "The Formation of the Catholic Minority in the United States, 1820–1860," *The Review of Politics* 10 (1948) 23.

83. McAvoy points out that the Irish members of the hierarchy were accustomed to religious and political persecution, and appealed to the guarantees in American law for their full rights more aggressively than previous groups (*A History of the Catholic Church,* 24–26). Liptak attributes to their facile use of English their sense of entitlement to leadership positions and their judgment on how well others adapted to American standards ("Immigrant Patterns," 68–69).

84. A number of American Catholic historians, including Ellis (1969), McAvoy (1969), Leckie (1970), and Maynard (1960) discuss the change of influence from Gallic to Gaelic as the American Church became inundated with Irish immigrants, and their English-speaking clergy began to replace the previously predominant French hierarchy.

85. Drinking seemed to be a special problem for the Irish. St. Paul's Parish in Manhattan, an Irish enclave, contained 487 saloons in 1885 (Dolan, *The American Catholic Experience,* 149). M. M. Reher stipulates, "As far as the Germans were concerned, intemperance was an Irish vice, not theirs" (*Catholic Intellectual Life in America: A Historical Study of Persons and Movements* [New York: Macmillan, 1989] 71).

86. McAvoy, *A History of the Catholic Church,* 24.

87. Maynard, *Story of American Catholicism,* 1:314–315.

88. McAvoy, *A History of the Catholic Church,* 157–161.

89. *A History of the Councils of Baltimore, 1791–1884,* 168–169.

90. Robert Emmett Curran, "Rome, the American Church and Slavery," in *Building the Church in America* (Washington: Catholic University Press, 1999) 40.

91. Ellis, *American Catholicism,* 90–96.

92. McAvoy, *A History of the Catholic Church,* 199–200.

93. James Hennesey, S.J., *American Catholics: A History of the Roman Catholic Community in the United States* (New York: Oxford University Press, 1981) 165.

94. Ibid., 166.

95. James Hennesey, S.J., "The Baltimore Council of 1866: An American Syllabus," *Records of the American Catholic Historical Society* 76 (1965) 167.

96. The resources of the southern bishops were particularly strained, with 750,000 persons of color in the Charleston diocese alone, of whom only 20,000 were Catholic (Ellis, *American Catholicism,* 101). Maynard speculates that Irish prejudice may have been among

the factors that contributed to the Church's failure to minister to so many potential converts (*Story of American Catholicism,* 2:36–42).

97. A. Neidermayer, *The Council in Baltimore, 7–21st October, 1866: A Picture of American Church Life* (Frankfurt: G. Hanacher, 1867) 50.

98. Ibid., 11.

99. Niedermayer reminds readers of the nation's mission status as he depicts the difference in lifestyle between American and European bishops: "In the Union the mitre is only a heavy burden and is not surrounded by a halo as in other countries; the prelates in America are in most dioceses still veritable beggars. . . . The bishop of a new diocese in America is forever traveling on foot and on horseback, in snow and in rain, he must preach at all hours, often hear confessions until midnight, visit the sick and pray. . . . [T]he life of an American prelate . . . is marked by the greatest physical strain like that of a missionary (*The Council in Baltimore,* 34–35).

100. Guilday, *A History of the Councils of Baltimore, 1791–1884,* 121.

101. Vincent P. DeSantis, "Catholicism and Presidential Elections, 1865–1900," *Mid-America* 42 (1960) 76.

102. Leckie, *American and Catholic,* 183. Cardinals are called "Princes of the Church" and rank higher than other bishops.

103. Dolan, *The American Catholic Experience,* 130.

104. Robert D. Cross, *The Emergence of Liberal Catholicism in America* (Cambridge: Harvard University Press, 1958) 45.

105. Bokenkotter, *A Concise History of the Catholic Church,* 329–332.

106. According to Maynard, the only American, and one of the only two bishops to vote against the measure, Edward Fitzgerald, bishop in Arkansas, spawned the joke, based on the concept of the pope as the successor to Peter, that it was a case of the Little Rock against the Big Rock (Maynard, *Story of American Catholicism,* 2:46).

107. In James E. Dougherty, *The Bishops and Nuclear Weapons: The Catholic Pastoral Letter on War and Peace* (Hamden, Conn.: Archon Books, 1984) 91.

108. McAvoy, *A History of the Catholic Church,* 38–39. The German motto was "Language saves the faith" (Liptak, *Immigrants and Their Church,* 94).

109. Dolan, *The American Catholic Experience,* 145.

110. Liptak, *Immigrants and Their Church,* 61.

111. Dougherty, *The Bishops and Nuclear Weapons,* 19. By 1900, two-thirds of the council of bishops were Irish or Irish-American (Liptak, *Immigrants and Their Church,* 62).

112. *Public Catholicism,* 102. O'Brien points out that the urgency for assimilation and education was created by equating individual success with social acceptability and respectability. He highlights the change in pastoral exhortations. In 1829 the bishops had urged thrift: "be frugal"; in 1840 they advocated against greed: "be content"; but by 1866 it was merely don't be profligate: "do not exhaust your means" (ibid., 102).

113. Dolan, *The American Catholic Experience,* 172–173.

114. Gillis, *Roman Catholicism in America,* 40.

115. In Richard M. Linkh, *American Catholicism and European Immigrants, 1900–1924* (New York: Center for Migration Studies, 1975) 38.

116. Liptak, *Immigrants and Their Church,* 74. Liptak identifies Irish Catholicism with rigid morality, plain liturgical worship, oratorical display, a silent congregation, numerous types of devotion, and lacking "spontaneity, beauty, and charm" (ibid., 88–89).

117. McAvoy, *A History of the Catholic Church,* 232–236.

118. The more than one million Catholics immigrating every year nullified the concept of an American Church and fostered divisiveness. It also heightened the need to seek further American acceptance, which was hampered by the diversity of newcomers (Liptak, *Immigrants and Their Church,* 61–65).

119. Ibid., 73.

120. Dolan, *The American Catholic Experience,* 191.

121. Thomas McAvoy, C.S.C., *The Great Crisis in American Catholic History, 1895–1900* (Chicago: Henry Regnery, 1957) 10–11.

122. Gerald P. Fogarty, *The Vatican and the American Hierarchy from 1870–1965* (Wilmington, Del.: Michael Glazier, 1985) 27–30.

123. Dolan, *The American Catholic Experience,* 353.

124. In Guilday, *A History of the Councils of Baltimore, 1791–1884,* 245. The emphasis on doctrinal uniformity and Christian education by the Third Plenary Council led to the creation of the famous Baltimore Catechism in 1885, used by generations of parochial schoolchildren (Philip Gleason, *Keeping the Faith: American Catholicism Past and Present* [Notre Dame: University Press, 1987] 119). That council was also responsible for calling for the establishment of a parochial school in every parish and the Catholic University of America in Washington (Glazier and Hellwig, *Modern Catholic Encyclopedia,* 68).

125. Dolan, *The American Catholic Experience,* 149.

126. Masonic groups with secret rites had been banned for two centuries, as were nationalistic anarchic groups such as the Fenians and Carbonari (McAvoy, *The Great Crisis in American Catholic History, 1895–1900,* 132). Societies which were condemned by Rome in 1894, making membership a matter for excommunication, included the Knights of Pythias, the Odd Fellows, and the Sons of Temperance (McAvoy, *A History of the Catholic Church,* 315–316). The Knights of Labor, at the behest of Cardinal Gibbons, narrowly avoided being condemned in 1886 (ibid., 276).

127. Joseph McShane points out that the bishops also wished to avoid condemnation of Catholicism because of the participation of their members in strikes, sabotage, and anarchy (*Sufficiently Radical: Catholicism, Progressivism, and the Bishops' Program of 1919* [Washington: Catholic University of America, 1986] 359). McAvoy makes a similar claim, reporting that the bishops may have been motivated less by social justice than by a desire to keep workers within the Church (*The Great Crisis in American Catholic History, 1895–1900,* 359).

128. *Pastoral Letters of the United States Catholic Bishops,* 1:171.

129. Bokenkotter, *A Concise History of the Catholic Church,* 324–325.

130. In Dolan, *The American Catholic Experience,* 310.

131. Ibid.

132. Patrick M. Carey "Catholic Religious Thought in the U.S.A.," in *Perspectives on the American Catholic Church, 1789–1989* (Westminster, Md.: Christian Classics, 1989) 152–153.

133. Spalding was a proponent of female education as a means of developing the habit of inquiry. He suggested that a women's college (Trinity) be established near all-male Catholic University. The Vatican disliked the idea, but Gibbons and Spalding argued that women in the U.S. were superior in their desire for self-improvement (Reher, *Catholic Intellectual Life in America,* 72).

134. In Dolan, *The American Catholic Experience,* 309.

135. The United States did not have a primate, a bishop designated as head of all the bishops. However, due to Baltimore's status as the first and oldest diocese, its archbishop was generally accorded seniority in rank.

136. Dolan, *The American Catholic Experience,* 310–311.

137. Ibid., 311–312.

138. Ibid.

139. Thomas McAvoy has written a detailed account of the development of the controversy in *The Great Crisis in American Catholic History* (see note 121 above).

140. McAvoy, *The Great Crisis in American Catholic History,* 274.

141. Ibid., 380–381.

142. *Testem Benevolentiae,* in McAvoy, *The Great Crisis in American Catholic History,* 381–382.

143. Ibid., 275–279.

144. Mark S. Massa, *Catholics and American Culture: Fulton Sheen, Dorothy Day and the Notre Dame Football Team* (New York: Crossroad, 1999) 34.

145. Ibid., 352.

146. Ellis, *American Catholicism,* 119.

NOTES TO CHAPTER 2, PAGES 34–68

1. David J. O'Brien, *Public Catholicism* (New York: Macmillan, 1989) 152; Timothy A. Byrnes, *Catholic Bishops in American Politics* (Princeton: Princeton University Press, 1991) 25.

2. Elizabeth McKeown, "The National Bishops' Conference: An Analysis of Its Origins," *Catholic Historical Review* 66 (1980) 567.

3. Thomas T. McAvoy, *A History of the Catholic Church in the United States* (Notre Dame: University Press, 1969) 372.

4. Don Brophy and Edythe Westenhaver, *The Story of Catholics in America* (New York: Paulist Press, 1978) 100.

5. McKeown, "The National Bishops' Conference," 570; Joseph McShane, *Sufficiently Radical: Catholicism, Progressivism, and the Bishops' Program of 1919* (Washington: Catholic University of America, 1986) 73.

6. Brophy and Westenhaver, *The Story of Catholics in America,* 107.

7. McKeown, "The National Bishops' Conference," 566.

8. McAvoy, *A History of the Catholic Church in the United States,* 370.

9. Elizabeth McKeown, "The Seamless Garment: The Bishops' Letter in the Light of the American Catholic Pastoral Tradition," in *The Deeper Meaning of Economic Life: Critical Essays on the U.S. Catholic Bishops' Pastoral Letter on the Economy* (Washington: Georgetown University, 1986) 574.

10. O'Brien, *Public Catholicism,* 121.

11. Brophy and Westenhaver, *The Story of Catholics in America,* 107.

12. McKeown, "The Seamless Garment," 583.

13. Ibid., 577.

14. John Tracy Ellis, *American Catholicism* (Chicago: University of Chicago Press, 1969) 141; McShane, *Sufficiently Radical,* 87.

15. "The Seamless Garment," 583.

16. *American Catholicism,* 141–142.

17. In O'Brien, *Public Catholicism,* 155.

18. Ellis, *American Catholicism,* 142; McAvoy, *A History of the Catholic Church in the United States,* 380–382.

19. Richard M. Linkh, *American Catholicism and European Immigrants, 1900–1924* (New York: Center for Migration Studies, 1975) 194.

20. The significance of this move is underscored by Dolores Liptak: "So close were ethnicity and religious consciousness joined in the minds of American Catholics as the new century dawned, and so often was ethno-religious identification spelled out in the social context that it became increasingly impossible to discuss twentieth-century Catholicism without situating the particular diocese, parish . . . or special issue under study within its ethnic framework" (*Immigrants and Their Church* [New York: Macmillan, 1989] 74).

21. McShane, *Sufficiently Radical*, 87.

22. Ibid., 88.

23. McAvoy, *A History of the Catholic Church in the United States,* 161–162.

24. Mel Piehl, "American Catholics and Social Reform," in *Perspectives on the American Catholic Church, 1789–1989* (Westminster, Md.: Christian Classics, 1989) 319. A fair representation of the stance of bishops on abolition was articulated by Bishop John England of Charleston in his Catholic newspaper: "I have been asked . . . whether I am friendly to the existence or continuation of slavery? I am not—but also see the impossibility of abolishing it here. Whether it can and ought to be abolished is a question for the legislature and not for me" (*United States Miscellany,* February 17, 1841, in Piehl, ibid., 320).

25. Aaron I. Abell, *American Catholic Thought on Social Questions* (New York: Bobbs-Merrill, 1968) xxii.

26. Piehl, "American Catholics and Social Reform," 322.

27. Jay Dolan, *The American Catholic Experience: A History from Colonial Times to the Present* (Garden City, N.Y.: Doubleday, 1985) 325.

28. Ibid., 324.

29. Piehl, "American Catholics and Social Reform," 323.

30. Robert D. Cross, *The Emergence of Liberal Catholicism in America* (Cambridge: Harvard University Press, 1958) 25.

31. O'Brien, *Public Catholicism,* 132–133; McShane, *Sufficiently Radical,* 278.

32. Piehl, "American Catholics and Social Reform," 318–319.

33. Dolan, *The American Catholic Experience,* 340.

34. McShane, *Sufficiently Radical,* 16–19.

35. Piehl, "American Catholics and Social Reform," 328–329.

36. Dolan, *The American Catholic Experience,* 340–343; McShane, *Sufficiently Radical,* 18–26.

37. O'Brien, *Public Catholicism,* 137.

38. Piehl, "American Catholics and Social Reform," 329–330; Dolan, *The American Catholic Experience,* 323–325.

39. McShane, *Sufficiently Radical,* 136.

40. Dolan, *The American Catholic Experience,* 329.

41. Piehl, "American Catholics and Social Reform," 328.

42. McShane, *Sufficiently Radical,* 144.

43. From the April 13, 1918, minutes of the NCWC Committee on Special War Activities, Catholic University Archives, in McShane, *Sufficiently Radical,* 144.

44. Ibid.

45. McAvoy, *A History of the Catholic Church in the United States,* 375; Ellis, *American Catholicism,* 144. According to McShane, Ryan was in the process of critiquing other reconstruction proposals and creating his own solutions within a framework that claimed economics is a moral issue (*Sufficiently Radical,* 158).

46. *Sufficiently Radical,* 144–156. Far from resenting the usurpation of his work, Ryan wrote to his sister: "The Bishops' names are on the Reconstruction program because they have made it their own and we all want it to have the authority that it derives from this fact. My name attached to it would defeat this purpose entirely. Most people who are acquainted with these matters know that I am sufficiently radical. What they did not realize is that such doctrines pass muster with the bishops. I think that this action of our bishops has given me more satisfaction than anything that has ever happened with my work" (letter of May 12, 1919, in O'Brien, *Public Catholicism,* 151).

47. McShane, *Sufficiently Radical,* 167.

48. Margaret Mary Reher, *Catholic Intellectual Life in America: A Historical Study of Persons and Movements* (New York: Macmillan, 1989) 112.

49. McShane, *Sufficiently Radical,* 147.

50. Larkin Mead, a professional publicist was hired, after some hesitation over his large fee of $15,000 (McShane, *Sufficiently Radical,* 80–81).

51. Ibid., 175.

52. Ibid., 209–210.

53. Abell, *American Catholic Thought on Social Questions,* 326.

54. McShane, *Sufficiently Radical,* 175.

55. Abell, *American Catholic Thought on Social Questions,* xxix.

56. Raymond Swing, "The Catholic View of Reconstruction," *The Nation* 108 (March 29, 1919) 467–468.

57. One bishop in 1939 touted a scorecard for the program, noting that of its eleven proposals, ten had been enacted into legislation during the New Deal (McShane, *Sufficiently Radical,* 275). However, Abell points out that the *Program* was less anticipatory of the New Deal than it was a reflection of the Progressive platform as it had been prior to the World War, focusing on voluntary cooperatives and state actions rather than federal mandates (*American Catholic Thought on Social Questions,* xxxi; 326).

58. McShane, *Sufficiently Radical,* 159–168.

59. Abell, *American Catholic Thought on Social Questions,* xxxi.

60. McShane, *Sufficiently Radical,* 173.

61. Hugh J. Nolan, ed., *Pastoral Letters of the United States Catholic Bishops* (Washington: United States Catholic Conference, 1984) 1:244.

62. Ibid., 1:243.

63. McShane, *Sufficiently Radical,* 247.

64. McAvoy, *A History of the Catholic Church in the United States,* 387.

65. Ibid., 400.

66. Brophy and Westenhaver, *Catholics in America,* 101–102; Linkh, *Catholicism and European Immigrants,* 195.

67. James E. Dougherty, *The Bishops and Nuclear Weapons: The Catholic Pastoral Letter on War and Peace* (Hamden, Conn.: Archon Books, 1984) 92.

68. Reher, *Catholic Intellectual Life in America,* 119.

69. Nolan identifies this as the first letter that addresses a problem outside the country, one that received "worldwide attention" (*Pastoral Letters,* 1:246). However, he overlooks earlier pastorals addressing issues involving persecutions in the international Church. It is true, however, that this missive is the first to be solely devoted to such a topic.

70. McAvoy, *A History of the Catholic Church in the United States,* 404.

71. For example, Father Charles Coughlin, whose radio speeches commanded a large audience but eventually degenerated into anti-Semitic diatribes until he was silenced by his bishop; Dorothy Day, one of the founders of the Catholic Worker Movement; Jesuit John LaFarge, founder of the Catholic Interracial Council; Catherine De Hueck's Friendship Houses (Brophy and Westenhaver, *Catholics in America*, 112–114).

72. "American Catholics and Social Reform," 330.

73. *A History of the Catholic Church in the United States*, 431.

74. James Hennesey, *American Catholics: A History of the Roman Catholic Community in the United States* (New York: Oxford University Press, 1981) 271.

75. *Pastoral Letters of the United States Catholic Bishops*, 2:11.

76. Earl Boyea notes that the bishops' first statement on events was a letter to German colleagues in 1937, in which, without mentioning Jews, they condemn Nazi destruction of religion. Aside from mention in the 1941 and 1942 pastorals, he notes, "Although these statements were important, there is a wonder that the bishops were not more forceful in their condemnation of the horror of the Holocaust" ("Archbishop Edward Mooney and the Rev. Charles Coughlin's Anti-Semitism, 1938–40," in *Building the Church in America*, ed. J. C. Linck and R. J. Kupke (Washington: Catholic University Press, 1999) 198–199.

77. A reminder of the "Zoot-suit" riots in Los Angeles that year (Hennesey, *American Catholics*, 277).

78. *A History of the Catholic Church in the United States*, 439.

79. Ibid., 442.

80. Nolan, *Pastoral Letters of the United States Catholic Bishops*, 2:111.

81. Mark S. Massa, *Catholics and American Culture: Fulton Sheen, Dorothy Day and the Notre Dame Football Team* (New York: Crossroad, 1999) 34.

82. *Public Catholicism*, 139.

83. Nolan, *Pastoral Letters of the United States Catholic Bishops*, 2:111.

84. Ibid., 2:112.

85. Ibid.

86. Ibid., 2:114–115.

87. Ibid., 2:115.

88. Ibid., 2:120.

89. Dolan, *The American Catholic Experience*, 368.

90. Michael Farquhar, "At Gonzaga High, Crossing the Great Divide: How a Church Helped Change the State of Race Relations," *Washington Post*, June 7, 1999: A1.

91. Nolan, *Pastoral Letters of the United States Catholic Bishops*, 2:123–125.

92. Ibid., 2:127.

93. Massa, *Catholics and American Culture*, 34.

94. E.g., the *Washington Post* and the *Syracuse Herald Journal*, December 1, 1959, and the *New York Herald Tribune*, December 3, 1959.

95. Massa, *Catholics and American Culture*, 128–132.

96. Nolan, *Pastoral Letters of the United States Catholic Bishops*, 2:234–240.

97. Ibid., 2:136.

98. Thomas Bokenkotter, *A Concise History of the Catholic Church* (Garden City, N.Y.: Image Books, 1979) 411–412.

99. *Pastoral Letters of the United States Catholic Bishops*, 3:8.

100. *Chronicle of America* (Mount Kisco, N.Y.: Chronicle Publications, 1989) 798–800.

101. Nolan, *Pastoral Letters of the United States Catholic Bishops,* 3:8–9. *On Racial Harmony* was issued in August 1963, and Nolan treats it as the annual pastoral. However, the regular November statement is *Bonds of Unity.* I believe that Nolan is in error, as *Bonds of Unity* fits more of the criteria for a pastoral: it is a longer statement, is the more reasoned and eloquent statement, and was issued at the normal annual conference time in November.

102. Pastoral Constitution on the Church in the Modern World, no. 40, in Austin Flannery, O.P., ed., *Vatican Council II: The Basic Sixteen Documents* (Northport, N.Y.: Costello Publishing Co., 1996) 207.

103. After this reorganization, Nolan notes, the bishops ceased the custom of signing their statements (3:69). This removed the last element of the original form of the pastoral "letter."

104. Nolan, *Pastoral Letters of the United States Catholic Bishops,* 3:48.

105. *Catholic Bishops in American Politics,* 40.

106. Ibid., 41.

107. Pastoral Constitution on the Church in the Modern World, no. 4.

108. Nolan, *Pastoral Letters of the United States Catholic Bishops,* 3:50.

109. Nolan cites the loss of fifteen thousand sisters, mostly teachers, in 1968 and 1969 (*Official Catholic Directory* [New York: P. J. Kenedy & Sons, 1969]).

110. Nolan, *Pastoral Letters of the United States Catholic Bishops,* 3:54.

111. Ibid., 3:62.

112. S. J. Adamo, "Scolding the Press," *America* (December 7, 1968) 605–606.

113. See the following chapter for an explanation of the Church's "just war" doctrine.

114. William A. Au, *The Cross, the Flag, and the Bomb: American Catholics Debate War and Peace, 1960–1983* (Westport, Conn.: Greenwood, 1985) 180.

115. From an interview with M. Winiarski in "Bishops Ahead of Catholic Mainstream," *National Catholic Reporter,* November 12, 1976.

116. Piehl, "American Catholics and Social Reform," 338.

NOTES TO CHAPTER 3, PAGES 69–98

1. Theologian John Courtney Murray, S.J., was highly influential in articulating this position. His theory, collected in *We Hold These Truths: Catholic Reflections on the American Proposition* (New York: Sheed and Ward, 1960), argued that Christian teaching is based on natural law compatible with American democratic values of freedom and justice. Thus Catholicism offers a heritage of reasoning and doctrine that supports the shared basis on which civil society rests. The Second Vatican Council authorized this view in its Pastoral Constitution on the Church and the Modern World. This position legitimized the bishops' authority to comment on social issues. (David J. O'Brien, "American Catholics and American Society," in *Catholics and Nuclear War: A Commentary on "The Challenge of Peace," The U.S. Catholic Bishops' Pastoral Letter on War and Peace,* ed. Philip Murnion [New York: Crossroad, 1983] 22–24.)

2. O'Brien, "American Catholics and American Society," 24–25.

3. Catholic News Service press release, January 28, 1982, CNS Archives, Washington, D.C. Citations regarding CNS refer to materials produced by the Catholic News Service and filed in their archives at the Bishops' Conference headquarters in Washington, D.C.

4. Philip F. Lawler, *The Ultimate Weapon* (Chicago: Regnery Gateway, 1984) 18. James E. Dougherty provides an extensive review of theological developments prior to the pastoral by Catholic just war and pacifist advocates in the third chapter of *The Bishops and Nuclear Weapons: The Catholic Pastoral Letter on War and Peace* (Hamden, Conn.: Archon Books, 1984).

5. Jim Castelli, *The Bishops and the Bomb* (Garden City, N.Y.: Image Books, 1983) 21.

6. The origin of the just war doctrine is attributed to St. Augustine of Hippo, whose writings distinguish between private violence, which is always wrong, and the duty of public authority which, under certain conditions motivated by necessity rather than revenge or hatred, could avenge injustice in a spirit of charity (Louis J. Swift, "Search the Scriptures: Patristic Exegesis and the *Ius Belli*," in *Peace in a Nuclear Age: The Bishops' Pastoral Letter in Perspective* [Washington: Catholic University of America, 1986] 60–67). St. Thomas Aquinas in 1270 consolidated these into three criteria necessary for a war to be considered just: legitimate sovereignty, justified cause, and virtuous aims. Later a fourth condition, proportionality, was added (James A. Brundage, "The Limits of the War-Making Power: The Contributions of the Medieval Canonists," in *Peace in a Nuclear Age: The Bishops' Pastoral Letter in Perspective* [Washington: Catholic University of America Press, 1985] 87–91). Lawler presents five requirements to justify conducting warfare: just cause, right intention, exhaustion of peaceful means, reasonable prospect of success, and legitimate authority (*The Ultimate Weapon,* 71–73).

7. David Hollenbach, "*The Challenge of Peace* in the Context of Recent Church Teachings," in *Catholics and Nuclear War: A Commentary on "The Challenge of Peace," The U.S. Catholic Bishops' Pastoral Letter on War and Peace* (New York: Crossroad, 1983) 12.

8. Castelli, *The Bishops and the Bomb,* 22–23.

9. Jeffrey D. Brand, "Negotiating Peace Activism in the Catholic Church: Responding to Anti-Nuclear Protest" (paper presented at the National Communication Association Conference, Chicago, November 1997) 16.

10. Ibid.; "Cardinal Cooke on Nuclear Arms," *Ecumenist: Journal for Promoting Christian Unity* (March–April 1982) 40.

11. Dougherty, *The Bishops and Nuclear Weapons,* 85–86.

12. Richard A. McCormick, "Nuclear Deterrence and the Problem of Intention: A Review of the Positions," in *Catholics and Nuclear War: A Commentary on "The Challenge of Peace"* (New York: Crossroad, 1983) 170.

13. "Anti-Nuclear Catholics," transcript 1590, "McNeil-Lehrer Report," October 30, 1981.

14. Lawler, *The Ultimate Weapon,* 19–20; Dougherty, *The Bishops and Nuclear Weapons,* 118–119.

15. "Instruments of Peace, Weapons of War," *Origins* 11 (October 15, 1981) 285.

16. "Archbishop's 'Nuclear Madness' Talk," October 5, 1981.

17. "Becoming a Church of Peace Advocacy," *Origins* 11 (January 21, 1982) 507.

18. Castelli, *The Bishops and the Bomb,* 13–14.

19. P. Murnion, *Catholics and Nuclear War,* xxi. Pax Christi is an international organization of Catholic peace activists, of which seventeen American bishops were members in 1980, but fifty-seven by 1982 (Castelli, *The Bishops and the Bomb,* 26, 60).

20. Castelli, *The Bishops and the Bomb,* 13–19.

21. "Address to Scientists and Scholars," February 25, 1981, *Origins* 12 (October 28, 1982) 313.

22. "Bishops Endorse Nuclear Freeze," April 22, 1982.

23. Castelli, *The Bishops and the Bomb,* 19, 65–75; Lawler, *The Ultimate Weapon,* 19–25.

24. Thomas J. Reese, *A Flock of Shepherds: The National Conference of Catholic Bishops* (Kansas City: Sheed and Ward) 126.

25. John T. Pawlikowski and Donald Senior, *Biblical and Theological Reflections on "The Challenge of Peace"* (Wilmington, Del.: Michael Glazier, 1984) 10–11.

26. Castelli, *The Bishops and the Bomb,* 45.

27. Ibid., 16.

28. Ibid., 81.

29. Ibid., 78–79.

30. United States Catholic Conference (USCC) news release, April 23, 1982; Castelli, *The Bishops and the Bomb,* 81–82.

31. Matthew F. Murphy, *Betraying the Bishops: How the Pastoral Letter on War and Peace Is Being Taught* (Washington: Ethics and Policy Center, 1987) 43.

32. Dennis P. McCann, "Communicating Catholic Social Teaching: The Experience of the Church in the United States of America," in *Rerum Novarum: A Hundred Years of Catholic Social Teaching* (Philadelphia: Trinity Press International, 1991) 130.

33. James L. Franklin, "Prelates Critical of Nuclear Arms as a Trump," October 26, 1982.

34. McCann, "Communicating Catholic Social Teaching," 129.

35. "Nuclear Weapon Use Immoral, Bishops Say," *Washington Post,* June 19, 1982.

36. Castelli, *The Bishops and the Bomb,* 91.

37. Dougherty, *The Bishops and Nuclear Weapons,* 128.

38. Castelli, *The Bishops and the Bomb,* 87.

39. Ibid., 88–90.

40. Ibid., 92.

41. Ibid., 91–92.

42. Lawler, *The Ultimate Weapon,* 25–26.

43. Castelli, *The Bishops and the Bomb,* 97–98; "Consultation Period Extended on War-Peace Pastoral Letter," USCC news release, August 2, 1982, NCCB Library Archives.

44. Dougherty, *The Bishops and Nuclear Weapons,* 120.

45. Published in *Origins* 12 (October 28, 1982) 305–328.

46. Castelli, *The Bishops and the Bomb,* 104.

47. Bruce M. Russett, "The Doctrine of Deterrence," in *Catholics and Nuclear War: A Commentary on "The Challenge of Peace"* (New York: Crossroad, 1983) 163.

48. Dougherty, *The Bishops and Nuclear Weapons,* 123.

49. Ibid.

50. Ibid., 124–125.

51. Lawler, *The Ultimate Weapon,* 53–60.

52. Charles E. Curran, *Directions in Catholic Social Ethics* (Notre Dame: Notre Dame University Press, 1985) 181.

53. James V. Schall, ed., *Out of Justice, Peace: Joint Pastoral of the West German Bishops/Winning the Peace: Joint Pastoral Letter of the French Bishops* (San Francisco: Ignatius Press, 1984).

54. Dougherty, *The Bishops and Nuclear Weapons,* 187–190.

55. "The Challenge of Peace: God's Promise and Our Response," *Origins* 12 (April 14, 1983) 697–728.

56. John E. Linnan, "Perspectives on the Church in the Challenge of Peace," in *Biblical and Theological Reflections on "The Challenge of Peace"* (Wilmington, Del.: Michael Glazier, 1984) 170.

57. Gordon C. Zahn, "Pacifism and the Just War," in *Catholics and Nuclear War: A Commentary on "The Challenge of Peace"* (New York: Crossroad, 1983) 118.

58. Dougherty, *The Bishops and Nuclear Weapons,* 131.

59. George Weigel, "The Bishops' Pastoral Letter and American Political Culture: Who Was Influencing Whom?" in *Peace in a Nuclear Age: The Bishops' Pastoral Letter in Perspective* (Washington: Catholic University of America Press, 1986) 183.

60. Curran, *Directions in Catholic Social Ethics,* 192.

61. 728, footnote 78; Lawler, *The Ultimate Weapon,* 46.

62. Curran, *Directions in Catholic Social Ethics,* 182.

63. Castelli, *The Bishops and the Bomb,* 137.

64. Jerry Filteau, "Speech Time Over at Bishops' Meeting," Catholic News Service, April 22, 1983.

65. Jerry Filteau, "Bishops Will Have Nation's Attention in Chicago," Catholic News Service, May 2, 1983.

66. "Bishops Endorse Stand Opposed to Nuclear War: Approve Third Draft of Pastoral Letter 238–9," *New York Times,* May 4, 1983.

67. Castelli, *The Bishops and the Bomb,* 158–167; Lawler, *The Ultimate Weapon,* 35–38.

68. Eugene Kennedy, "America's Activist Bishops," *New York Times Magazine,* August 12, 1984:47.

69. Hollenbach, "Recent Church Teachings," 4.

70. Murnion, *Catholics and Nuclear War,* xv; Jerry Filteau, "Vote for Peace Pastoral Tops Other Pastorals," Catholic News Service, May 4, 1983.

71. Page numbers refer to the final document as appended to Castelli's account (185–283).

72. Timothy G. McCarthy, *The Catholic Tradition: Before and After Vatican II, 1878–1993* (Chicago: Loyola University Press, 1994) 249.

73. McCann, "Communicating Catholic Social Teaching," 126.

74. Alan Geyer, "Two and Three-Fourths Cheers for the Bishops' Pastoral: A Peculiar Protestant Perspective," in *Peace in a Nuclear Age: The Bishops' Pastoral Letter in Perspective* (Washington: Catholic University of America Press, 1986) 29.

75. Castelli, *The Bishops and the Bomb,* 106.

76. James L. Franklin, "U.S. Bishops Raise Nuclear Alarm," November 14, 1982.

77. Broadcast October 26, 1982.

78. John C. Bennett, "The Bishops' Pastoral: A Response," *Christianity and Crisis* (May 30, 1983) 203.

79. Franklin, "U.S. Bishops Raise Nuclear Alarm."

80. Castelli, *The Bishops and the Bomb,* 118.

81. Lawler, *The Ultimate Weapon,* 45.

82. Ibid., 43–44.

83. "The U.S. Catholic Bishops and Nuclear Arms," *Wall Street Journal,* November 15, 1982.

84. Among these were Alexander Haig, Secretary of State; Richard Allen, first National Security Advisor; William Clark, Allen's successor; William J. Casey, director of the CIA; and John Lehman, Secretary of the Navy (Kenneth Woodward, "Challenging the Bishops," *Newsweek* [November 8, 1982] 78).

85. Jerry Filteau, "24 Catholic Congressmen Oppose Bishops' 'Peace Pastoral,'" Catholic News Service, December 23, 1982.

86. "Prelates Backed in Dispute on Arms: 24 Academics and Ex-officials Say Bishops Should Take a Stand," *New York Times,* November 18, 1982.

87. *BusinessWeek* verified this in 1984, depicting National Security Advisor William Clark as working "feverishly to head the bishops off from labeling the U.S. policy of nuclear deterrence as 'immoral'" ("The Church and Capitalism," 105), about which the final document was indeed silent.

88. Ibid.

89. Curran, *Directions in Catholic Social Ethics,* 182.

90. "Administration Hails New Draft of Arms Letter—Says Bishops 'Improved' the Nuclear Statement," *New York Times,* April 7, 1983; Lawler, *The Ultimate Weapon,* 51.

91. Castelli, *The Bishops and the Bomb,* 151.

92. "Didn't Bow to Reagan, Bishops Say," *Chicago Tribune,* April 10, 1983; "Bishops Stand Firm," *Time* (April 11, 1983, under "Religion").

93. Congress seemed more appreciative. Senator Edward Kennedy thanked the bishops for their achievement and requested that the full text of the pastoral be entered into the *Record,* which was so ordered (*Congressional Record* 129 [May 16, 1983] 66).

94. NCCB statement, Catholic News Service, April 12, 1983.

95. Rev. Kenneth K. Doyle, "No Major Changes Foreseen in War and Peace Pastoral," Catholic News Service, January 24, 1983.

96. Castelli, *The Bishops and the Bomb,* 131–133.

97. Reese, *Flock of Shepherds,* 113.

98. Lawler, *The Ultimate Weapon,* 32; Timothy A. Byrnes, *Catholic Bishops in American Politics* (Princeton: Princeton University Press, 1991) 114.

99. Lawler, *The Ultimate Weapon,* 53–60.

100. Conrad Komorowski, "To Uphold Human Values," *New York Daily World,* December 14, 1982.

101. Hollenbach, "Recent Church Teachings," 4.

102. Charles Curran, *Tensions in Moral Theology* (Notre Dame: Notre Dame University Press, 1988) 181.

103. Jonathan Schell, "Reflections—Nuclear Arms, Part I," *The New Yorker,* January 2, 1984:66.

104. "Bishops Vitally Linked to Democratic Process," NCCB Library Archives, n.p., n.d.

105. Castelli, *The Bishops and the Bomb,* 100.

106. Michael Novak, "Moral Clarity in the Nuclear Age," *National Review* (April 1, 1983) 354–392.

107. Francis X. Winters, "The Cultural Context of the Pastoral Letter on Peace," in *Peace in a Nuclear Age: The Bishops' Pastoral Letter in Perspective* (Washington, D.C.: Catholic University of America Press, 1986) 340.

108. Ibid.

109. "Will the Pope Stop Nuclear Heresy?" *Washington Post,* November 8, 1982.

110. Komorowski, "To Uphold Human Values."

111. E.g., William F. Buckley, "When the Bishops Speak," *Washington Post,* November 29, 1982; William Safire, "Bullies in the Pulpit" *New York Times,* March 14, 1983.

112. "God and the Bomb: Catholic Bishops Debate Nuclear Morality," *Time* (November 29, 1982) 76.

113. "God and the Bomb," 74.

114. Ibid., 77.

115. On "CBS Evening News with Dan Rather," November 15, 1982.

116. Gommar A. DePauw, *The Challenge of Peace Through Strength: God's Plan and Our Defense of It: The Stripping of a Bishops' Pastoral Letter* (Westbury, N.Y.: CTM, 1989).

117. "More Danger from the Catholic Left," April 20, 1983: E 1721.

118. "For the Catholic Bishops—The Full Implication," *Congressional Record,* April 21, 1983: E 1790.

119. "Bishops in the Wrong Pew," *Detroit News,* November 24, 1982.

120. Herman Kahn, December 9, 1982.

121. "U.S. Catholics on the Brink," *National Review* (November 26, 1982) 1476.

122. "The Bishops and the Bomb," October 29, 1982.

123. Curran, *Directions in Catholic Social Ethics,* 180.

124. Florence L. Herman, "Archbishop Hannan Finds Major Problems in War and Peace Pastoral," Catholic News Service, April 27, 1983. As auxiliary bishop of Washington, D.C., Bishop Hannan had argued against proposals condemning the threat of nuclear weapons as a deterrent during Vatican II in 1964 (Dorothy Dohen, *Nationalism and American Catholicism* [New York: Sheed and Ward, 1967] 161).

125. "When the Bishops Speak," *Washington Post,* November 29, 1982.

126. "A Call to Conscience," May 16, 1983.

127. "Bishops Debate an Attack on Arms Policy," November 18, 1982.

128. "The Catholic Conversion on Peace," *Newsday* (November 21, 1982).

129. "God and the Bomb," 71.

130. Ibid.

131. Jerry Filteau, "Bishops Will Have Nation's Attention in Chicago," Catholic News Service, April 22, 1983.

132. Both dated November 8, 1982.

133. With Bryant Gumbel on "Today," NBC.

134. With David Hartman on "Good Morning America," ABC.

135. WRC-TV broadcast, November 20, 1982.

136. "All Things Considered," National Public Radio, November 18, 1982; "Newsbreak," CBS Radio, November 19, 1982.

137. USCC press release, May 10, 1983, NCCB Library Archives.

138. Eugene Kennedy, August 12, 1984:14–30.

139. Castelli, *The Bishops and the Bomb,* 126.

140. For example, *National Review,* December 24, 1982; *Dallas Morning News,* May 10, 1983.

141. "God and the Bomb," 68.

142. Ibid.

143. Kenneth A. Briggs, "Bishops to Finish Atom Arms Letter," May 1, 1983.

144. Jerry Filteau, "An Evolution of Teaching: Pastoral Drafts Compared," Catholic News Service, April 4, 1983.

145. McCann, "Communicating Catholic Social Teaching," 128.

146. Ibid., 130.

147. "God and the Bomb," 77.

148. "The Bishop's Letter: Moral Leadership," April 14, 1983.

149. Cardinal James Hickey, "To Be Peacemakers," *Origins* 12 (October 7, 1982) 270.

150. *Directions in Catholic Social Ethics,* 195.

151. *Challenge of Peace,* in Castelli, *The Bishops and the Bomb,* 201.

152. Hickey, "To Be Peacemakers," 271.

153. "A Document of Faith and Hope," *Boston Globe,* November 17, 1982.

154. Bennett, "The Bishops' Pastoral: A Response," 203.

155. "The Bishops' Velvet Glove," April 9, 1983.

156. Dean C. Curry, *Evangelicals and the Bishops' Pastoral Letter* (Grand Rapids, Mich.: Wm. B. Eerdmans, 1984) 19.

157. Curran, *Directions in Catholic Social Ethics,* 195.

158. "Intersection of Public Opinion and Public Policy," address to the NCCB General Meeting, *Origins* 14 (November 29, 1984) 387.

159. Castelli, *The Bishops and the Bomb,* 113.

160. Roy Larson, "It's Bishops' Duty to Join Nuclear Debate," *Chicago Sun-Times,* November 20, 1982.

161. *New York Daily World,* December 14, 1982.

162. "Prelates Backed in Dispute on Arms: 24 Academics and Ex-officials Say Bishops Should Take a Stand," *New York Times,* November 18, 1982.

163. Larson, "It's Bishops' Duty to Join Nuclear Debate."

164. "A Tolerant Invitation" (7 April 1983).

165. "Resisting All Nuclear War, the Bishops' Welcome Cry," May 6, 1983.

166. "A Document of Faith and Hope," November 17, 1982.

167. "Reflections—Nuclear Arms, Part I," 43. Schell concurred with the concept of a clergy of experts: "So widely accepted in our country had the doctrine [of deterrence] become, that some likened it to a religious faith and referred to its experts as a 'priesthood.'" Ibid., 64.

168. William E. Murnion, "The Role and Language of the Church in Relation to Public Policy," in *Catholics and Nuclear War: A Commentary on "The Challenge of Peace," The U.S. Catholic Bishops' Pastoral Letter on War and Peace* (New York: Crossroad, 1983) 58.

169. "Studying War and Peace," NCCB committee report, *Origins* 11 (December 3, 1981) 404.

170. Dated October 26, 1982, NCCB Library Archives.

171. "The Role and Language of the Church in Relation to Public Policy," in *Catholics and Nuclear War: A Commentary on "The Challenge of Peace," The U.S. Catholic Bishops' Pastoral Letter on War and Peace,* ed. P. J. Murnion (New York: Crossroad, 1983) 65.

172. Byrnes, *Catholic Bishops in American Politics,* 102.

173. "The Next Step: Acting on Faith?" *Nuclear Times* (February 1983) 9.

174. "A Call to Conscience," May 16, 1983.

175. "The Next Step: Acting on Faith?" *Nuclear Times* (February 1983) 10.

176. "Reflections—Nuclear Arms, Part I," 38.

177. In Castelli, *The Bishops and the Bomb,* 228.

178. Robert F. Baldwin, "Avoid Secular Interpretations of Pastoral, Bishop Says," Catholic News Service, April 18, 1983.

179. Richard Reeves, "Simple Moral Words," *San Francisco Chronicle* (November 25, 1982).

180. *The Challenge of Peace,* in Castelli, *The Bishops and the Bomb,* 228–229.

181. Barry Bearak, "Pro-Peace Spirit Grows in Catholics," *Los Angeles Times* (June 25, 1984).

182. Kenneth A. Briggs, "Bishops Gratified, Prepare to Teach Pastoral on Peace," *New York Times* (May 5, 1983).

183. "Is the Pastoral Letter on Nuclear Weapons Only a Beginning?" *New York Times* (May 8, 1983).

184. Bearak, "Pro-Peace Spirit Grows in Catholics."

185. Catherine Inez Adlesic, "The Effort to Implement the Pastoral Letter on War and Peace," in *Peace in a Nuclear Age: The Bishops' Pastoral Letter in Perspective* (Washington, D.C.: Catholic University of America Press, 1986) 387.

186. Ibid., 391.

187. Ibid., 388–396.

188. "NBC News One Hour Special," Catholic News Service (May 9, 1983).

189. Washington: Center of Concern, 1983.

190. Office of Catholic Education, Indianapolis, 1983.

191. Ramsey, N.J.: Paulist Press, 1983.

192. Washington: NCCB, 1983.

193. Collegeville, Minn.: The Liturgical Press, 1986.

194. Albuquerque: Hosanna, 1986.

195. Akron: Akron Catholic Committee, 1984.

196. Chicago: Liturgy Training Publications, 1987.

197. *The Challenge of Peace,* in Castelli, *The Bishops and the Bomb,* 193.

198. Kevin J. Cassidy, "Who Is Responsible? Bringing the Light to G.E.?" *Commonweal* (May, 17, 1985) 295–297.

199. Andrew Greeley, "The Church and the Poor" *New York Times* (June 17, 1985).

200. May 11, 1983, NCCB Library Archives.

201. May 16, 1983.

202. "Apathy Slows Disarmament, Says Cardinal Bernardin Accepting Peace Prize," Catholic News Service, November 8, 1983.

203. "Pastoral Letter Projects Named to Share Einstein Peace Award," USCC press release, January 6, 1984, NCCB Library Archives.

204. Curry, *Evangelicals and the Bishops' Pastoral Letter,* 18.

205. Ibid., xii.

206. "Reform Judaism Launches Nuclear Freeze Drive," Catholic News Service, April 26, 1983.

207. Jim Castelli, "Nuclear Pastoral May Be Watershed for U.S. Bishops," *Our Sunday Visitor,* May 22, 1983.

208. Synagogue Council press release.

209. Bennett, "The Bishops' Pastoral: A Response," 203.

210. Pat McCullough, "The Bishops' Pastoral Letter—Issues and Responses" (Louisville: Center for Christian and Ethical Concerns, 1988).

211. Bearak, "Pro-Peace Spirit Grows in Catholics."

212. Murphy, *Betraying the Bishops,* 61.

213. Lawler, *The Ultimate Weapon,* 10–15.

NOTES TO CHAPTER 4, PAGES 99–121

1. Dale Francis, "Economic Justice," *The Catholic Post* (November 1986) 4.

2. Eugene Kennedy, *Re-Imagining American Catholicism: The American Bishops and Their Pastoral Letters* (New York: Random House, 1985) 58.

3. "Bishops Guard Pastoral But Leak Rumors Persist," *Cleveland Plain Dealer,* October 20, 1984.

4. David J. O'Brien, "The Economic Thought of the American Hierarchy," in *The Catholic Challenge to the American Economy: Reflections on the U.S. Bishops' Pastoral Letter on Catholic Social Teaching and the U.S. Economy* (New York: Macmillan, 1987) 31–33.

5. These included the National Labor Relations Act of 1935, the Social Security Act of 1935, and the Fair Wages and Hours Law of 1938 (O'Brien, "Economic Thought," 33).

6. O'Brien traces this development in his chapter, cited above, on the involvement of the American bishops in critiques of the economic system.

7. Ibid.

8. John J. O'Connor, "Catholic Social Teaching and the Limits of Authority," in *Challenge and Response* (Washington: Ethics and Public Policy Center, 1985) 75.

9. O'Brien, "Economic Thought," 33.

10. "On Human Work," *Origins* 11 (September 24, 1981) 230.

11. Brien J. Hallett, "Pope John Paul's Challenge to the American Bishops," *America* (May 4, 1985) 372.

12. Eugene Kennedy, "America's Activist Bishops," *New York Times Magazine* (August 12, 1984) 16.

13. "Great Lakes Appalachian Project on the Economic Crisis," December 9, 1984.

14. Vincent Carrafiello, "Bishops Lash U.S. Economy," *The Month* (February 1985) 45. In 1977, Lykes Corporation's decision to close their steel mill in Youngstown had cost the region five thousand jobs ("How Effective is the Church's Social Doctrine?" *Origins* 11 [November 26, 1981] 373).

15. "Catholic Lay Group Preempts," *New York City Tribune,* December 4, 1984.

16. "Insufficiently Radical," *New Oxford Review* (March 1985) 4.

17. "The Bishops and Capitalism," *St. Louis Post-Dispatch,* editorial, November 16, 1984.

18. "Bishops' Bold Pleas Deserve Our Backing," *USA Today,* November 15, 1984.

19. Jodie T. Allen, "Someone Has to Swim Against the Political Tide," *Washington Post,* November 18, 1984.

20. James R. Crotty and James R. Stormes, "The Bishops on the U.S. Economy," *Challenge: The Magazine of Economic Affairs* (March–April 1985) 36.

21. "Take Two," broadcast November 12, 1984.

22. "Bishops Coming to Grips with the Prophetic Role," November 18, 1984.

23. "Document Praised at Bishops' Parley," *New York Times,* November 15, 1984.

24. John J. LaFalce, "Catholic Social Teaching and Economic Justice," *America* (May 4, 1985) 357.

25. *Origins* (December 8, 1983) 447.

26. Kennedy, "America's Activist Bishops," 24.

27. Eugene Kennedy, *Re-Imagining American Catholicism: The American Bishops and Their Pastoral Letters* (New York: Random House, 1985) 80.

28. Robert N. Bellah, "Economics and the Theology of Work," *New Oxford Review* (November 1984) 14–17.

29. Philip F. Lawler, *How Bishops Decide: An American Catholic Case Study* (Washington: Ethics and Public Policy Center, 1986) 10–11.

30. "The U.S. Bishops' Pastoral on Social Justice," *Doctrine and Life* (March 1985) 142.

31. "Church and Capitalism: Report by Catholic Bishops on U.S. Economy Will Cause a Furor," *BusinessWeek* (November 11, 1984) 105; "Evening News," CNN, November 13, 1984.

32. In *Origins* 14 (November 15, 1984) 337–383.

33. "Chapter 5 of the Economic Pastoral: Food and Agricultural Policies," *Origins* 15 (May 23, 1985) 1–8.

34. "Archbishop Says Pastoral Might Use a Bit More Optimism," Catholic News Service, November 14, 1984.

35. "Document Praised at Bishops' Parley," *New York Times,* November 15, 1984.

36. "Three Day Conference at Notre Dame Served as Coming-out Party," December 17, 1983.

37. "How Many Divisions Do They Have?" April 25, 1983:50.

38. *Dun's Business Month* (March 1984) 31–35.

39. Dick Dowd, "The Hidden Agenda," *Long Island Catholic,* November 5, 1984.

40. "Catholics and Economics: In the Right Church but the Wrong Pew?" November 22, 1984.

41. "Catholic Church Is Weighing into Political Scene," November 16, 1984.

42. Sheila Collins, "Pastoral Welcome, Long Overdue," *The Witness* 67 (November 6, 1984).

43. "Capitalism and the Bishops," November 13, 1984.

44. LaFalce, "Catholic Social Teaching," 356.

45. "Address on Christian Unity in a Technological Age," *Origins* 14 (October 4, 1984) 248.

46. "The Church and Capitalism," November 12, 1984.

47. "Catholic Lay Letter Defends Capitalist Ethics," *Detroit Free Press,* November 7, 1984.

48. Colman McCarthy, "The Bishops Can't Win with Novak," *Newsday,* November 25, 1984.

49. *BusinessWeek,* "The Church and Capitalism," 106.

50. "More Must be Asked of Poor, Poverty Experts Tell Lay Group," *Louisville Record*, July 17, 1984.

51. Donald Warwick, "Four Views of the Bishops' Pastoral, the Lay Letter and the U.S. Economy," *This Word* (Winter 1985) 108.

52. Michael Novak, *Toward the Future: Catholic Social Thought and the U.S. Economy: A Lay Letter* (New York: Lay Committee on Catholic Social Teaching and the U.S. Economy, 1984).

53. "Church and Capitalism," *BusinessWeek,* 106.

54. "Catholic Lay Group Preempts Bishops in Economic Sermon," December 4, 1984.

55. "Special Report," *Religion and Society Report* (March 1985) B1.

56. "Bishops Need Some Scissors," November 18, 1984.

57. "The Bishops' Moral Capital," *Sojourner* (January 1985) 5–6.

58. Channel 2, November 8, 1984.

59. Leonard Silk, "Pastoral Letter Gets Attention of Political, Economic Leaders," November 15, 1984.

60. James Shannon, "Bishops' Letter on Economy Generates Right Kind of Controversy," December 2, 1984.

61. "Bishops' Letter Expected to Spark Debate," *Chicago Sun-Times,* November 15, 1984.

62. "Morning Edition," National Public Radio, November 13, 1984.

63. "Catholic Bishops Criticized on Poor," *New York Times,* November 5, 1986.

64. Harvey Cox, "Vision for a Bright Economic Future," *New York Times,* November 18, 1984.

65. "Corporate Giving Fails to Offset Cuts by U.S.," *New York Times,* February 15, 1985.

66. Leon Wielseltier, "The Poor Perplex," *The New Republic* (January 7–14, 1985) 11–12.

67. "The Bishops on Poverty," *Norfolk Virginia-Pilot,* November 13, 1984.

68. "The Nation's Have-nots: How Long Will They Wait?" November 15, 1984.

69. Richard Dujardin, "Letter on Poor Puts Bishops in Conflict with Guardians of Affluence," *Providence Journal-Bulletin,* November 17, 1984.

70. "Let's Replace Prejudice with Facts," both in *USA Today,* November 15, 1984.

71. "Critics Missed Bishops' Stand on Poverty, Consultant Says," *San Diego Tribune,* December 15, 1984.

72. *San Diego Tribune,* September 28, 1985.

73. "Economic Policy: Creation, Covenant and Community," *America* (May 4, 1985) 365–369.

74. "Four Views of the Bishops' Pastoral," *This Word,* 111.

75. "Catholic Bishops' Economic Sermon," November 14, 1984.

76. Robert McAfee Brown, "Appreciating the Bishops' Letter, *The Christian Century* (February 6–13, 1985) 129.

77. Transcript, November 14, 1986, NCCB Library Archives.

78. Dujardin, "Letter on Poor Puts Bishops in Conflict."

79. "All Things Considered," National Public Radio, November 16, 1984.

80. Transcript, November 12, 1984, NCCB Library Archives.

81. Dale Francis, "Bishops Seek Range of Views," *St. Louis Review,* December 14, 1984.

82. "Pocketbook Theology," November 15, 1984.

83. "Critics Missed Bishops' Stand on Poverty," December 15, 1984.

84. Tom Bethell, "Prophecy at the Hilton," *National Review* (December 14, 1984).

85. "Pope John Paul's Challenge to the American Bishops," *America* (May 4, 1985) 372–373.

86. "Poverty Is Not as Bad Here as the Bishops Believe," *Los Angeles Times,* December 26, 1984.

87. June 6, 1986.

88. House Subcommittee on Economic Stabilization, March 19, 1985, in *America* (May 4, 1985) 359.

89. Ibid., 363.

90. *Orlando Sentinel,* November 18, 1986.

91. Leonard Silk, "Three Messages of Challenge," *New York Times,* December 28, 1984.

92. "The Bishops and Cliches," *Washington Post,* November 14, 1984.

93. "Perils of the Prophet Motive," in *Challenge and Response* (Washington: Ethics and Public Policy Center, 1985) 13.

94. "The Vanity of Bishops," *Washington Post,* November 15, 1984; "U.S. Bishops Sing Old Liberal Hymns," *Washington Post,* November 16, 1984.

95. Dinesh D'Souza, "Whose Pawns Are the Bishops?" *Policy Review* (Fall 1985) 55.

96. "The Work of Bishops," *Washington Post,* November 23, 1984.

97. "Porridge from the Bishops," *Washington Post,* November 30, 1986.

98. "Bishops and Poverty: Two Different Worlds," *Daily News,* November 13, 1984.

99. "Poverty Letter Author Thrives on Getting Involved," November 13, 1984.

100. "Am I My Brother's Keeper?" November 6, 1984.

101. "Whose Pawns are the Bishops?" June 4, 1986.

102. *New York City Tribune,* n.t., November 11, 1986.

103. "The Bishops' Pastoral Letter—The True Christmas Spirit," November 17, 1986.

104. "Economy: U.S. Bishops Speak on Behalf of the Poor," November 17, 1986.

105. *Oregonian,* December 4, 1984.

106. *Philadelphia Inquirer,* November 26, 1984.

107. *St. Louis Post-Dispatch,* December 10, 1984.

108. Ibid.

109. Carrafiello, "Bishops Lash U.S. Economy," 49.

110. *Miami Herald,* n.t., November 21, 1984.

111. "God as a Social Democrat," November 19, 1984:97–98.

112. Although Archbishop Weakland, confronted with constant references to the father of economics, did retort that Adam Smith had never met Imelda Marcos ("U.S. Catholic Bishops Urge Sweeping Economic Reform," *Chicago Tribune,* November 18, 1986).

113. Letter to the editor, *Richmond Times-Dispatch,* November 24, 1984.

114. "Conservatives to Be Heard, Bishop Says," *Cleveland Plain Dealer,* November 15, 1984.

115. "Bishops See Economy Pastoral as Help in Living the Gospel," USCC news release, May 21, 1985.

116. "Commentary and Response to First Draft," *Chicago Call to Action,* Coalition of Laity, Religious and Clergy, March 1, 1985.

117. "Toward a Second Draft of the Economic Pastoral," *Origins* 15 (June 27, 1985) 93–95.

118. *Origins* 15 (October 10, 1985) 257–296.

119. Jerry Filteau, "Bishops on Economy: Invitation, Not Confrontation," Catholic News Service, October 3, 1985.

120. Ibid.

121. Ibid.

122. John Buchanan, "Multi-pastoral?" *Chicago Catholic,* March 1, 1985.

123. Roy Larson, "Biblical Illiteracy Hampers Bishops' Economic Pastoral," *Chicago Sun-Times,* November 24, 1984.

124. "Reagan Hit for Bible Defense," *Baltimore Evening Sun,* February 6, 1985.

125. "Does the Bishops' Pastoral Letter Adequately Address the Economy?" *Hartford Advocate,* March 6, 1985.

126. "Insufficiently Radical," *New Oxford Review* (March 1985) 7.

127. "Reform Jews Hail Bishops Plea to Fight Poverty," *Jewish Week,* November 27, 1986.

128. Michael J. McManus, "Catholic Bishops' Pastoral on the Economy," *Ethics and Religion* (November 26, 1986) n.p.

129. Albert L. Schweitzer, "U.S. Bishops Working on New Pastoral," *Globe-Democrat,* December 31, 1983.

130. *New York Times,* December 15, 1983; *Washington Post,* December 17, 1983. John W. Houck and Oliver F. Williams, *Catholic Social Teaching and the U.S. Economy: Working Papers for a Bishops' Pastoral* (Washington: University Press of America, 1984) 15.

131. December 19, 1983.

132. "The Church and Capitalism," November 12, 1984.

133. November 15, 1984.

134. "Vision for a Bright Economic Future," *New York Times,* November 18, 1984.

135. James Shannon, "Bishops' Letter on Economy Generates Right Kind of Controversy," December 2, 1984.

136. John Corry, "Pressing Issues Politely Debated," *New York Times,* December 9, 1984.

137. November 11, 1984.

138. November 26, 1984.

139. November 16, 1984.

140. "Pope John Paul's Challenge," April 5, 1985:372.

141. "Kennedy, "America's Activist Bishops," 14

142. Ibid., 17.

143. Ibid.

144. Ibid., 30.

145. "Economic Justice for All," *Origins* 16 (June 5, 1986) 33–76.

146. "Bishops See Economy Pastoral as Help in Living the Gospel," press release, USCC, May 21, 1985.

147. "Catholic Bishops Say U.S. Must Do More for the Poor," November 14, 1986.

148. "Catholic Hierarchy's Growing Activist Role in Public Affairs Is Defended," *Providence Journal,* November 13, 1984.

149. "Bishops Coming to Grips with the Prophetic Role," *Los Angeles Times,* November 18, 1984.

150. *Center Focus,* n.t. (November 1984) n.p.

151. Dennis P. McCann, "The Pastoral Letter Process," DePaul University, Chicago, n.d., NCCB Library Archives.

152. *BusinessWeek* (November 1984) 110.

153. Warwick, "Four Views of the Bishops' Pastoral," 115.

154. "U.S. Bishops vs. Reagonomics: A Growing Furor," *U.S. News and World Report* (November 26, 1984) 59.

155. "Catholics Debate Morality of Capitalism, U.S. Style," *New York Times,* November 29, 1986.

156. "U.S. Bishops Sing Old Liberal Hymns," *Washington Post,* November 16, 1984.

157. "Bishops' Economic Views Due," *Cleveland Plain Dealer,* November 10, 1984.

158. "A Bombshell From the Bishops," *Cleveland Plain Dealer,* November 13, 1984.

159. "Excerpts from the Final Draft of the Bishops' Letter on the Economy," *New York Times,* November 14, 1986.

160. "Poverty Amid Plenty is a Scandal," *USA Today,* November 26, 1986.

161. "U.S. Bishops, in Face of Criticism, Back Draft of Letter on Economy," *New York Times,* June 15, 1985.

162. "The Invisible Poor," November 16, 1984.

163. "The Pastoral," *Catholic New York,* November 29, 1984.

164. Carrafiello, "Bishops Lash U.S. Economy," 50.

NOTES TO CHAPTER 5, PAGES 122–147

1. Jim Castelli, "Bishops' Committee Asks Staff Office for Women's Concerns," Catholic News Service, November 19, 1975.

2. Jerry Filteau, "Bishops' Conference Will Not Have Special Office for Women," Catholic News Service, May 7, 1976.

3. "Task Force Recommends Shaping Public Opinion on Women," Catholic News Service, June 14, 1976.

4. "Bishops' Committee Surveying Women's Role in Church," Catholic News Service, May 26, 1977.

5. Jim Castelli, "Survey Shows More Women in Decision-making Roles," Catholic News Service, November 16, 1977.

6. Jim Castelli, "Bishops Considering Support for ERA," Catholic News Service, March 8, 1978.

7. "Missouri Bishop Testifies in Support of ERA," Catholic News Service, January 21, 1980.

8. Maureen Aggeler, *Mind Your Metaphors: A Critique of Language in the Bishops' Pastoral Letters on the Role of Women* (New York: Paulist Press, 1991) 127.

9. Ibid., 9–10.

10. "Dialogue on Women in the Church, Interim Report," *Origins* 11 (June 25, 1981) 81.

11. Ibid., 91.

12. Jerry Filteau, "Bishops' Committee Urges More Roles for Women, 'Perhaps Diaconate,'" Catholic News Service, April 28, 1982.

13. "The Future of Women in the Church," *Origins* 12 (May 20, 1982) 1–9.

14. "Women's Roles in Church Elicit Pastoral Commission, Conferences," Catholic News Service, September 26, 1983.

15. Ibid.

16. "Bishop Imesch to Chair Committee on Women's Pastoral," Catholic News Service, May 7, 1984.

17. "Bishops Agree to Write Pastoral on Women," Catholic News Service, November 17, 1983.

18. "Bishop Imesch to Chair Committee on Women's Pastoral," Catholic News Service, May 7, 1984.

19. The bishops members were Bishops Matthew H. Clark of Rochester, N.Y.; Thomas J. Grady of Orlando, Fla.; Bishop Joseph L. Imesch of Joliet, Ill.; Auxiliary Bishop William J. Levada of Portland, Oreg.; Bishop John J. McRaith of Owensboro, Ky.; and Auxiliary Bishop Amedee W. Proulx of Portland, Maine. The women were Mary Brabeck and Pheme Perkins of Boston College; Toinette Eugene of Colgate Rochester Divinity School; Ronda Chervin of St. John's Seminary (Calif.); Sister Sara Butler of the Missionary Sisters of the Most Blessed Trinity; Sister Mariella Frye, staff consultant; and Susan Muto of Duquesne University. The first three women members resigned after the consulting process ("Members, Consultants to Women's Committee Listed," Catholic News Service, April 2, 1990).

20. "Women's Statement Affirms Support for Church Teachings," Catholic News Service, December 19, 1984.

21. "Leader of Nuns Ask Bishops to Delay Women's Pastoral," Catholic News Service, March 5, 1985.

22. "LCWR Board Urges Change of Course," *Origins* 14 (March 21, 1985) 656.

23. Ibid., 655.

24. Jerry Filteau, "Write Letters on Sexism and Men, Bishops Committee Told," Catholic News Service, March 6, 1985.

25. Jerry Filteau, "Sexism, Patriarchy Issues Given New Prominence in Church," Catholic News Service, March 11, 1985.

26. Jeanine Jacob, "'Writing Pastoral on Women Tough Task for Bishops,' CPA Told," Catholic News Service, May 21, 1985.

27. "Women Treated as Second Class Citizens, Hearings Told," Catholic News Service, June 27, 1985.

28. "Women in the Church Want Recognition, Orlando Hearings Told," Catholic News Service, July 9, 1985.

29. Mary Claire Eart, "Bishops' Committee Hears Women's Concerns, Plans Pastoral Response," Catholic News Service, August 27, 1985.

30. "Columbus Hearings Urge Pastoral to Focus on Sexism, Women's Talents," Catholic News Service, September 13, 1985.

31. Mark Zimmerman, "Proposed Pastoral on Women May Not Be Written, Adviser Says," Catholic News Service, August 6, 1985.

32. "Committee Writing Women's Pastoral to Shift Focus," Catholic News Service, September 20, 1985.

33. "Understand Women's Role in Creation, Says Bishop Welsh," Catholic News Service, October 8, 1985.

34. Jerry Filteau, "'Pastoral Response' to Catholic Women Now Being Written," Catholic News Service, March 27, 1986.

35. Julie Asher, "Work on Women's Pastoral Is Proceeding, Bishop Says," Catholic News Service, March 27, 1986.

36. "Women's Pastoral Doing Well," Catholic News Service, April 28, 1986.

37. Jerry Filteau, "Reviews of Women's Pastoral 'Positive' to Document as Whole," Catholic News Service, June 16, 1987.

38. "Archbishop Mahony Urges Placing Women in Policy-Making Jobs," Catholic News Service, August 14, 1987.

39. "Persistent Questions, Faithful Witness," *Origins* 12 (October 14, 1982) 273–286.

40. Jerry Filteau, "Women's Pastoral Draft: A Call to Male Responsibility," Catholic News Service, April 8, 1988.

41. *Origins* 17 (April 21, 1988) 758–788.

42. Ibid., 761.

43. Ibid., 763.

44. Ibid., 765–766.

45. Ibid., 772–775.

46. Ibid., 781.

47. Ibid.

48. "Address to the NCCB," Catholic News Service, June 27, 1988.

49. "Bishops Ask for Expansion of Pastoral on Women," Catholic News Service, June 24, 1988.

50. Daniel Medinger, "Baltimore Auxiliary Calls for Study of Women's Ordination," Catholic News Service, June 20, 1988.

51. "Bishops Ask for Expansion of Pastoral on Women," Catholic News Service, June 24, 1988.

52. Pat Morrison, "Man Behind Women's Pastoral Sees Realistic, Forceful Document," Catholic News Service, April 18, 1988.

53. "Women's Pastoral Biased Toward Feminists, Groups Write," Catholic News Service, June 24, 1988.

54. Rick Wade, "Notion That Church Oppresses Women Called 'Ridiculous,'" Catholic News Service, September 26, 1988.

55. Cindy Wooden, "Pastoral Draft on Women Gets Mixed Reaction," Catholic News Service, April 18, 1988.

56. "Consultations on Women's Pastoral Draft Begin Amid Praise, Criticism," Catholic News Service, September 12, 1988.

57. "Bishops' Pastoral on Women Disappoints LCWR Panel," Catholic News Service, September 6, 1988.

58. Morrison, "Man Behind Women's Pastoral Sees Realistic, Forceful Document," April 18, 1988.

59. Teresa Coyle, "Bishops Imesch Rejects Feminist Label in Bishops' Pastoral," Catholic News Service, October 6, 1988.

60. Sister Mary Ann Walsh, "Speakers Call for Healing Polarization in Church," Catholic News Service, September 21, 1988.

61. Imesch, "Address to the NCCB," Catholic News Service, June 27, 1988.

62. Catherine Haven, "Bishop Says Men Must Be Concerned About What Pastoral on Women Says," Catholic News Service, September 26, 1988.

63. Gordon Watson, "Diocesan Task Force Asks for More Women in Church Decision-Making," Catholic News Service, December 29, 1988.

64. Ibid.

65. Imesch, "Address to the NCCB," Catholic News Service, June 27, 1988.

66. "Pope Praises U.S. Draft Pastoral on Women," Catholic News Service, September 2, 1988.

67. Jerry Filteau, "Pope's Letter Seen Defending Women," Catholic News Service, October 3, 1988.

68. "Committee Anticipates Different Tone in Women's Pastoral Second Draft," Catholic News Service, January 24, 1989.

69. Cindy Wooden, "Solidarity Among Men, Women to Be Urged in New Pastoral Draft," Catholic News Service, January 26, 1989.

70. Cindy Wooden, "Pastoral Needs of Women Will Be Church's Priority, Bishop Says," Catholic News Service, January 25, 1989.

71. Cindy Wooden, "Women Sharing Pain, Stories Is Good for Church, Bishop Says," Catholic News Service, January 27, 1989.

72. Cindy Wooden, "Diocesan Women's Groups Must Include More Minorities," Catholic News Service, January 26, 1989.

73. Cindy Wooden, "Bishops' Draft Letter on Women to Undergo 'Radical Change,'" Catholic News Service, January 30, 1989.

74. Cindy Wooden, "Alleviating Women's Pain Part of Pastoral Process, Bishop Says," Catholic News Service, February 10, 1989.

75. "Nationwide Vigils Held to Protest Sexism in Church," Catholic News Service, February 15, 1989.

76. Laurie Hansen, "Women's Ordination Issue Plagues Writers of Proposed Pastoral," Catholic News Service, April 2, 1990.

77. Laurie Hansen, "Feminists, Altar Society Members Seen Expressing Same Concerns," Catholic News Service, November 15, 1990.

78. Richard Higgins, "Bishops Decry 'Sexism,' Defend Male Priesthood," *Boston Globe,* April 3, 1990.

79. *Origins* 19 (April 5, 1990) 718–740.

80. Hansen, "Women's Ordination Issue Plagues Writers of Proposed Pastoral."

81. *Origins* 19 (April 5, 1990) 721.

82. Ibid., 722.

83. Ibid., 728.

84. Ibid., 730.

85. Ibid., 730.

86. Ibid., 734.

87. Ibid., 721–723.

88. Ibid., 721.

89. Laurie Hansen, "Second Draft of Women's Pastoral Prompts Enthusiasm, Dismay," Catholic News Service, April 6, 1990.

90. "Women's Ordination Group Urges Bishops to Drop Women's Pastoral," Catholic News Service, September 11, 1990.

91. "Writer of Proposed Women's Pastoral Calls it History-Making," Catholic News Service, April 16, 1990.

92. Laurie Hansen, "Center of Concern Urges Bishops to Scrap Letter on Women," Catholic News Service, July 27, 1990.

93. "LCWR Urges Bishops to Scrap Proposed Pastoral on Women," Catholic News Service, August 13, 1990.

94. "Pastoral on Women 'Not Inspired,'" *Milwaukee Catholic Herald,* May 10, 1990.

95. Ibid.

96. Laurie Hansen, "Some Bishops Say Pastoral on Women Should be Scrapped for Now," Catholic News Service, August 24, 1990.

97. Mark Pattison, "Pastoral 'Alive and Well' but 'On Life Support,'" Catholic News Service, December 4, 1990.

98. "Bishop Grady Warns Against Abandoning Pastoral on Women," Catholic News Service, September 20, 1990.

99. "Women's Ordination Group Urges Bishops to Drop Women's Pastoral," Catholic News Service, September 11, 1990.

100. Hansen, "Some Bishops Say Pastoral on Women Should be Scrapped for Now."

101. Jerry Filteau, "Women's Pastoral Vote Delayed; Vatican Suggests More Consultation," Catholic News Service, September 13, 1990.

102. Laurie Hansen, "Consulting Seen Apt to Show Women's Concerns Not Confined to U.S.," Catholic News Service, September 14, 1990.

103. Ines Pinto Alicea, "Demonstrators Praise Bishops for Postponing Vote on Pastoral," Catholic News Service, November 12, 1990.

104. Cindy Wooden, "Vatican Arranges Meeting on U.S. Pastoral on Women," Catholic News Service, May 7, 1991.

105. John Thavis, "Women's Pastoral Consultation Highlights U.S. Church Leadership," Catholic News Service, May 14, 1991.

106. Ibid.

107. Ibid.

108. Cindy Wooden, "NCCB Head: Other Nations Must Deal with Women's Issues Eventually," Catholic News Service, May 29, 1991.

109. Thomas J. Reese, *A Flock of Shepherds: The National Conference of Catholic Bishops* (Kansas City: Sheed and Ward, 1992) 215.

110. Cindy Wooden, "U.S. Bishops Urged to Be Careful Drafting Women's Pastoral," Catholic News Service, May 30, 1991.

111. Ibid.

112. Ibid.

113. Cindy Wooden, "Vatican Women's Meetings Won't Betray Tradition, Official Says," Catholic News Service, May 28, 1991.

114. James L. Franklin, "Church Letter on Women to be Pursued," June 3, 1991.

115. Cindy Wooden, "U.S. Bishops Urged to Be Careful Drafting Women's Pastoral."

116. "Bishop Imesch 'Frustrated' by Vatican Consult on Women's Letter," Catholic News Service, June 21, 1991.

117. Laurie Hansen, "Third Draft of Women's Pastoral Influenced by Vatican Meeting," Catholic News Service, April 9, 1992.

118. Office of Media Relations, "Bishops to Consider Third Draft of Pastoral Letter on Women's Concerns," United States Catholic Conference.

119. The drafting committee was aware that the Church was emphatic about the ban on ordination for women and had also been made aware of the depth of feeling the issue raised with American Catholic women. Thus a statement of Church teaching was incorporated

without elaboration (L. Hansen, "Treating Topic of Women's Ordination Confounds U.S. Bishops," Catholic News Service, April 9, 1992).

120. Even the bishops' National Advisory Council called the latest draft "defensive and authoritarian rather than pastoral" and wanted it replaced with a brief statement calling for more study (Jerry Filteau, "Bishops' Advisory Council Opposes Women's Pastoral," Catholic News Service, September 18, 1992).

121. "NCCW Says Pastoral Draft on Women Opens Door to More Dialogue," Catholic News Service, April 21, 1992.

122. "Center of Concern Urges Bishops to Put Aside Women's Pastoral," Catholic News Service, June 25, 1992.

123. "Bishops Urged to Hold New Hearings on Women's Concerns in June," Catholic News Service, May 27, 1992.

124. Ibid.

125. Jerry Filteau, "Bishops Take 'Straw Vote' to Forge Ahead with Women's Pastoral," Catholic News Service, June 19, 1992.

126. Ibid.

127. Jerry Filteau, "Fourth Draft of Pastoral on Women Sent to Bishops' Committee," Catholic News Service, August 19, 1992.

128. "One in Christ Jesus," *Origins* 22 (September 10, 1992) 221–240.

129. Peter Steinfels, "Catholic Panel Rewrites Letter on Female Role," *New York Times,* August 30, 1992.

130. "One in Christ Jesus," *Origins* 22 (September 10, 1992) 232–235.

131. Jerry Filteau, "New Draft of Pastoral Defends Male-Only Priesthood," Catholic News Service, August 31, 1992.

132. Jerry Filteau, "New Draft Pastoral Draws Strong but Varied Reaction from Bishop," Catholic News Service, September 15, 1992.

133. "Bishop Lucker Wants Bishops to Drop Women's Pastoral," Catholic News Service, October 13, 1992.

134. "Richmond Bishop Says 'No' to Pastoral on Women," Catholic News Service, October 26, 1992.

135. Jerry Filteau, "Baltimore Auxiliary Bishop Says Justice Demands Ordaining Women," Catholic News Service, September 18, 1992.

136. P. Francis Murphy, "Let's Start Over," *Commonweal* (September 25, 1992) 11–15.

137. "Archbishop Weakland Sees Vatican Hurting Bishops' Conference," Catholic News Service, November 2, 1992.

138. Jerry Filteau, "Like Bishops, Catholic Editors Divided on Pastoral," Catholic News Service, October 15, 1992.

139. "Just Say No to the Women's Pastoral," *St. Anthony's Messenger* (November 1992) 56.

140. Jerry Filteau, "Early Discussion on Women's Pastoral Indicates Bishops' Concerns," Catholic News Service, November 16, 1992.

141. Laurie Hansen, "Women's Pastoral Unlikely to be Approved, Say Committee Members," Catholic News Service, November 16, 1992.

142. Jerry Filteau, "Cardinal Moves Women's Pastoral Be Remanded to Executive Committee," Catholic News Service, November 17, 1992.

143. Filteau, "Early Discussion on Women's Pastoral Indicates Bishops' Concerns."

144. "Document on Women's Concerns Debated," *Origins* 22 (December 3, 1992) 422.

145. Ibid., 418.

146. Jerry Filteau, "Cardinal Bernardin Led Solution to Women's Pastoral Stalemate," Catholic News Service (19 November 1992) .

147. "Document on Women's Concerns," *Origins* 22 (December 3, 1992) 420.

148. Jerry Filteau, "Pastoral on Women Fails to Get Necessary Two-Thirds Vote," Catholic News Service, November 18, 1992.

149. "One in Christ Jesus," *Origins* 22 (December 31, 1992) 489–508.

150. Nancy Frazier O'Brien, "Bishops Called Uncomfortable with Ban on Discussing Women Priests," Catholic News Service, November 18, 1992.

151. Linda M. Harrington, "Catholic Bishops Reject Letter on Role of Women," *Chicago Tribune* (November 23, 1992) 1.

152. "Document on Women's Concerns," *Origins* 22 (December 3, 1992) 420.

153. John Deedy, *American Catholicism: And Now Where?* (New York: Plenum Press, 1987) 70.

NOTES TO CHAPTER 6, PAGES 148–159

1. Patrick W. Carey, *Pastoral Letters of the United States Bishops,* vol. 6 (Washington: United States Catholic Conference, 1998) 5.

2. As of December 2000, the NCCB's roster of publications contained Pastoral Responses (*Domestic Violence Against Women,* September 1992); Pastoral Message to Families (September 1993); Pastoral Reflection (*Strengthening the Bonds of Peace,* September 1994); Pastoral Plan (*Ministry with Young Adults,* November 1996); and other less common appellations. The proliferation of both the number and status of documents reflected the bureaucratic complexity of the National Conference of Catholic Bishops and the output of its research/lobbying arm, the United States Catholic Conference.

3. Carey, *Pastoral Letters,* 4.

4. Patricia Zapor, "Bishops Overwhelmingly Approve Pastoral Message on Role of Women," Catholic News Service, November 16, 1994.

5. *Living the Gospel of Life: A Challenge to American Life* (Washington: United States Catholic Conference, 1998) 2–3.

6. *Faithful Citizenship: Civic Responsibility for a New Millennium: A Statement on Political Responsibility* (Washington, D.C.: United States Catholic Conference, 1999) 4.

7. Avery Dulles, "What Is the Role of a Bishops' Conference?" *Origins* 17 (April 28, 1988) 795.

8. Rembert Weakland, "Catholics as Social Insiders," *Origins* 22 (May 28, 1992) 38.

9. "What Is the Role of a Bishops' Conference?" 794.

10. James W. Malone, "Intersection of Public Opinion and Public Policy," *Origins* 14 (November 29, 1984) 386.

11. Ibid., 388.

12. "Catholics as Social Insiders," 38.

13. John Courtney Murray, *We Hold These Truths: Catholic Reflections on the American Proposition* (Kansas City, Mo.: Sheed and Ward, 1988) 80.

14. Ibid., 120.

15. Joseph Bernardin, "Religion and Politics: The Future Agenda," *Origins* 14 (November 8, 1984) 326.

16. *Living the Gospel of Life,* 1998, 9.

17. John Paul II, "Teachers of Moral Truth," *Origins* 28 (October 1, 1998) 282–284.

18. *Living the Gospel of Life,* 11.

Works Cited

Abbot, Walter M., S.J., ed. Pastoral Constitution on the Church in the Modern World. *The Documents of Vatican II.* New York: Crossroad, 1996.

Abell, Aaron I., ed. *American Catholic Thought on Social Questions.* New York: Bobbs-Merrill, 1968.

Adlesic, Catherine Inez. "The Effort to Implement the Pastoral Letter on War and Peace." In *Peace in a Nuclear Age: The Bishops' Pastoral Letter in Perspective,* ed. Charles J. Reid, Jr. Washington, D.C.: Catholic University of America Press, 1986: 387–398.

Aggeler, Maureen, R.S.C.J. *Mind Your Metaphors: A Critique of Language in the Bishops' Pastoral Letters on the Role of Women.* New York: Paulist Press, 1991.

Agonito, Joseph. *The Building of an American Catholic Church: The Episcopacy of John Carroll.* New York: Garland, 1988.

Au, William A. *The Cross, The Flag, and The Bomb: American Catholics Debate War and Peace, 1960–1983.* Westport, Conn.: Greenwood, 1985.

_____. "Papal and Episcopal Teaching on War and Peace: The Historical Background to The Challenge of Peace: God's Promise and Our Response." In *Peace in a Nuclear Age: The Bishops' Pastoral Letter in Perspective,* ed. Charles J. Reid, Jr. Washington, D.C.: Catholic University of American Press, 1986: 98–119.

Bellah, Robert N. "Economics and the Theology of Work." *New Oxford Review* (November 1984): 13–18.

Benestad, J. Brian. *The Pursuit of a Just Social Order: Policy Statements of the U.S. Catholic Bishops, 1966–1980.* Washington, D.C.: Ethics and Public Policy Center, 1982.

Bennett, John C. "The Bishops' Pastoral: A Response." *Christianity and Crisis* (May 30, 1983): 203.

Bernardin, Cardinal Joseph. "Religion and Politics: The Future Agenda." *Origins* 14 (November 8, 1984): 321–328.

Berryman, Phillip. *Our Unfinished Business: The U.S. Catholic Bishops' Letters on Peace and the Economy.* New York: Pantheon, 1989.

Billington, Ray Allen. *The Protestant Crusade, 1800–1860: A Study in the Origins of American Nativism*. Chicago: Quadrangle Books, 1938, rpt. 1964.

"Blast from the Bishops, A." *Time* (November 8, 1982): 16–18.

Block, Walter. *U.S. Bishops and Their Critics: Economic and Ethical Perspectives*. Vancouver: Fraser Institute, 1986.

Bokenkotter, Thomas. *A Concise History of the Catholic Church*. Garden City, N.Y.: Image Books, 1979.

Boyea, Earl. "Archbishop Edward Mooney and the Rev. Charles Coughlin's Anti-Semitism, 1938–40." In *Building the Church in America: Studies in Honor of Monsignor Robert F. Trisco on the Occasion of His Seventieth Birthday*, ed. Joseph C. Linck and Raymond J. Kupke. Washington, D.C. : Catholic University of America Press, 1999: 196–211.

Brand, Jeffrey D. "Negotiating Peace Activism in the Catholic Church: Responding to Anti-Nuclear Protest." Paper presented at the National Communication Association Conference, Chicago, November, 1997.

Brophy, Don, and Edythe Westenhaver. *The Story of Catholics in America*. New York: Paulist Press, 1978.

Brown, Robert McAfee. "Appreciating the Bishops' Letter." *The Christian Century* (February 6–13, 1985): 129–130.

Brundage, James A. "The Limits of the War-Making Power: The Contributions of the Medieval Canonists." In *Peace in a Nuclear Age: The Bishops' Pastoral Letter in Perspective*, ed. Charles J. Reid, Jr. Washington, D.C.: Catholic University of America Press, 1986: 69–85.

Buetow, Harold A. "The United States Catholic School Phenomenon." In *Perspectives on the American Catholic Church, 1789–1989*, ed. S. J. Vicchio and V. Geiger. Westminster, Md.: Christian Classics, 1989: 197–222.

Burns, Gene. *The Frontiers of Catholicism: The Politics of Ideology in a Liberal World*. Berkeley: University of California, 1992.

Byrnes, Timothy A. *Catholic Bishops in American Politics*. Princeton: Princeton University Press, 1991.

"Cardinal Cooke on Nuclear Arms." *Ecumenist: Journal for Promoting Christian Unity* (March/April 1982): 39–42.

Carey, Patrick M. "Catholic Religious Thought in the U.S.A." In *Perspectives on the American Catholic Church, 1789–1989*, ed. S. J. Vicchio and V. Geiger. Westminster, Md.: Christian Classics, 1989: 143–166.

Carey, Patrick W. *Pastoral Letters of the United States Bishops*, vol. 6. Washington, D.C.: United States Catholic Conference, 1998.

Carrafiello, Vincent. "Bishops Lash U.S. Economy." *The Month* (February 1985): 45–50.

Cassidy, Kevin J. "Who Is Responsible? Bringing the Light to G.E.?" *Commonweal* (May 17, 1985): 295–297.

Castelli, Jim. *The Bishops and the Bomb*. Garden City, N.Y.: Image Books, 1983.

Cheney, George. *Rhetoric in an Organizational Society: Managing Multiple Identities*. Columbia: University of South Carolina, 1991.

————. "Speaking of Who 'We' Are: The Development of the U.S. Catholic Bishops' Pastoral Letter 'The Challenge of Peace' as a Case Study in Identity, Organization, and Rhetoric." Ph.D. diss., Purdue University, 1985.

"Church and Capitalism: Report by Catholic Bishops on U.S. Economy Will Cause a Furor." *BusinessWeek* (November 12, 1984): 104–112.

Clark, Thomas D. "An Exploration of Generic Aspects of Contemporary Christian Sermons." *Quarterly Journal of Speech* 63 (1977): 384–394.

Cogley, John. *Catholic America*. Garden City, N.Y.: Doubleday, 1973.

Coleman, J., and Gregory Baum, eds. *Rerum Novarum: One Hundred Years of Catholic Social Teaching*. Philadelphia: Trinity Press International, 1991.

Cross, Robert D. *The Emergence of Liberal Catholicism in America*. Cambridge: Harvard University Press, 1958.

Crotty, James R., and James R. Stormes, S.J. "The Bishops on the U.S. Economy." *Challenge: The Magazine of Economic Affairs* (March/April 1985): 36–41.

Curran, Charles E. *Directions in Catholic Social Ethics*. Notre Dame: University of Notre Dame Press, 1985.

————. *Tensions in Moral Theology*. Notre Dame: University of Notre Dame Press, 1988.

Curran, Robert Emmett. "Rome, the American Church and Slavery." In *Building the Church in America: Studies in Honor of Monsignor Robert F. Trisco on the Occasion of His Seventieth Birthday*, ed. Joseph C. Linck and Raymond J. Kupke. Washington, D.C.: Catholic University of America Press, 1999: 30–49.

Curry, Dean C., ed. *Evangelicals and the Bishops' Pastoral Letter*. Grand Rapids, Mich.: Wm. B. Eerdmans, 1984.

Deedy, John. *American Catholicism: And Now Where?* New York: Plenum Press, 1987.

DePauw, Gommar A. *The Challenge of Peace Through Strength: God's Plan and Our Defense of It: The Stripping of a Bishops' Pastoral Letter*. Westbury, N.Y.: CTM, 1989.

DeSantis, Vincent P. "Catholicism and Presidential Elections, 1865–1900." *Mid-America* 42 (1960): 67–79.

Dohen, Dorothy. *Nationalism and American Catholicism*. New York: Sheed and Ward, 1967.

Dolan, Jay. *Catholic Revivalism: The American Experience, 1830–1900*. Notre Dame: University of Notre Dame Press, 1978.

_____. "New Horizons in American Studies." In *An American Church: Essays on the Americanization of the Catholic Church,* ed. David J. Alvarez. Moraga, Calif.: St. Mary's College, 1979: 63–87.

_____. *The American Catholic Experience: A History from Colonial Times to the Present.* Garden City, N.Y.: Doubleday, 1985.

Dougherty, James E. *The Bishops and Nuclear Weapons: The Catholic Pastoral Letter on War and Peace.* Hamden, Conn.: Archon Books, 1984.

Douglass, R. Bruce, ed. *The Deeper Meaning of Economic Life: Critical Essays on the U.S. Catholic Bishops' Pastoral Letter on the Economy.* Washington, D.C.: Georgetown University, 1986.

D'Souza, Dinesh. "Whose Pawns Are the Bishops?" *Policy Review* (Fall 1985) 50–56.

Duff, Edward, S.J. "The Church and American Public Life." In *Contemporary Catholicism in the United States,* ed. P. Gleason. Notre Dame: University of Notre Dame Press, 1969: 97–125.

Dulles, Avery, S.J., "What Is the Role of a Bishops' Conference?" *Origins* 17 (April 28, 1988: 789–796.

Ellis, John Tracy. *American Catholicism.* 2nd ed. Chicago: University of Chicago Press, 1969.

Finn, James, ed. *Private Virtue and Public Policy: Catholic Thought and National Life.* New Brunswick: Transaction Books, 1990.

_____. "American Catholics and Social Movements." In *Contemporary Catholicism in the United States,* ed. P. Gleason. Notre Dame: University of Notre Dame Press, 1969: 127–146.

Fogarty, Gerald P. *The Vatican and the American Hierarchy from 1870–1965.* Wilmington, Del.: Michael Glazier, 1985.

Fontenot, Julie. "A Content Analysis on NCCB's *One in Christ Jesus:* A Communication Perspective." Thesis, Texas at El Paso, 1994.

Gannon, Thomas, S.J., ed. *The Catholic Challenge to the American Economy: Reflections on the U.S. Bishops' Pastoral Letter on Catholic Social Teaching and the U.S. Economy.* New York: Macmillan, 1987.

Geyer, Alan. "Two and Three-Fourths Cheers for the Bishops' Pastoral: A Peculiar Protestant Perspective." In *Peace in a Nuclear Age: The Bishops' Pastoral Letter in Perspective,* ed. Charles J. Reid, Jr. Washington, D.C.: Catholic University of America Press, 1986: 291–304.

Gillis, Chester. *Roman Catholicism in America.* New York: Columbia University Press, 1999.

Glazier, Michael, and Monika K. Hellwig. *Modern Catholic Encyclopedia.* Collegeville, Minn.: The Liturgical Press, 1994.

Gleason, Philip. *Keeping the Faith: American Catholicism Past and Present.* Notre Dame: University of Notre Dame Press, 1987.

_____, ed. *Documentary Reports on Early American Catholicism.* New York: Arno Press, 1978.

_____, ed. *Contemporary Catholicism in the United States.* Notre Dame: University of Notre Dame Press, 1969.

_____. "The Crisis of Americanization." In *Contemporary Catholicism in the United States,* ed. P. Gleason. Notre Dame: University of Notre Dame Press, 1969: 3–31.

"God and the Bomb: Catholic Bishops Debate Nuclear Morality." *Time* (November 29, 1982): 68–78.

Goldzwig, Steven, and George Cheney. "The U.S. Catholic Bishops on Nuclear Arms: Corporate Advocacy, Role Redefinition, and Rhetorical Adaptation." *Central States Speech Journal* 35 (Spring 1984): 8–23.

Grasso, K. L., G. U. Bradley, and R. P. Hunt, eds. *Catholicism, Liberalism and Communitarianism: Catholic Intellectual Traditions and Moral Foundations of Democracy.* Lanham, Md.: Rowman and Littlefield, 1995.

Greeley, Andrew M. *The Catholic Experience: An Interpretation of the History of American Catholicism.* Garden City, N.Y.: Doubleday and Company, 1967.

Guilday, Peter. *A History of the Councils of Baltimore, 1791–1884.* New York: Macmillan Co., 1932; New York: Arno Press, 1969.

_____. *The National Pastorals of the American Hierarchy (1792–1919).* Washington, D.C.: National Catholic Welfare Council, 1923.

Hallett, Brien J. "Pope John Paul's Challenge to the American Bishops." *America* (May 4, 1985): 371–374.

Hart, Roderick P. "The Rhetoric of the True Believer." *Communication Monographs* (November 1971): 249–261.

Hehir, J. Bryan. "There's No Deterring the Catholic Bishops." *Ethics and International Affairs* 3 (1989): 277.

Hennesey, James, S.J. *American Catholics: A History of the Roman Catholic Community in the United States.* New York: Oxford University Press, 1981.

_____. "The Baltimore Council of 1866: An American Syllabus." *Records of the American Catholic Historical Society* 76 (1965): 157–173.

Hitchcock, Helen Hull. "The Pastoral That Wasn't." *Crisis* (January 1, 1993): 37–41.

Hobgood, Mary E. *Catholic Social Teaching and Economic Theory: Paradigms in Conflict.* Philadelphia: Temple University Press, 1991.

Hogan, J. Michael. "The Bishops as 'Revolutionaries': An Ideological Debate?" *Quarterly Journal of Speech* 76 (1990): 312–314.

_____. "Managing Dissent in the Catholic Church: A Reinterpretation of the Pastoral Letter on War and Peace." *Quarterly Journal of Speech* 75 (1989): 400–415.

Hollenbach, David. "*The Challenge of Peace* in the Context of Recent Church Teachings." In *Catholics and Nuclear War: A Commentary on "The Challenge of Peace," The U.S. Catholic Bishops' Pastoral Letter on War and Peace*, ed. Philip J. Murnion. New York: Crossroad, 1983: 3–15.

Houck, John W., and Oliver F. Williams, eds. *Catholic Social Teaching and the U.S. Economy: Working Papers for the Bishops' Pastoral.* Washington, D.C.: University Press of America, 1984.

Huber, Raphael J. *Our Bishops Speak (1919–1951).* Milwaukee: Bruce Publishing, 1952.

Jablonski, Carol J. "*Aggiornamento* and the American Catholic Bishops: A Rhetoric of Institutional Continuity and Change." *Quarterly Journal of Speech* 75 (1989): 416–432.

_____. "Promoting Radical Change in the Roman Catholic Church: Rhetorical Requirements, Problems and Strategies of the American Bishops." *Central States Speech Journal* 31 (1980): 282–289.

Jubilee Group. *The Bishops and the Economy: A Symposium of Responses to the American Roman Catholic Bishops' Pastoral Letter on Catholic Social Teaching and the U.S. Economy.* London: Jubilee Group, 1985.

Keightley, Georgia Masters. "Women's Issues are Laity Issues." *America* (August 6–13, 1988): 77–83.

Kennedy, Eugene. *Re-Imagining American Catholicism: The American Bishops and Their Pastoral Letters.* New York: Random House, 1985.

_____. "America's Activist Bishops." *New York Times Magazine* (August 12, 1984): 14–30.

Kennedy, Maida Larew. "A Rhetorical Analysis of the Catholic Bishops' Pastoral Letter on War and Peace: An Examination of the Metaphor of Nuclear Evil." M.A. thesis, Washington State University, 1984.

Krauthammer, Charles. "Perils of the Prophet Motive." In *Challenge and Response*, ed R. Royal. Washington, D.C.: Ethics and Public Policy Center, 1985: 56–58.

LaFalce, John J. "Catholic Social Teaching and Economic Justice." *America* (May 4, 985): 356–358.

Lanagan, John. "The American Context of The U.S. Bishops' Pastoral Letter on the Economy." In *The Deeper Meaning of Economic Life: Critical Essays on the U.S. Catholic Bishops' Pastoral Letter on the Economy,* ed. Douglass, R. Bruce. Washington, D.C.: Georgetown University Press, 1986: 1–19.

Lawler, Philip F. *How Bishops Decide: An American Catholic Case Study.* Washington, D.C.: Ethics and Public Policy Center, 1986.

_____. *The Ultimate Weapon*. Chicago: Regnery Gateway, 1984.

_____, ed. *Justice and War in the Nuclear Age*. Washington, D.C.: University Press of America, 1983.

Leckie, Robert. *American and Catholic*. Garden City, N.Y.: Doubleday, 1970.

Linkh, Richard M. *American Catholicism and European Immigrants, 1900–1924*. New York: Center for Migration Studies, 1975.

Linnan, John E., C.S.V. "Perspectives on the Church in *The Challenge of Peace*." In *Biblical and Theological Reflections on "The Challenge of Peace,"* ed. J. T. Pawlikowski and D. Senior. Wilmington, Del.: Michael Glazier, 1984:

Liptak, Dolores, R.S.M. "Catholic Immigrant Patterns, 1789–1989." In *Perspectives on the American Catholic Church, 1789–1989*, ed. S. J. Vicchio and V. Geiger. Westminster, Md.: Christian Classics, 1989: 63–84.

_____. *Immigrants and Their Church*. New York: Macmillan, 1989.

Lutz, Charles P., ed. *God, Goods and the Common Good: Eleven Perspectives on Economic Justice in Dialog with the Roman Catholic Bishops' Pastoral Letter*. Minneapolis: Augsburg, 1987.

MacInnis, John E. "Catechesis in the United States: Church Texts in the Catholic Context, The National Documents of the U.S. Bishops in Light of Catechetical Developments in the U.S.A. and Official Texts of the Holy See, 1792–1979." Ph.D. diss., Pontificia Universita Gregoriana, 1984.

Mahony, Roger. "The Catholic Conscience and Nuclear War." *Commonweal* (March 12, 1982): 137–143.

Malone, Bishop James W. "Intersection of Public Opinion and Public Policy." *Origins* 14 (November 29, 1984): 384–390.

Massa, Mark S. *Catholics and American Culture: Fulton Sheen, Dorothy Day and the Notre Dame Football Team*. New York: Crossroad, 1999.

May, William W., ed. *Vatican Authority and American Catholic Dissent*. New York: Crossroad, 1987.

Maynard, Theodore. *The Story of American Catholicism*. 2 vols. Garden City, N.Y.: Image Books, 1960.

McAvoy, Thomas T., C.S.C. *A History of the Catholic Church in the United States*. Notre Dame: University of Notre Dame Press, 1969.

_____. *The Great Crisis in American Catholic History, 1895–1900*. Chicago: Henry Regnery, 1957.

_____. "The Formation of the Catholic Minority in the United States, 1820–1860." *The Review of Politics* 10 (1948): 13–34.

McCann, Dennis P. "Communicating Catholic Social Teaching: The Experience of the Church in the United States of America." In *Rerum Novarum: A Hundred*

Years of Catholic Social Teaching, ed. J. Coleman and G. Baum. Philadelphia: Trinity Press International, 1991.

McCarthy, Timothy G. *The Catholic Tradition: Before and After Vatican II, 1878–1993.* Chicago: Loyola University Press, 1994.

McCormick, Richard A. "Nuclear Deterrence and the Problem of Intention: A Review of the Positions." In *Catholics and Nuclear War: A Commentary on "The Challenge of Peace,"* ed. P. Murnion. New York: Crossroad, 1983: 168–182.

_____. "The Chill Factor: Recent Roman Interventions." *America* (June 30, 1984): 475–481.

McKeown, Elizabeth. "The Seamless Garment: The Bishops' Letter in the Light of the American Catholic Pastoral Tradition." In *The Deeper Meaning of Economic Life: Critical Essays on the U.S. Catholic Bishops' Pastoral Letter on the Economy,* ed. R. Bruce Douglass. Washington, D.C.: Georgetown University, 1986: 117–138.

_____. "The National Bishops' Conference: An Analysis of Its Origins." *Catholic Historical Review* 66 (1980): 565–576.

McShane, Joseph, S.J. *Sufficiently Radical: Catholicism, Progressivism, and the Bishops' Program of 1919.* Washington, D.C.: Catholic University of America, 1986.

Murnion, Philip J., ed. *Catholics and Nuclear War: A Commentary on "The Challenge of Peace," The U.S. Catholic Bishops' Pastoral Letter on War and Peace.* New York: Crossroad, 1983.

Murnion, William E. "The Role and Language of the Church in Relation to Public Policy." In *Catholics and Nuclear War: A Commentary on "The Challenge of Peace," The U.S. Catholic Bishops' Pastoral Letter on War and Peace,* ed. P. J. Murnion. New York: Crossroad, 1983: 57–70.

Murphy, Matthew F. *Betraying the Bishops: How the Pastoral Letter on War and Peace Is Being Taught.* Washington, D.C.: Ethics and Policy Center, 1987.

Murray, John Courtney, S.J. *We Hold These Truths: Catholic Reflections on the American Proposition.* Kansas City, Mo.: Sheed and Ward, 1960, rpt. 1988.

Neidermayer, A. *The Council in Baltimore, 7–1st October, 1866: A Picture of American Church Life.* Frankfurt: G. Hanacher, 1867. Translated and published Baltimore, 1914.

Nolan, Hugh J., ed. *Pastoral Letters of the United States Catholic Bishops.* 5 vols. Washington, D.C.: United States Catholic Conference, 1984.

_____. *Pastoral Letters of the American Hierarchy, 1792–1970.* Huntingdon, Ind.: Our Sunday Visitor, 1971.

Novak, Michael. "The Authority of National Conferences of Bishops: Catholic Social Thought." *America* (January 6, 1990): 10.

_____. "Realism, Dissuasion, and Hope in the Nuclear Age." In *Peace in a Nuclear Age: The Bishops' Pastoral Letter in Perspective,* ed. C. J. Reid, Jr. Washington, D.C.: Catholic University of America Press, 1986: 123–136.

_____. "Moral Clarity in the Nuclear Age," *National Review* 35 (April 1, 1983) 354–392.

O'Brien, David J., and Thomas A. Shannon, eds. *Catholic Social Thought: The Documentary Heritage.* Maryknoll: Orbis, 1992.

_____. *Public Catholicism.* New York: Macmillan, 1989.

_____. The Economic Thought of the American Hierarchy." In *The Catholic Challenge to the American Economy: Reflections on the U.S. Bishops' Pastoral Letter on Catholic Social Teaching and the U.S. Economy,* ed. Thomas Gannon. New York: Macmillan, 1987: 27–41.

_____. "American Catholics and American Society." In *Catholics and Nuclear War: A Commentary on "The Challenge of Peace," The U.S. Catholic Bishops' Pastoral Letter on War and Peace,* ed. P. J. Murnion. New York: Crossroad, 1983: 16–29.

_____. *The Renewal of American Catholicism.* New York: Oxford University Press, 1972.

O'Connor, John J. "Catholic Social Teaching and the Limits of Authority." In *Challenge and Response,* ed. R. Royal. Washington, D.C. : Ethics and Public Policy Center, 1985: 75–82.

Overberg, Kenneth R. *An Inconsistent Ethic: Teachings of the American Catholic Bishops.* Washington, D.C.: University Press of America, 1980.

Pawlikowski, John T., O.S.M., and Donald Senior, C.P., eds. *Biblical and Theological Reflections on "The Challenge of Peace."* Wilmington, Del.: Michael Glazier, 1984.

Piehl, Mel. "American Catholics and Social Reform." In *Perspectives on the American Catholic Church, 1789–1989,* ed. S. J. Vicchio and V. Geiger. Westminster, Md.: Christian Classics, 1989: 317–339.

Rasmussen, Douglas, and James Sterba. *The Catholic Bishops and the Economy: A Debate.* New Brunswick, N.J.: Transaction Books, 1987.

Rasmussen, Lawrence. "Economic Policy: Creation, Covenant and Community." *America* (May 4, 1985): 365–369.

Reese, Thomas J. *A Flock of Shepherds: The National Conference of Catholic Bishops.* Kansas City: Sheed and Ward, 1992.

_____. "The Bishops and the Economy." *America* (November 3, 1984): 269–271.

Reher, Margaret Mary. *Catholic Intellectual Life in America: A Historical Study of Persons and Movements.* New York: Macmillan, 1989.

Reid, Charles, J., Jr., ed. *Peace in a Nuclear Age: The Bishops' Pastoral Letter in Perspective.* Washington, D.C.: Catholic University of America, 1986.

Riley, Maria. "One in Christ Jesus?: Women Critique the Pastoral." *The Catholic World* (November/December 1991): 282–286.

_____. "Women, Church and Patriarchy" *America* (May 5, 1984): 333–338.

Royal, Robert, ed. *Challenge and Response*. Washington, D.C. : Ethics and Public Policy Center, 1985.

Russell, Frederick H. "The Historical Perspective of the Bishops' Pastoral Letter: The View of One Medievalist." In *Peace in a Nuclear Age: The Bishops' Pastoral Letter in Perspective*, ed. Charles J. Reid, Jr. Washington, D.C.: Catholic University of America Press, 1986: 86–97.

Russett, Bruce M. "The Doctrine of Deterrence." In *Catholics and Nuclear War: A Commentary on "The Challenge of Peace,"* ed. P. Murnion. New York: Crossroad, 1983: 149–167.

Schall, James V., ed. *Out of Justice, Peace: Joint Pastoral of the West German Bishops/ Winning the Peace: Joint Pastoral Letter of the French Bishops*. San Francisco: Ignatius Press, 1984.

Schell, Jonathan. "Reflections—Nuclear Arms, Part I." *The New Yorker* (January 2, 1984): 36–74.

Schultz, David P. "Retrieving the Importance of Social Justice Themes in the Pastoral Letters of the United States Catholic Bishops. Ph.D. diss., Marquette University, 1998.

Shannon, William H. "Bishop' Pastoral Letter on Women." *America* (August 6–13, 1988): 84–86.

Shepard, Anne K. "An Adventure in Process: An Inquiry into the Process of Drafting 'The Challenge of Peace' and How the Bishops Were Educated in That Process." Ph.D. diss., Columbia University, 1991.

Strain, Charles R., ed. *Prophetic Visions and Economic Realities: Protestants, Jews and Catholics Confront the Bishops' Letter on the Economy*. Grand Rapids, Mich.: Wm. Eerdmans, 1989.

Sunshine, Edward R. "Moral Argument and American Consensus: An Examination of Statements by U.S. Catholic Bishops on Three Public Policy Issues, 1973–1986." Ph.D. diss., Graduate Theological Union, 1988.

Swift, Louis J. "Search the Scriptures: Patristic Exegesis and the *Ius Belli*." In *Peace in a Nuclear Age: The Bishops' Pastoral Letter in Perspective*, ed. Charles J. Reid, Jr. Washington, D.C.: Catholic University of America Press, 1986: 48–68.

Swing, Raymond. "The Catholic View of Reconstruction." *Nation* 108 (March 29, 1919): 467–468.

U.S. Congress. *Economic Implications of Bishops' Pastoral Letter on the American Economy*. Hearing before the Subcommittee on Economic Stabilization of the Committee on Banking, Finance and Urban Affairs, House of Representatives, Ninety-ninth Congress, first session, March 19, 1985.

Vicchio, Stephen J. "The Origins and Development of Anti-Catholicism in America." In *Perspectives on the American Catholic Church, 1789–1989*, ed. S. J. Vicchio and V. Geiger. Westminster, Md.: Christian Classics, 1989: 85–103.

_____, and Virginia Geiger, S.S.N.D., eds. *Perspectives on the American Catholic Church, 1789–1989*. Westminster, Md.: Christian Classics, 1989.

von Kuehnelt-Leddihn, Erik. "U.S. Catholics on the Brink." *National Review* (November 26, 1982): 1470–1476.

Walch, Timothy. *Catholicism in America: A Social History*. Malabar, Fla.: Robert E. Kriegler, 1989.

Warner, Michael. *Changing Witness: Catholic Bishops and Public Policy, 1917–1994*. Washington, D.C.: Ethics and Public Policy Center, 1995.

_____. "A New Ethic: The Social Teaching of the American Catholic Bishops, 1960–1986." Ph.D. diss., University of Chicago, 1990.

Weakland, Rembert. "Catholics as Social Insiders." *Origins* 22 (May 28, 1992): 33–39

Weigel, George. "The Bishops' Pastoral Letter and American Political Culture: Who Was Influencing Whom?" In *Peace in a Nuclear Age: The Bishops' Pastoral Letter in Perspective*, ed. Charles J. Reid, Jr. Washington, D.C.: Catholic University of America Press, 1986: 171-189.

Williams, D., and J. Houck, eds. *Catholic Social Thought and the New World Order: Democratic Capitalism and Catholic Social Teaching*. Washington, D.C.: Ethics and Public Policy Center, 1993.

Winters, Francis X., S.J. "The Cultural Context of the Pastoral Letter on Peace." In *Peace in a Nuclear Age: The Bishops' Pastoral Letter in Perspective*, ed. Charles J. Reid, Jr. Washington, D.C.: Catholic University of America Press, 1986: 336–341.

Woods, Walter J. "Pastoral Care, Moral Issues, Basic Approaches: The National Pastoral Texts of the American Bishops from the Perspective of Moral Theology." Ph.D. diss., Pontificia Universita Gregoriana, 1979.

Woodward, Kenneth L. "Challenging the Bishops." *Newsweek* (November 8, 1982): 78.

Zahn, Gordon C. "Pacifism and the Just War." In *Catholics and Nuclear War: A Commentary on "The Challenge of Peace,"* ed. P. Murnion. New York: Crossroad, 1983: 119–131.

DATE DUE
